THE TALES OF
HENRY JAMES

LITERATURE AND LIFE SERIES
(Formerly Modern Literature and World Dramatists)

Selected list of titles:

JAMES BALDWIN	Carolyn Wedin Sylvander
ANTHONY BURGESS	Samuel Coale
TRUMAN CAPOTE	Helen S. Garson
WILLA CATHER	Dorothy Tuck McFarland
T.S. ELLIOT	Burton Raffel
E.M. FORSTER	Claude J. Summers
ERNEST HEMINGWAY	Samuel Shaw
JOHN IRVING	Gabriel Miller
CHRISTOPHER ISHERWOOD	Claude J. Summers
HENRY JAMES, THE NOVELS OF	Edward Wagenknecht
KEN KESEY	Barry H. Leeds
ARTHUR KOESTLER	Mark Levene
D.H. LAWRENCE	George J. Becker
MARY MCCARTHY	Willene Schaefer Hardy
NORMAN MAILER	Philip H. Bufithis
JOHN O'HARA	Robert Emmet Long
EUGENE O'NEILL, THE PLAYS OF	Virginia Floyd
GEORGE ORWELL	Roberta Kalechofsky
EDGAR ALLAN POE	Bettina L. Knapp
MURIEL SPARK	Velma Bourgeois Richmond
JOHN STEINBECK	Paul McCarthy
LIONEL TRILLING	Edward Joseph Shoben, Jr.
MARK TWAIN	Robert Keith Miller
GORE VIDAL	Robert F. Kiernan
ROBERT PENN WARREN	Katherine Snipes
EDMUND WILSON	David Castronovo
THOMAS WOLFE	Elizabeth Evans
VIRGINIA WOOLF	Manly Johnson

Complete list of titles in the series available from publisher on request.

THE TALES
OF
HENRY JAMES

Edward Wagenknecht

FREDERICK UNGAR PUBLISHING CO.
New York

For
WAYNE and ELIZABETH BRANDSTADT

faithful friends through uncounted years

Library of Congress Cataloging in Publication Data

Wagenknecht, Edward, 1900-
    The tales of Henry James.

    (Literature and life series)
    Includes bibliographical references and indexes.
    1. James, Henry, 1843-1916—Criticism and interpre-
tation. I. Title. II. Series.
PS2124.W284 1984   813'.4   84-34
ISBN 0-8044-2957-X

Author's Note

The Tales of Henry James complements The Novels of Henry James (Ungar, 1983), and completes the present writer's survey of James's fiction. Leon Edel's twelve-volume collection, The Complete Tales of Henry James (Lippincott, 1961-1964), contains the text of 112 stories, which cover James's fictional output outside the productions he himself called novels, with the single exception of "The Married Son," his contribution to the 1908 Harper composite novel, The Whole Family. He chose to include only fifty-five of his shorter fictions in the definitive New York Edition (Scribners, 1907-1909, 1917) of his writings, however, and the discussion in the eleven chapters which make up the body of this book is confined to them. Since the order in which they are considered is not topical but chronological, it has not been possible to assign covering titles to these chapters:

The tales not included in the New York Edition are considered in Appendix A, where they are arranged alphabetically for convenient reference. Information concerning the original appearance of all tales is given in connection with the discussions thereof, and by reference to Appendix B the reader may easily determine when and where any given piece first appeared between hard covers. Notes, Index of Names, and Index of James's Writings follow:

There is one exception to what I have written. The stories published in 1910 in *The Finer Grain* were produced too late to be considered for the New York Edition, but they are sufficiently distinctive so that I did not think it possible to consign them to Appendix A, where, quite naturally, early material predominates. Chapter XI is therefore devoted to these five *Finer Grain* tales.

E.W.
West Newton, Massachusetts
Spring 1984

THE TALES OF
HENRY JAMES

I

So far as is now known, "A Tragedy of Error," which appeared unsigned in *The Continental Monthly* for February 1864, was James's first published tale. Before the end of the sixties, the young writer would be represented in the magazines by thirteen more narratives: "The Story of a Year," "A Landscape-Painter," "A Day of Days," "My Friend Bingham," "Poor Richard," "The Story of a Masterpiece," "The Romance of Certain Old Clothes," "A Most Extraordinary Case," "A Problem," "De Grey: A Romance," "Osborne's Revenge," "A Light Man," and "Gabrielle de Bergerac," none of which would be taken up into the New York Edition.

During the first half of the 1870s, James's production of fiction was abundant. Besides his first novel, *Watch and Ward*, which he afterwards wished to forget, and which was serialized in *The Atlantic Monthly* in 1871 but not republished in book form until seven years later, he placed twelve stories in the magazines: "Travelling Companions," "A Passionate Pilgrim," "At Isella," "Master Eustace," "Guest's Confession," "The Madonna of the Future," "The Sweetheart of M. Briseux," "The Last of the Valerii," "Madame de Mauves," "Adina," "Professor Fargo," and "Eugene Pickering." Three of these—"A Passionate Pilgrim" (*Atlantic*, March-April 1871), "The Madonna of the Future" (*Atlantic*, March 1873), and "Madame de Mauves" (*Galaxy*, February-March 1874) became the earliest stories to appear in the New York Edition.

Whether or not the "Pilgrim" and the "Madonna" were essentially superior to all the rejected tales might be debated at some length. James's special interest in them was due partly, as he acknowledges in his preface

1

to Volume XIII of the New York Edition, to the circumstances under which they were written. His interest is
not difficult to understand, however, for these tales
represent his discovery of the international theme of
which he was to make so much, "sops instinctively
thrown to the international Cerberus formidably posted
where I doubtless then didn't quite make him out."[1] The
"Madonna" focuses more perfectly than the "Pilgrim,"
but both are narrated in the first person by an observer
disinterested save through sympathy. In both, too, the
reader's interest in the central character is limited by his
aberrant if not unbalanced behavior. Both protagonists,
again, die at the end, and Clement Searle, the Pilgrim, is
sick from the beginning.

Theobald, the aspiring artist of the "Madonna," is
the one who has set his sights higher. Like Searle, he is
afflicted with what in "Four Meetings" his creator
would describe as "the great American disease," a
romantic infatuation for Europe (Italy in his case, not,
as with Searle, England).[2] He differs from Searle, however, in being consumed by a creative passion—to paint
the perfect Madonna, in which the best qualities of all
the others would be combined—while Searle comes to
England armed with only a shadowy claim upon an
English estate. Aided by the narrator, an enthusiastic
friend whom he has picked up at his inn, he goes down
to Middlesex, where he falls in love with his middle-
aged cousin and she with him. "She had no arts, no
impulses nor graces—scarce even any manners; she was
queerly, almost frowsily dressed," yet there was "an
antique sweetness" about her, "a homely fragrance of
old traditions." Because her nephew, the child of the
present possessor, her tyrannical brother, has died, she
is now the apparent heir. The brother, at first frigidly
polite to Searle, soon denounces and then insults him,
whereupon the visitor returns to the inn, where he sees
the ghost of the mistress of the Searle who had founded

the American branch of the family and who had herself met a tragic death.[3] The ending is deeply, one might even say crassly, ironical, for Miss Searle arrives at the inn as the American claimant dies; her brother has been killed, and the estate, now hers, might have been Searle's also if he had lived.

Theobald is a nobler figure, but he has lost his hold upon reality to an even greater extent. He can talk about his artistic aspirations very impressively, even boasting that he has never sold a picture nor added anything to the world's accumulation of rubbish, yet the fact remains that he has dreamed his life away without putting brush to canvas until it has become too late to develop such powers as he might have manifested had he ever learned to understand what Browning cele-brated as the glory of the imperfect.[4] Meanwhile the common woman of easy morals whom he had idealized as the perfect model has grown old and fat and coarse— "a bourgeois Egeria" with "a vulgar stagnation of mind"—and when the narrator blunderingly opens Theobald's eyes by calling his attention to these facts ("You've *dawdled!* She's an old, old woman—for a maiden mother"), the shock kills him.

Theobald's story is told to a group of men around a dinner table, one of whom introduces it briefly. Bal-zac's *Le Chef d'oeuvre Inconnu* and de Musset's *Loren-zaccio*, both of which are referred to in the course of the narrative (the former without being named), seem to have contributed to it, and there is much to admire in the telling. Mrs. Coventry, herself later shown up as somewhat uncomprehending, is used to supplement the narrator's initial view of Theobald and thus prevent him and the reader from being too much taken in, but the artist is made more attractive by being juxtaposed to the loathsome "successful" sculptor, probably the paramour of the wonderful model, who has made a very good thing out of figurines of cats and monkeys in suggestive or obscene attitudes: "Cats and monkeys, monkeys and cats—all human life is there!"

The most important tale of this period is unquestionably "Madame de Mauves." It was written in "a dampish, unsunned room, cool, however, to the relief of the fevered muse," at an inn in Bad Homburg in the summer of 1873, and in later years that was all James professed to be able to remember about its origins. Both Flaubert's *Madame Bovary* and *The Princess of Clèves* (1678) by Madame de La Fayette have been nominated as possible influences. The case for the *Princess* is much the stronger of the two, but positive evidence is lacking, and there can be little point in invoking either *The Scarlet Letter* or James's own acquaintance with Sarah Butler Wister or anybody else.[5]

The story concerns an international marriage between Euphemia Cleve, an American who has been reared in a French convent, where she had nurtured her imagination on "various Ultramontane works of fiction," and a cynical, debt-ridden sprig of the aristocracy who made no distinction between women and "those very lavender gloves that are soiled in an evening and thrown away." The Comte de Mauves marries Euphemia for her money, and since she is "essentially incorruptible" and "in the prime purity of her moral vision," her response to him implies no snobbery on her part; in her eyes he is simply "an historic masterpiece" to which she arbitrarily assigns all the virtues that belong to the naive romances she has read and to her own idealistic imagination. By the time Longmore meets her, however, the romanticism of her youth has been replaced by the "hard prose" of reality, and she is like a singer who has lost her high notes, living what Thoreau called a life of quiet desperation. Madame de Mauves is a Christian, and her husband is a pagan with no virtues save an unfailing politeness and an unbreakable shell of fine manners, who thinks her morbid and finds it a strain to be with her. About all she has left is "a dogged obstinate clinging conscience," which, in her own words, may prevent her "from doing anything very base" but will probably also keep her from attempting anything very fine.

Longmore is a well-to-do American, about thirty years old, who, having met Madame de Mauves and understood her plight, soon comes to feel for her a pity that ripens into love. This is far from displeasing to the Count, who would be glad to see his wife take a lover, since this would signalize her acceptance of the code under which his society operates and leave him that much freer to pursue his own infidelities. Perhaps, more significantly, it would also relieve him of the painful sense of inferiority he now experiences in her presence. His feelings in the matter are shared by his equally corrupt widowed sister, Madame Clairin, who was with Euphemia in the convent school and through whom her first contact with the de Mauves was made. Longmore always thinks of Madame Clairin as "that dreadful woman—that awful woman," and though she makes an open play for him, he tells her to her face that she is "the most immoral person I've lately had the privilege of conversing with." He would have liked to deliver Madame de Mauves from her bondage, and if she had been of a different temperament—or if he had been—this might have been achieved. But he is like her, idealistic and capable of devotion but better at endurance than action, and when she begs him not to laugh at his conscience ("That's the only blasphemy I know") and pleads with him not to disappoint her ("If I were to find you selfish where I thought you generous, narrow where I thought you large, vulgar where I thought you rare, I should think worse of human nature"), there is nothing for him to do, being what he is, but to follow her lead and "assent to destiny."

Though Longmore's is the central consciousness

enlisted in the telling of the tale, the omniscient narrator makes important additions, and Mrs. Draper, Longmore's friend and Euphemia's, fills in occasionally. Longmore is himself deeply involved in the action and therefore much more than a mere device for getting the story told. Yet although we see a great deal more of him than of Madame de Mauves and get deeper into his mental and emotional processes, the story is rightly named for her, for we see him only in a specialized relationship. At the beginning we see her "through a thickening twilight," and even at the end Longmore views her "for the last time at the hour of long shadows and pale reflected amber lights, as he had almost always seen her." She is slight, fair, and pale, with beautiful, gentle gray eyes, a high forehead, thick brown hair, a slender throat, and a mouth "all expression and intention." She speaks very little at first, and when we do hear her voice, her utterance is rather formal, couched in language one might more naturally associate with literature and the stage than, say, with the innkeeper and the idyllic young unmarried lovers whom Longmore encounters in the country and whose behavior, which attracts him at first, and which certainly has its charm, perhaps in their milieu even its rightness, some of her critics seem to believe Madame de Mauves should have emulated.[6]

J.A. Ward rightly observes that James's admiration for Euphemia and his "disapproval of the duplicity and adultery of Richard de Mauves establish" in this story "an absolute moral dualism" and moreover that the evil she encounters is presented as "endemic to a civilization" and "inseparable from the European past," to which he adds, however, that the lady's "unflinching rectitude offends the modern reader" which would, I should think, make the evil endemic to modern readers also.[7]

These objections might never have gone to their

present length without the ambiguous epilogue James appended to his tale. Even Ward added to his statement about absolute moral dualism the words "possibly qualified by the ambiguous ending of the story." After Longmore has left Madame de Mauves and returned to America, he hears nothing about her for two years. Then Mrs. Draper comes back with startling tidings. After Longmore's departure, Euphemia had left her husband and gone to live in the country. Some correspondence between her and Mrs. Draper had been succeeded by a year of silence; then, at Vichy, Mrs. Draper had encountered "a clever young Frenchman whom I accidentally learned to be a friend of that charming sister of the Count's, Madame Clairin." He had told her that M. de Mauves had repented of his sins, amended his way of life, fallen in love with his wife and begged her forgiveness, and that she had refused. "She was stone, she was ice, she was outraged virtue," and the Count had taken this so much to heart that he had gone into seclusion, lost his health, and finally taken his own life. To which James adds that, though Longmore's first impulse, upon hearing this news, was to go to Euphemia, he had not done so: "The truth is that, in the midst of all the ardent tenderness of his memory of Madame de Mauves, he has become conscious of a singular feeling—a feeling of wonder, of uncertainty, of awe."

Most commentators seem to have taken all this at face value, important exceptions being Benjamin C. Rountree and Charles Kaplan.[8] Yet it comes to us at the third remove, and, like everything connected with Madame Clairin—Longmore's "dreadful" and "awful" woman—it seems highly suspect. Mrs. Draper's view of this lady as "the Count's charming sister" shows how little she knows her, and the young Frenchman's friendship with her suggests that *he* knows her only too well. Moreover, the wild extravagance of his reference to Euphemia as "the terrible little woman who killed her husband" may well have been intended to put the reader on guard.

James seems here to be going out of his way deliberately to create ambiguity. Except that what is related brings a kind of completion to what must otherwise have been left hanging in the air, this achieves nothing save to deepen the reader's sense of the complexity of human character and the difficulty of believing that one can really know anybody. The suicide itself does not seem impossible; men who live as the Count has lived must always be in some danger of being overtaken by disgust with life itself. But that he could have been capable of true repentance and amendment of life, I for one simply do not believe, and if James intended me to believe it, all I can say is that at this point I think his art failed him. As for the believability of Longmore's final—or fatal—hesitation, it is certainly puzzling but perhaps not, for him, incredible. What had he done but hesitate ever since the tale began?[9]

II

If James's production of fiction had been, as noted, prolific during the first half of the 1870s, it was phenomenal during the second half. In 1875 he published the first novel he cared to acknowledge, *Roderick Hudson*, which was followed by *The American* in 1877, by both *The Europeans* and the first book publication of *Watch and Ward* in 1878, and by *Confidence* in 1879. His first two collections of short stories—*A Passionate Pilgrim and Other Tales* and *The Madonna of the Future and Other Tales*—came along in 1875 and 1879 respectively, nor should we forget that he was also writing and publishing nonfiction during this period.

What is more our concern here, however, is that there were eleven new tales in the magazines: "Benvolio," "Crawford's Consistency," "The Ghostly Rental," "Four Meetings," "Théodolinde" (later renamed "Rose-Agathe"), "Daisy Miller," "Longstaff's Marriage," "An International Episode," "The Pension Beaurepas," "The Dairy of a Man of Fifty," and "A Bundle of Letters." Only five of these—"Four Meetings," "Daisy Miller," "An International Episode," "The Pension Beaurepas," and "A Bundle of Letters"—were destined to "make" the New York Edition and therefore come in for consideration here. With them must be considered "The Point of View," which, though it did not appear until 1882, is very closely connected with the last two tales named.

The first meeting between the narrator of "Four Meetings" (*Scribner's Monthly*, November 1879) and the heroine, Caroline Spencer, occurs at a party in a New England home, where because he is familiar with Europe, he is asked by their hostess to guide the young schoolteacher through some photographs of well-known

European sites. He finds that she is suffering from an acute attack of "the great American disease" and has for some time been saving up her money for a trip abroad. He does not encounter her again until three years later, when he comes upon her sitting in a sidewalk café rapturously drinking in European atmosphere in one of its less attractive manifestations and awaiting the return of her cousin, an "art student" who has gone off to exchange her money for her. When this character returns, he impresses the narrator—and the reader—as obviously sleazy and untrustworthy, but the trio breaks up without our having learned anything more than that the young man has something "bad" to tell Miss Spencer. But at the third meeting, which follows shortly, the narrator learns that she has given him all the money she had saved for her trip to Europe, retaining just enough to cover her fare home, and that she is returning at once, having enjoyed only thirteen hours of the Old World in the port of Le Havre.

The last meeting occurs five years later, when the narrator calls upon Miss Spencer at her home in North Vernon and finds that she has been saddled for two years and four months with the "Countess," now her cousin's "widow," a coarse, dominating creature whose title is obviously as bogus as her marriage lines, who, by the sheer force of an overbearing personality, has virtually reduced her hostess to servant status while she devotes herself to ensnaring a stupid, wealthy youth whom she is supposed to be teaching French but whose main interest, like hers, clearly lies elsewhere. There is a prologue of a single paragraph, written some seventeen years after the first meeting, from which we learn that Caroline Spencer has lately died. "I'm sorry to hear of her death, and yet when I think of it, why should I be? The last time I saw her she was certainly not——."

It would be difficult to write a simpler or clearer story than "Four Meetings," nor would one suppose that

Miss Spencer's fate could call for much more comment than Othello's "the pity of it, Iago." The tale has, however, come in for a surprising amount of attention during recent years. Long ago, Ford Madox Ford (then Ford Madox Hueffer) made the ridiculous statement that it was "unsurpassed in the literature of any language or of any age."[1] (With friends like that a writer does not need enemies.) Recent critics, however, have been mainly concerned with the problems they have found in it, and since, for the most part, these have been of their own making, their lucubrations have not on the whole proved very enlightening.

Most of the animus that has appeared has been directed against the narrator; Caroline Spencer herself has acquired only one enemy, John A. Clair, who advances the astonishing view that she had not been a schoolteacher at all but "at least a clever confidence woman if not...a shameless prostitute," the confederate of both her cousin and the "Countess," with whom, at the time of the last meeting recorded, she has lived for ten years. To Leo Gurko, however, the narrator is an unconscious villain who kills Miss Spencer by forcing her "beyond her emotional means" and imposing more life upon her than she can bear (by showing her some pictures of Europe, I presume). Somewhat similarly, Roger Seamon finds that the story is not about Caroline at all but "about the narrator and the significance of the meetings for *him*," and he is a man whose divided impulse is "to respond deeply" to her needs but also to flee from any obligation such sympathy may involve and with whom "politeness, alienation and safety win out over candor, intimacy and risk." Finally in a footnote to Seamon's article, W.R. Martin sees the "Countess" as "a reflection of the narrator, though of course a grossly distorted one," but presents no evidence whatever to support this extraordinary interpretation.[2]

A neglected writer during his lifetime, Henry

James used to say that publishing books was like taking them out and dropping them into the mud. If he were alive now, he would know that neglect is not the worst fate a writer can suffer. I must confess that I find it a little difficult to determine just what those who lambaste the narrator for his failure to save Miss Spencer think he ought to have done. Should he have taken an axe to the "Countess" and thrown Miss Spencer over his charger's neck so that he might ride off with her like young Lochinvar come out of the West? And, for that matter, what help can anybody, least of all a stranger quite without authority in the matter, give to an adult human being who is sufficiently the lamb to allow herself to be victimized and exploited by people who have no claim whatever upon her, as Miss Spencer does?[3]

Our next tale is "Daisy Miller," the story of the little Western flower so cruelly cropped in Rome.[4] "Take all the other men that have written novels in English and match their women with [those of Henry James]," wrote William Dean Howells, "and they seem not to have written of women at all." "Daisy Miller" contained the first of his many supreme portraits of women, and it was also his greatest popular success, even if it was partly, incredible as it now seems, a *succès de scandale*. What irony it was that it should have been given to this most fastidious of writers to create the American "flapper" in literature so long before she manifested in life!

James wrote "Daisy Miller" in London in the spring of 1878 and sent it first to *Lippincott's Magazine*, which, to his surprise, rejected it without explanation (he learned afterwards that it had been regarded as "an outrage on American girlhood"). But when Virginia Woolf's father, Leslie Stephen, printed it in England in the *Cornhill Magazine*, (June-July 1878), both *Littell's Living Age* and the *Home Journal* of New York promptly pirated it in America—"a sweet tribute,"

James called it, "that I hadn't yet received and was never again to know"—and an unauthorized American paper edition, which likewise failed to yield the author a penny, is said to have sold 20,000 copies in a few weeks.[5]

When he wrote his preface to Volume XVIII of the New York Edition, which contains "Daisy Miller," James professed not to be able to remember why he had originally used the subtitle "A Study," which he now abandoned, nor anything about his sources except that the tale had been suggested by what a friend had told him in the autumn of 1877 about a girl like Daisy who had innocently scandalized Rome. Since in the story itself he causes Mrs. Costello to ask Winterbourne to bring her a copy of *Paule Méré* by the Swiss novelist Victor Cherbuliez, it seems odd that he did not mention this work, but perhaps he did not wish to call attention to the similarities between the two stories.[6] What he did do, both in his preface and in his now famous letter to Mrs. Lynn Linton,[7] was to tell exactly how he intended his readers to understand Daisy and to commit himself irrevocably to her cause as against that of her critics. "The keynote of her character," he said, was her "innocence." She had no idea of defying social mores or creating a scandal; she was merely a "natural" creature who was sacrificed to "a social rumpus that went on quite over her head."

Frederick Winterbourne encounters Daisy first at Vevey and later at Rome. She attracts him at once, but like a true Jamesian hero, he spends most of his time until nearly the end of the story trying to make up his mind whether she is worthy to be loved. His frosty aunt Mrs. Costello is sure that she is not. Daisy has an extremely graceful, refined prettiness, she is not in any way rough or coarse, and her every movement is charming. Her manner is quiet and tranquil and her voice soft, well modulated, and agreeable. She dresses beautifully and always in perfect taste. But she has no "form." She chatters incessantly, makes a friend of the family courier, boasts that she has always had "a great deal of gentleman's society," and goes unattended about Rome at all hours with a young Italian who is obviously not a gentleman. Mrs. Walker sums up the indictment against her: she flirts[8] with any man she can pick up; she sits in corners with mysterious Italians; she dances all evening with the same partner; she receives visitors alone at eleven o'clock at night.

Mrs. Walker treats Daisy both more and less severely than Mrs. Costello. The latter, who regards her as a "horror," simply declines to meet either her or her lymphatic mother, and when her nephew tells her that the Millers are only ignorant, not "bad," she replies that "they're hopelessly vulgar. Whether or not being hopelessly vulgar is being 'bad' is a question for the metaphysicians. They're bad enough to blush for at any rate; and for this short life that's quite enough." Mrs. Walker, on the other hand, tries to teach Daisy how to behave and actually goes in her carriage to rescue her from the Pincian Gardens, where she is walking with her friend Giovanelli, "so that the world may see she's not running absolutely wild—and then take her safely home." Daisy, however, declines to be rescued and refuses to get into the carriage. What she tells Mrs. Walker is that she is more than five years old, that if she could not walk she would die, and that if what she is doing is not the custom in Rome, it ought to be. Not until later do we learn that she did not wish to hurt Giovanelli's feelings by leaving him abruptly after he had so looked forward to this excursion. From this time forward the American colony in Rome is through with Daisy—or would be if it had ever taken her up—though she still has coming what in a play we should call her great scene, when she sails in very late at Mrs. Walker's party, "in radiant loveliness, smiling and chattering, carrying a large bou-

quet and attended by Mr. Giovanelli." She had been
coaching him in some songs she wanted him to sing for
the company, and she actually succeeds in bringing this
off before Mrs. Walker both literally and figuratively
turns her back on her.

Admittedly such a person must remain difficult to
fit into categories, especially for people who live by
forms. Daisy Miller is a child of nature who lives spon-
taneously, as girls may have lived in the Golden Age but
cannot live now. To be sure, even in these matters, she is
not altogether a fool. She shows more intelligence and
penetration than her critics give her credit for when she
says that "they're only pretending to be shocked. They
don't really care a straw what I do." But James makes it
clear that she has never confronted nor realized evil.
When Mrs. Walker invites her into her carriage to save
her from being talked about, she replies wonderingly,
"Talked about? What do you mean?" and when the
other says, "Come into my carriage and I'll tell you," she
comes back at her with "I don't think I want to know
what you mean. I don't think I should like it." It is both
her tragedy and theirs that when the American colony
in Rome rejects her, they are making the wrong choice
between the forms of goodness and its reality, and if the
mistake costs her her life, they pay for it with moral
blindness.

It is remarkable that James could make all this so
clear to the reader as he does yet at the same time filter
so much of what we know about Daisy through the stiff,
prissy consciousness of Frederick Winterbourne, for
though "Daisy Miller" is written in the third person, his
are the eyes through which the reader for the most part
looks. If Winterbourne does not reject Daisy so quickly
or so easily as Mrs. Costello and Mrs. Walker, this is
partly because he is a man who is strongly attracted to
her (or would be if he could let himself go) and partly
because he has great difficulty in making up his mind

about anything. He does not quite give her up until he finds her at night alone with Giovanelli in the Colosseum, for no more improper reason, it turns out, than that she wanted to see the ruin by moonlight, and it is characteristic of his self-centered egotism that even at this point he should feel not only "final horror" but also "final relief." It was something to have cleared up "the ambiguity of the poor girl's appearance and the whole riddle of her contradictions" and to be sure at last that "she was a young lady about the *shades* of whose perversity a foolish puzzled gentleman need no longer trouble his head or his heart."

No, there is no longer a need, either for him or for her, for this time the girl's rashness and disregard for appearances have really undone her; she has picked up the germs of Roman fever in the Colosseum, and in a little while she is dead. Before the end Winterbourne learns that she had indeed cared for him, that he had hurt her deeply by his behavior in the Colosseum, and at last that, as he puts it so elegantly and restrainedly to Mrs. Costello, "she would have appreciated one's esteem." But he needed Giovanelli, who was so much his inferior in so many ways, to open his eyes. "'She was the most beautiful young lady I ever saw.'" says Giovanelli, " 'and the most amiable.' To which he added in a moment, 'Also—naturally—the most innocent.'" At this point even Winterbourne cannot but realize that he was "booked to make a mistake," having "lived too long in foreign parts." Essentially, however, he is now—or still—committed to Costelloism, and James tells us in conclusion that "he soon went back to live at Geneva," the city above all others most identified with John Calvin and Calvinism, where he was reported to be "much interested in a very clever foreign lady."[9]

Some of Daisy's admirers, not content to love her for what she is, would make her not only an Isabel Archer or a Milly Theale but a high priestess of American Transcendentalism or even a Christian martyr. James himself may be guilty of misleading us in this connection by permitting Winterbourne to find her in the Colosseum at the foot of the cross erected in honor of the Christians who were martyred there. I have already rejected Motley Deakin's conception of her as a rebel.[10] In this aspect she could only be a rebel without a cause, for if she is martyred, it is for nothing nobler or higher than being herself and doing as she likes regardless of circumstances, conditions, or consequences; to see more than this in her fate not only blurs distinctions but also robs her of her innocence and much of her charm. Nor does the fact that she declares, after Winterbourne has "cut" her in the Colosseum, that she does not care now whether she has Roman fever or not make her a martyr of love. Winterbourne might indeed have saved her if—well, if he had not been Winterbourne, but we have all said something like what she says without meaning it. It was not Daisy's words that gave her the Roman fever, and Bret Harte was quite right when he declared that she might have gone to the Colosseum under perfectly proper escort and still have died as she did.

On the other hand, I think Howells exaggerated somewhat when he wrote that what Daisy did in Rome would never have been criticized or provoked comment in Schenectady or Cleveland or Buffalo or Richmond or Louisville. Although European chaperonage has never prevailed in America, surely Daisy's manners could never have been accepted as standard among genteel people even here, and it is no compliment to her to try to make her over into something she was not. The girl's mother is a fool, her father is shut up in his business establishment in America making money for his family to spend in Europe, and her little brother is an *enfant terrible*. The point is not at all that everything Daisy does is right but rather that those who cannot see through her surface shortcomings to the purity and goodness beneath are far more seriously handicapped than she. As James himself tells us, what he asked of his readers was to muster "a sufficiently brooding tenderness" to "extract a shy incongruous charm" from "an object scant and superficially vulgar."

It is for this reason too, I believe, that Daisy's death is reported so summarily at the end of the story. "Daisy Miller" has its tragic elements, but it is not a full-fledged tragedy because its heroine does not attain truly tragic stature. Like Ophelia's, her fate is more pathetic than tragic. The element of social comedy in the tale remains a large one, and the net result is a skillful and delicate blend.[11]

Though "An International Episode" (*Cornhill Magazine*, December 1878-January 1879) is somewhat longer than "Daisy Miller," it invites considerably less comment. At one point, indeed, James himself speaks of the possibility, "were it convenient," of presenting a record of the impressions of America entertained by Lord Lambeth and Percy Beaumont, "none the less soothing that they were not exhaustively analyzed." Though the young lord certainly has his virtues, neither he nor his friends are capable of nor reward much analysis, and both are presented, in the first part of the story, in what amounts almost to caricature, which the English did not enjoy.

After having met J.L. Westgate, an American businessman who seems rarely to leave his office, in New York, the English visitors are sent down to Newport to be royally entertained by his wife, where Beaumont, the older and more canny of the two, becomes fearful that Mrs. Westgate's sister, Bessie Alden, is setting her cap at Lord Lambeth and alerts his mother to call him home on the pretext that his father has been taken sick. In the second part of the tale, in which Bessie and her sister visit England, Lambeth does propose, but Bessie rejects him, not only because of the grossly and rudely condescending behavior of his mother and sister after he has dragooned them into calling upon her but also because she has been disappointed in him personally. He is largely indifferent to the historical associations that mean so much to the romantic young American, and since he never reads, her frequent references to English books and writers are so much Greek to him. Worst of all, however, from her point of view, he gives no sign of even desiring to become the civic leader that she thinks a peer of the realm should be.

In the most comprehensive study of this tale that has been made, Adeline R. Tintner has pointed out that Lord Lambeth's title, as well as the titles of both his mother and sister, the Duchess of Bayswater and the Countess of Pimlico, must seem, to readers of Thackeray, deliberately denigrating.[12] It is quite true that Mrs. Westgate, who chatters incessantly for pages at a stretch and is capable on occasion of both tartness and rudeness, has her own gaucherie, but on the whole the Americans certainly have the better of it in this story, and Bessie's rejection of Lord Lambeth suggests Isabel Archer's of Lord Warburton in *The Portrait of a Lady*.

"The Pension Beaurepas" (*Atlantic Monthly*, April 1879), "A Bundle of Letters" (*The Parisian*, December 1879), and "The Point of View" (*Century Magazine*, December 1882) all ignore plot completely in favor of concentration upon character-drawing. The second and third are in epistolary form, and the last carries over characters from both of the others. Since James mentions Balzac's *Père Goriot* on the very first page of "The Pension Beaurepas," he must obviously have been influenced by this work in choosing his scene,[13] and though nobody seems to think it worth mentioning, he was also of course quite familiar with *The Autocrat of the Breakfast Table* and its successors, in which Oliver Wendell Holmes used the same boardinghouse device to bring a variety of types together. Except for the landlady, her servant, and old M. Pigeonneau, who is not much developed beyond being a stereotypical Frenchman in his attitude toward women, all the characters are Americans: the narrator, Mr. and Mrs. Ruck and their daughter Sophy, and Mrs. Church and her daughter Aurora.

Except for Aurora all the women are loathsome. Mrs. Ruck and Sophy are heartless, voracious spendthrifts with not an idea in their heads except to possess themselves of all the loot they can carry out of the shops and too insensitive to notice or care that their hapless husband and father, one of James's few sympathetic portraits of an American businessman, is not only sick in body but also worrying himself to death over the fear of impending business failure (in "The Point of View" we are to learn that these fears were justified). Mrs. Church sees herself as a lofty, scholarly idealist, vastly superior to the Rucks; actually she is a brainless, pretentious "culture vulture" who lives in Europe only because it is cheaper there than in America and makes herself ridiculous by squabbling over every sou. Worse still, she is doing her best to ruin the life of her daughter—"this unfortunately situated, this insidiously mutinous young creature...in search of an effective preserver"—who is being dragged over Europe from one pension to another, with no opportunity to become either an American or a European and with nothing to do and no chance to develop whatever her capacities may be.

"A Bundle of Letters," which was written in a single session in the fall of 1879 for Theodore Child (who wanted a story for his magazine, *The Parisian*) is in much the same vein. This time the scene is what one of the characters calls "a second-rate boarding house" in Paris, from which Miss Miranda Hope, who is audaciously traveling alone in search of culture, writes to her mother in Bangor, Maine; Violet Ray, an American society girl and a snob, to her friend Agnes Rich in New York; Louis Leverett, a shallow Boston aesthete, who mouths fashionable jargon without really knowing what he is talking about, to Harvard Tremont (surely not one of James's subtlest names!); Evelyn Vane, a nice young English girl, sincerely shocked by American freedom, to the Lady Augusta Fleming at Brighton; Léon Verdier, a French gallant, to Prosper Gobain at Lille; and Dr. Rudolph Staub, who embodies everything James did not like about the Germans and who thinks as Allied war propaganda tried to make Americans believe all Germans thought in 1914, to Dr. Julius Hirsch at Göttingen. The general idea is to have these people comment upon each other and enable the reader to judge them by what they say. Miranda Hope is the one from whom we hear most and most wish to hear. Miranda is naive, ignorant if you like, but she is a sincere, basically sensible girl, with plenty of spunk, who does in Paris exactly what she had done in Bangor and finds that she has done exactly right.

In "The Point of View" we find that the dowerless Aurora Church has persuaded her silly mother to give her three months in American in search of a husband, though Mrs. Church is determined that if they find one, he must live in Europe with them. They do not find him in the East, and their departure for the West at the end of the tale is its closest approach to a plot. There are eight letters, of which Aurora writes the first and the last; she is the only person from whom we hear twice. Both the aesthetic Louis Leverett and the violently American Marcellus Cockerell, who regard each other as "sickly little ass" and "strident savage," respectively, are attracted to her, but she is too European for one and too American for the other.

There were evidently a good many Cockerells among the readers of the *Century* when "The Point of View" appeared there, for they are said to have found evidence in the story of James's anti-Americanism. They were of course wrong, for although some of the criticisms made by the foreigners are penetrating as far as they go, James makes it clear that there is much they do not see. Obviously we are intended to find what we would now call Cockerell's "100 percent Americanism" ridiculous, but we must still take it into consideration that M. Gustave Legeune, "the first French writer of distinction who has been in America since de Tocqueville," is a conventionally lecherous Latin and that the Right Honorable Edward Antrobus, M.P., whose radicalism (suggestive of Lord Warburton's) is baffled by what seems to him the extremism of American developments, is quite as dense an Englishman as those James had already created in "An International Episode." All in all, the American Miss Sturdy, who knows both Europe and America and is capable of weighing their respective merits and demerits against each other, is the only character who can be taken as even a limited spokesman for the author, as she is the only one except the unfortuante Aurora with whom either he or his readers could possibly be expected to sympathize.

III

During the 1880s James's published fiction comprised four novels—*The Portrait of a Lady*, his first unquestioned masterpiece (1881); *The Bostonians* and *The Princess Casamassima*, both major works (1886); *The Reverberator*, which was anything but a major work (1888)—plus, after "The Point of View," seventeen more tales: °"The Siege of London," "The Impressions of a Cousin," °"Lady Barbarina," °"The Author of Beltraffio," °"Pandora," "Georgina's Reasons," "A New England Winter," "The Path of Duty," "Mrs. Temperly," °"Louisa Pallant," °"The Aspern Papers," °"The Liar," "The Modern Warning," °"A London Life," °"The Lesson of the Master," °"The Patagonia," and "The Solution." Tales whose titles are marked with an asterisk were included in the New York Edition; the first four constitute the subject matter of this chapter, and the rest will be discussed in Chapter IV.

The international note is sounded again in "The Siege of London" (*Cornhill Magazine*, January-February 1883), a straightforward narrative, cool, even a bit cynical, in tone. The basic situation of "a man of honour who has to testify about the antecedents of a woman he has known in the past" derives from *Le Demimonde* of Alexandre Dumas *fils* (James's tale opens at the Comédie Française). Unlike Dumas's heroine, however, Nancy Beck, or Mrs. Headway, or whatever, was conceived as a comparatively "innocent adventuress," of "the newnesses, the freshnesses, the independence, the freedoms" suitable to a "well-known Texas belle" and "flower of the Pacific slope; ignorant, absurd, crude, but full of pluck and spirit," all of whose marriages have been "unfortunate." New York society has pretty definitely rejected her, and when, in Paris, with Sir Arthur

Demesne, M.P., in tow, she reencounters George Littlemore, an American rancher and mine owner, now
engaged in "doing nothing" with "a beautiful consistency," she has set her sights upon making it in London
and upon marrying Sir Arthur, who is seven years her
junior, both for its own sake and as a stepping stone
toward her goal. What she wants of Littlemore and his
friend Waterville, who is attached to the American legation in London, is that they should give her a clean bill of
health.

The action shifts midway from Paris to Warwick-
shire, where Waterville and Mrs. Headway are both
guests of Sir Arthur's mother, Lady Demesne, who
loathes Mrs. Headway but realizes that her only hope of
keeping her out of the family is to be able to give her son
authoritative word that the lady is not respectable.
Waterville parries her questions, but when Littlemore
returns from America to find that English society has
taken up Mrs. Headway as "great fun," the situation
grows more complicated. ("The people here do beat
the Dutch! There's no one they won't go after.")
Though Littlemore had previously committed himself
to the thesis that a gentleman must "lie nobly" when "a
woman's honour's at stake," he now plays it coy, without committing himself one way or the other, watching
the show for the pleasure it affords and not caring "a pin
for the fine old race" that Nancy Beck might contami-
nate by marrying into it. In the end she takes all the
tricks.

When he came to "touch up" the story for the New
York Edition,[1] the "poor little old thing" struck James as
"pretty dim and rococo," but he still apparently thought
it worthy of occupying over 125 pages. Though it is
certainly a successful story upon its own terms, its material is such that it makes no very deep appeal to the
reader. Mrs. Headway's enterprise is no doubt important to her, but since we have been guided to regard her

tolerantly at best, it does not greatly concern us. Except for Lady Demesne, English society seems quite as stupid about her as her lover is, and though one grants that Littlemore's position is at best uncomfortable, it is not of its nature calculated to enhance his dignity.

In "Lady Barbarina" (first published in *Century Magazine*, November-December 1883, as "Lady Barberina") James reverses the prevailing pattern in the much discussed Anglo-American marriages of the time of composition; instead of an impoverished English nobleman marrying a rich American girl for her money, we have Jackson Lemon, a wealthy American physician, choosing the second daughter of Lord Canterville, a marquis with a very large family. The scene on Rotten Row with which the story opens and in which not only Lady Barb and her father but even Dr. Lemon seem almost more equine than human so impressed Stevenson by its "instantaneous precision" that he acknowledged himself, in comparison to James, "a louse and slouch of the first water." It was Howells's observation that the ending was hurried that occasioned James's famous admission that "it's always the fault of my things that the head and trunk are too big and the legs too short."[2]

Though the tale is told by the omniscient author, there is no lack of reflectors in it. The Dexter Freers foreshadow the Assinghams in *The Golden Bowl*, and Dr. Feeder discusses matters both with them and with Dr. Lemon. Besides these, we have Lady Marmaduke and Lady Barb's sister, Lady Beauchemin, who are keen for international marriages as a means of uniting the English-speaking peoples; perhaps Jackson might not even have approached Lord Canterville when he did without Lady Beauchemin's encouragement.

Neither Lady Barb nor her lover (later her husband) are idealized. Hers was conceived as "a maiden nature that, after a fashion all its own, should show as fine and complete, show as neither coarse nor poor," but James admitted that he had more interest in Dr. Lemon with "his comparative sense for shades." Lemon was "neither handsome nor distinguished, but only immensely rich and quite original," and though he is pretty slow to make up his mind that he loves Lady Barb, once he has done so, he behaves very much as if there were no other minds to be considered. He has much of the naiveté of Christopher Newman in *The American*. "How can he dislike me?" he asks when Lady Barb expresses uncertainty as to what her father will say to his suit, and when Lady Canterville invites him to luncheon and "dares" to say her husband will be at home, he assures her that "it will be worth his while!" As for Lady Barb, she was clearly, "in her perfection ... one of the rarest of types," but her "character, like her figure, appeared mainly to have been formed by riding across country." She "wasn't strikingly clever" nor "particularly quick in the give and take of conversation," and "there was very little that was explanatory about her." "She wasn't light, she wasn't supple," and after six months of marriage, her husband has made up his mind that she wasn't intelligent either. It is rather a surprise that James should tell us, after she has been transferred to New York at the beginning of the fifth division, that she is "eminently good-natured." She certainly has an odd way of showing it, for not only is she wholly unadjusted to her surroundings but she takes no pains to conceal her unwillingness to make an effort for either her husband or his friends.

It would be an exaggeration to say that James treats his two principals quite impartially. Dr. Lemon is as pig-headed as you like about his refusal to make a "settlement" upon his bride because this is not the American way, but he yields at last, though perhaps almost as much because he cannot bear to have one of his plans fall through as because he loves the girl.

Nevertheless the fact remains that he does yield, and he yields again at the end, when his sister-in-law, Lady Agatha, who has become thoroughly and absurdly Americanized during her stay in New York, elopes with a Western adventurer, Herman Longstraw, a "mere moustache" and "a slightly mitigated cowboy." Lady Barb seizes the opportunity to return home to comfort her mother; her husband goes with her, and even at the end there seems no prospect that either of them will ever return to America. Jackson is now riding in the park every day with his wife and scanning the features of his little daughter "for the look of race—whether in hope or in fear today is more than my muse has revealed." He also now has the privilege of supporting Lady Agatha and her husband, but he is cut off from the practice of his profession, which troubles Lady Barb and her family not at all, for they had never regarded medicine as quite the thing for a gentleman, nor had Lady Barb been quite certain that she should not address everybody in America as "Doctor." She, it is clear, has never yielded in anything nor entertained any idea of doing so, and if there is anything in this story that is not quite convincing, it must be that we are never sure that she would have been capable of falling in love with Jackson in the first place. It may be added that "Mr. Longstraw's personality had immense success during the last London season"; he is very much the English idea of what an "American" is like; indeed, James himself had remarked when Lady Barb came over that "it is not in the least of American barbarism she was afraid; her dread had been all of American civilisation." No, decidedly, "Lady Barbarina" is not the place to look for evidence that James was "anti-American."

"The Author of Beltraffio" (*English Illustrated Magazine*, June-July 1884) is of course a far more significant story. When Edmund Gosse told James that Mrs. John Addington Symonds regarded her husband's writ-

ings as "immoral, pagan, hyper-aesthetic, etc.," James
immediately confided the tentative sketch of a tale to
his notebook, at the same time expressing his fear that
the situation indicated was "probably too gruesome—
the catastrophe too unnatural" for fiction.[3] Though the
piece is one of James's great stories about writers, it
does not deal with literature as such but rather with a
domestic crisis in a writer's life. The writer in question is
Mark Ambient, the author of *Beltraffio*, which his wife
has never read but which she considers, like all his
work, "most objectionable," as she does not hesitate to
tell the naive and at this point rather sycophantic
admirer who has come from America to see him and
who tells the story, in retrospect, after he has become
old and wise enough to be aware of his early mistakes.
Ambient and his wife are at swordpoints over their
exquisite seven-year-old son, Dolcino, whom both
adore and whom the wife makes enough of an effort to
keep away from his father—as if Ambient's very touch
were contamination—so that, as Ambient tells his
admirer, he fears they will kill the child between them.
Beatrice Ambient lives in such terror lest when Dolcino
grows up to read his father's books he will be corrupted
by them that when he contracts diphtheria, she deliberately withholds his medicine from him so that he may
die innocent.

   In one of the most penetrating studies of "The
Author of Beltraffio" that has been made,[4] Viola Hop-
kins Winner contends that "the fusion of the story
between the aesthetic idea and the moral, psychological conflict is imperfect" and that "the passages ex-
pounding [Ambient's] views on art seem imperfectly
associated with the action." Ms. Winner sees Ambient as
"a composite of Rossetti, Symonds, Pater, Flaubert,
and James himself"[5] and rightly dissociates him from
the extreme fin de siècle aesthetes. James, who despised Oscar Wilde, seems to have known about

Symonds's homosexuality, but he makes no use of it in his tale, in which he indeed goes out of his way to stress the decency and respectability of Ambient's private life. Yet he is perhaps not wholly without responsibility for the confusion that has arisen in this connection. Ambient holds off "from a direct profession of literary faith" even with the narrator, and he hopes in the future "to be truer than I've ever been," giving "the impression of life itself." He has always, he now thinks, "arranged things too much, always smoothed them down and rounded them off and tucked them in—done everything that life doesn't do," and he is trying to make his next book "a golden vessel, filled with the purest distillation of the actual." As he sees it, the difference between him and his wife is "the difference between Christian and Pagan," yet he dislikes the term "pagan" as "too sectarian" (as Ms. Winner says, he "does not represent 'Hellenism' pure and simple"). Mrs. Ambient's behavior seems more Philistine than Christian, but James's persistence in associating her beauty with such painters as Reynolds, Gainsborough, Lawrence, and Romney does not suggest Philistinism, and if she thinks, as her husband says, that "a work of art ought to have a 'purpose,' " there is a longer and more distinguished literary tradition behind that view than any the "art for art's sake" people have even been able to cite.

His mother's responsibility for Dolcino's death is undeniable, yet she is presented not as a monster but as a woman who, tragically divided between her emotions and her convictions, makes a terrible mistake that costs not only her son's life but ultimately her own. Moreover, an element of tragic irony is added to her fate by the fact that after the child is gone, she is even driven partially to revise her attitude toward her husband's work, so that before her death "she even dipped into the black 'Beltraffio.' "[6] It should not be forgotten, though it has seldom been taken into account, that since James

was nowhere more like Hawthorne than in his conviction that using human beings like things is the unpardonable sin, whether the husband or the wife was "right" is
not here the primary consideration; Mrs. Ambient has
sinned deeply in her attempt to monopolize her son
regardless of all such considerations.

A few critics have recently concerned themselves
with whether the other characters in any degree share
her responsibility, and Ambient seems to be the one
who comes off most lightly from this inquiry. Certainly
the narrator is involved.[7] He can hardly be blamed for
his youthful enthusiasm in crying up her husband's
work to Beatrice Ambient, but surely he oversteps the
privileges of hospitality when he sets out to convert her
to his view. ("So it shaped itself before me, the vision of
reconciling Mrs. Ambient with her husband, of putting
an end to their difference.") Certainly he did not know
that she would read the proof sheets of her husband's
work in progress, which he had pressed upon her, at the
bedside of her desperately sick child, yet the fact
remains that without this cruel juxtaposition, she might
never have made her terrible decision.

Strange as it may seem, Mark Ambient's eccentric
sister Gwendolen is a more doubtful quantity. As presented, she is virtually a caricature of the Pre-Raphaelite
lady (Pickering derives her from Jane Morris, whom
James had met), "a restless, romantic disappointed
spinster, consumed with the love of Michael-Angelesque
attitudes and mystical robes," and though the narrator
speaks of her "mysteries," there is no character in
James's fiction whose absurdities are more completely
set forth upon our first introduction to her. Indeed, the
teller of the tale even admits that he has a grudge against
her because "her affectations rubbed off on her brother's renown," so that those "who darkly disapproved of
him . . . could easily point to his sister as a person formed
by his influence," thus compromising him "with the

world at large." Yet as the story develops, Miss Ambient is certainly not a sinister figure, nor, whatever her affectations may be, does she seem wholly lacking in either humanity or insight.

James conceived "Pandora" (New York *Sun*, June 1, 8, 1884) as a kind of companion piece to "Daisy Miller" that would give him a chance to record his impressions of post-Civil War Washington, as seen especially from the salon of his friends Henry Adams and his ill-starred wife, Marian ("Clover") Hooper, who appear as the Bonnycastles. The tale, though written in the third person, is told largely from the point of view of Count Otto Vogelstein, a young diplomat of the new German Empire, just assigned to the German legation at Washington, "a highly upright young man, whose only fault was that his sense of comedy, or of the humor of things, had never been specifically disengaged from his several other senses." He first encounters Pandora Day on shipboard, where he happens to be reading "Daisy Miller," and he wonders at first whether she is the same kind of girl. She has a pair of "fat plain serious" burgherlike parents in tow (she had kept them three hours on the Acropolis, and she "guesses" they won't forget that), a dissipated nineteen-year-old brother who might be Randolph C. Miller grown up, and a little sister who could conceivably become another Daisy, and they all hail this time not from Schenectady but from Utica. But Pandora herself is older than Daisy and not so pretty, and she reads Renan and Sainte-Beuve in French, and turns to Alfred de Musset when she wishes to relax.

Count Otto does not encounter her again until his second year in Washington, when he finds her at the Bonnycastles' talking confidentially to the President, who had been invited only because the season was nearly over and the Bonnycastles wished to be vulgar and have a little fun.[8] Pandora and her family now live in New York City, and she exemplifies a new type, the "self-made girl," who has "crashed" society on her own without the support of family or background. "She [that is, both the individual and the type] was not fast, nor emancipated, nor crude, nor loud, and there wasn't in her . . . a grain of the stuff of which adventuresses are made. She was simply very successful, and her success was entirely personal." Her attitude toward her parents is in its way exemplary. She is devoted to them and speaks lovingly of them, but she has them completely under her control and keeps them for domestic consumption, which is the only thing she could do if she wished to live as she liked. Count Otto has nearly fallen in love with her when he learns that the "self-made girl" nearly always has somebody in her background to whom she is engaged. With Pandora it is D.F. Bellamy of Utica, who is considerably older than she is and to whom she has been bound since she was sixteen. It is in his behalf that she is canvassing the President when Count Otto meets her again at the Bonnycastles', though we do not learn this until the end of the tale, when Bellamy turns up with the ambassadorship to Holland in his pocket, and then we know that Pandora will probably control him, too. James had hoped to make this story "a little gem" if he tried hard enough,[9] and the result is a happy example of his lighter manner, but despite Pandora's obvious superiorities to Daisy Miller, and even with the circulation of the New York Sun to help her, the public never took her to its heart as it had taken that ourtageous, irresistible girl. Pandora was foreordained to success as clearly as Daisy was doomed, and in literature at least, success is comparatively dull. It is no accident that all the best Civil War romances glorify the "lost cause."

IV

The first of the New York Edition stories of the later eighties to see print was "Louisa Pallant" (*Harper's Magazine*, February 1888). Though not one of Jame's "difficult" stories, it is certainly one of the more enigmatic so far as the interpretation of the motives of the two female characters is concerned.[1] The action is simple. At Homburg, "nearly ten years ago," where he was waiting for his nephew Archie Parker so that he might "show" him Europe, the narrator reencountered the woman who in his youth had taken "back her given word" and broken "a fellow's heart for mere flesh-pots" by marrying a better-heeled man whom he considered greatly inferior to himself. Pallant had, after all, not left her very well off, and Louisa and her beautiful daughter Linda are now drifting about Europe, cultivating the art of living on very little a year and presumably keeping an eye open for a suitable husband for the girl.

Archie of course falls in love with Linda and she, to judge by appearances, with him. Amazed at his uncle's apparent willingness to accept the possible consequences, Mrs. Pallant warns her old admirer that Linda is "a bad hard girl—one who'd poison any good man's life!" as well as her own "punishment" and "stigma." In her daughter she sees herself as she was for years. "But she's worse . . . than I intended or dreamed."

> "There's not a tender spot in her whole composition. To arrive at a brilliant social position, if it were necessary, she would see me drown in this lake without lifting a finger, she would stand there and see it—she would push me in—and never feel a pang. That's my young lady!"

When the narrator fails to act on this warning, Mrs.

Pallant takes it upon herself to "save" Archie and send him packing by telling him "the terrible truth." This is her "reparation" or "expiation," and she declares that she does it not for the narrator but for herself.

But *does* she tell the truth, and if so, what is her real motive? Upon the answer to these questions the reader's whole understanding of both mother and daughter must rest. James does not give us all the materials we need to frame an authoritative answer; consequently, the best we can do is to sum up the considerations involved.

We have the narrator's word for it that he himself believes Mrs. Pallant to be sincere. If there is any story by James that contains what used to be called a "moral," it is stated here at the very beginning.

> Never say you know the last word about any human heart! I was once treated to a revelation which startled and touched me in the nature of a person with whom I had been acquainted—well, as I supposed—for years, whose character I had had good reasons, heaven knows, to appreciate and in regard to whom I flattered myself I had nothing more to learn.

But this is the narrator, not the author, and not the most perspicacious narrator *this* author ever created. Moreover, the narrator's own last words in the story certainly do not make the reader's task easier.

> My nephew has not even yet changed his state, my sister at last thinks it high time. I put before her as soon as I next saw her the incidents here recorded, and—such is the inconsequence of women—nothing can exceed her reprobation of Louisa Pallant.

The notebook entry[2] in which James records his initial idea for this story supports the view that the daughter "excels and surpasses" the mother in her degradation and that it is "some principle of goodness still left in her composition" that impels the latter to behave as she does. James adds too that Mrs. Pallant wishes to redeem herself in her old lover's eyes. But since the notebook entry does not correspond in all respects with the finished tale, this is not necessarily conclusive. In the notebook, for example, the narrator mistrusts the girl even before the mother has spoken; this survives in the story only in his uneasy feeling that she may be too much "a felicitous *final* product" to be quite real. When, after the tale had appeared in *Harper's Magazine*, a correspondent asked James what it was that Mrs. Pallant told Archie, he replied that he did not know what it was, nor whether it was true or false, though he did seem to commit himself that she thought her daughter "a monster of secret worldliness" and that she acted in "a fit of exaltation and penitence." She *might* have accused Linda of unchastity, and this accusation *could* conceivably have been true, but he thought it more likely that if Mrs. Pallant did say this, she lied.[3]

What it all comes down to finally is whether the reader feels more inclined to trust Mrs. Pallant or her daughter as he makes their acquaintance in the tale. The best argument in behalf of the girl is that the reader is permitted to see nothing in her that would justify her mother's charges; in all her behavior she seems a model of propriety. One is further inclined to disbelieve the mother because of her almost hysterical extremism; if she had been content to stop without describing her daughter as a monster, she might have been more convincing. On the other hand, we see much less of Linda than we do of her mother and consequently know less about her. According to Louisa, she and Linda understand each other so well that they have no need to confer with each other, but is she right about this? Certainly it would deepen Linda's infamy to be what her mother says she is and still behave as she does, but is it conceivable that at her age she could have been capable of such a feat? And if she really is so worldly as her mother claims, how can she seriously consider attaching herself to Archie Parker, who, after all, is no great catch?

Nevertheless it must be remembered that Mrs. Pallant is not only about as devious as they come but also very, very complicated. In life, surely, women of her general complexion have often manifested signs of repentance during their later years, but few of them have become less dangerous to themselves or others upon this account, and sometimes their behavior as penitents has been considerably worse than as sinners. Louisa Pallant may well have more than one motive for behaving as she does, may indeed have so many that she is not able to disentangle them all. It is too late in the day to atone for her own mistakes. Does she perhaps, consciously or unconsciously, put forth her daughter as a kind of scapegoat or sacrificial lamb in a form of vicarious atonement, and is this what Mrs. Parker felt when she indicated to her brother that nothing could "exceed her reprobation" of her?

"The Aspern Papers" (*Atlantic Monthly*, March-May, 1888) is generally rated very high among James's shorter works; Edel, for example, calls it "the most brilliant of all Henry's tales." A notebook entry of January 12, 1887, records the origin, relating how the Bostonian Captain Silsbee had learned that Byron's mistress, Mary Jane (or Claire) Clairmont lived on in Florence with her niece to a very advanced age. Because he believed she possessed important Byron and Shelley papers, Silsbee secured lodgings in Claire's house in the hope that she might soon die and that he might then gain possession of the materials. She did die, and the papers passed to her niece, but when Silsbee made overtures to her, she refused to turn them over to him unless he would marry her, a condition he refused to accept. As James recorded in his preface, the story interested him all the more because he realized that his own life had considerably overlapped Claire's and that he had "again and again all unknowing," passed "the door of her house, where she sat above, within call and in her habit as she lived."

He followed the general outline of the Silsbee story pretty closely, but he transferred the scene to Venice, thus achieving a more picturesque and richly historic setting and accenting his narrator-hero's quest to possess the past, and he made the Byronic figure one Jeffrey Aspern, a distinguished American poet. Claire became Juliana Bordereau and her niece Tita (changed to Tina in the New York Edition). Edel thinks Juliana was colored by an elder sister of his mother's grandmother whom James described in *A Small Boy and Others*, and Ora Segal finds the name Juliana recalling Donna Julia in Byron's *Don Juan*, while J. Gerald Kennedy, who thinks that, because Aspern was an American, James had Poe on his mind, believes that the picture of the old lady in her palazzo was derived from Thomas Wentworth Higginson's description of Poe's friend Sarah Helen Whitman during her declining years.[4]

Of the three important characters, "the divine Juliana" is the one of whom we see the least and who presents the fewest problems. The narrator calls her "a sarcastic profane cynical old woman," and we are told that "there hovered about her name a perfume of impenitent passion, an intimation that she had not been exactly as the respectable young person in general." She has hidden herself away from the world in the palazzo which she evidently rents for very little and which she never leaves. She is "very small and shrunken," and even when the narrator is allowed to converse with her, he does not really see her, for she hides her eyes under "a horrible green shade which served her almost as a mask," creating the "presumption of some ghastly death's-head lurking behind it" and turning her into "a grinning skull." There is no "property" anywhere in his work that James manages to make more sinister than that harmless shade. Juliana is as bored with life as was the aging Madame du Deffand, and, according to her niece, would like to die, if only for the change it would afford. "Besides all her friends had been dead for ages; either they ought to have remained or she ought to have gone." Even when the narrator sees her in bed, "the upper half of her face was covered by the fall of a piece of dingy lacelike muslin, a sort of extemporised hood which, wound round her head, descended to the end of her nose, leaving nothing visible but her white withered cheeks and puckered mouth, closed tightly and, as it were, consciously." The glorious orbs that Aspern had celebrated, the narrator is privileged to view only once, for a moment, at the very end. In a scene that would prove, if proof were needed, that James would have had no difficulty turning out Drury Lane melodramas, Juliana rises from her deathbed to catch him apparently attempting to rifle her desk, and "they glared at me; they were like the sudden drench, for a caught burglar, of a flood of gaslight; they made me horribly ashamed."

The passion Juliana herself reveals most clearly to the reader in the few scenes in which she appears is her hunger for money. She charges the narrator a thousand francs a month for lodging in her house and collects three months' rent in gold when he moves in; later she shows herself painfully anxious that he should prolong his stay and dangles Jeffrey Aspern's miniature before him without identifying it, outrageously pricing it at a thousand pounds. Juliana's avarice must be somewhat discounted, however, if we accept Tina's statement that she expects soon to die and is concerned for her niece's future. Everybody except Jacob Korg, who believes she has sentenced herself to voluntary imprisonment in lifelong penitence for her liaison with Aspern,[5] seems to believe that she cherishes his memory, and she herself asks the narrator whether he thinks it right to rake up the past. "The truth is God's; it isn't man's; we had better leave it alone."

The unnamed narrator is a more complicated character, even after one has sufficiently allowed for many commentators' having unnecessarily magnified the difficulties or manufactured them. He has been called a journalist, a publisher, an editor, and an antiquarian. What he actually is is a literary scholar; is it possible that the commentators do not even recognize their own profession?

There is of course a conflict, latent or actual, running far beyond the bounds of this story, between a human being's right to a reasonable privacy and the desire, even obligation, of the historian, the biographer, the scholar, or the critic to learn and make known the truth about the past, especially about those geniuses in whom the possibilities of human character and achievement have been most fully realized and explored, and our narrator is very emphatically caught up in this conflict.[6] He regards himself and his associate John Cumnor as cocustodians of the fame of Jeffrey Aspern, who now "hangs high in the heaven of our literature for all the world to see." But though the great poet has become "part of the light by which we walk," nobody else holds quite the "stock" in him that belongs to these two, and to that extent their investigations fail of being completely disinterested.

It is ridiculous to see the narrator, as one writer does, as seeking "a vicarious eroticism" in the Aspern papers and even more ridiculous to "thirst," with another, for his blood. He is no scandalmonger—what he admires and seeks fully to understand is Aspern's genius; if anything, he tends to judge the man's reported moral lapses too charitably. Even at the outset he admits that "hypocrisy" and "duplicity" furnish his "only chance" to get at the papers that both he and the scholarly world need. "There's no baseness," he says, "I wouldn't commit for Jeffrey Aspern's sake;" he even envisages "making love to the niece" as a possible part of his scheme. His worst moment is at the end when, believing Juliana to be asleep and probably on the verge of drifting into death, he confronts the desk in which he thinks the papers may be contained. Even then he declares that "it wasn't in my mind that I might proceed to thievery," but who can be sure that if he had found them there and Juliana had not discovered him and denounced him as a "publishing scoundrel" he would not have done so? In retrospect he regards this as "the worst thing I did"; yet, he adds, "there were extenuating circumstances." Many of the commentators do not allow much for extenuation. Thus Barbara Bell finds that the narrator fails "to arrive at any redeeming awareness of his own corruption," though Anna Salne Brylowski is more charitable when she declares that though he fails to understand either Tina or Juliana, his creator still invites the reader "to withhold judgment for the understanding of this fascinating man who loves the arts to the exclusion of human concerns."[7]

Disagreements concerning the narrator seem mild, however, compared to those about Tina. She is introduced to us as "a long lean pale person" of indeterminate age, "habited . . . in a dull-coloured dressing gown." "Her face was not young, but it was candid; it was not fresh, but it was clear. She had large eyes which were not bright, and a great deal of hair which was not dressed, and long fine hands which were—possibly—not clean," and she gives "an effect of irresponsible incompetent youth comically at variance with the faded facts of her person." All in all, one might say, she is quite the person whose "transparent honesty borders on downright stupidity" that Matthiessen and Murdock indicated in their edition of James's *Notebooks*.

At her first meeting with the narrator in the garden, she is "the oddest mixture of shyness and straightness." He gives her the first clue to the mystery of why he has sought lodging in her aunt's house by admitting that he reads Jeffrey Aspern. She admits her aunt knew him and asks, "Do you write about *him*—do you pry into his life?"

She says she has not told her aunt about this before Juliana next asks to see him, and it is on this occasion that Juliana suggests that he take "that girl" out in his gondola. When Tina admits that Juliana "has everything!" he rashly asks, "Couldn't you get them away from her?" to which she replies with another question: "And give them to you?" But she finally promises, "I'll do what I can to help you."

Later she tells him that the letters have been removed from the trunk in which they had been kept, and when he asks whether she would have given them to him if she had found them, she replies that she does not know what she would have done. After Juliana's death, she admits that she has the papers but seems torn between her desire to help the narrator and her obligation to her aunt. Finally, she in effect asks him to marry her by telling him that if he were a member of the family, it would be all right for him to see the papers. Feeling that it "wouldn't do" to "marry a ridiculous pathetic provincial old woman" for "a bundle of tattered papers," he first flees from Venice, but upon his return, he finds Tina so transfigured that he wonders for a moment whether he had made the right decision. "She stood in the middle of the room with a face of mildness bent upon me, and her look of forgiveness, of absolution, made her angelic. It beautified her; she was younger; she was not a ridiculous old woman." When, however, she tells him that she has "done the great thing" and "destroyed the papers" and that she shall not see him again and doesn't "want to," she becomes "a plain dingy elderly person" again, though there is "no resentment, nothing hard or vindictive" in her final look.

To Daniel J. Schneider, who plays down the sense of the past in this tale and sees its theme as "freedom versus enslavement," Tina is a helpness pawn between two antagonists. James W. Gargano also sees her as a "faded and feckless spinster" at the beginning but believes that in the course of the narrative she is transformed into "a woman rejuvenated by love and matured by a vision of necessity and renunciation." To James W. Crowley, on the other hand, she is "a clever manipulator" who is "far more resourceful and complex" than the narrator imagines and who is finally "enmeshed in the web of her own deceit." She feels intense resentment against Juliana and conspires against her to gain control of the papers. Sam S. Baskett also sees her as loyal to the narrator, not to Juliana.

It was left to William Bysshe Stein to go to the opposite extreme. To him Tina is "a feminine Christ, the means of redemption for the pathological curiosity of her friend," and when he rejects her, he rejects "emotional salvation" along with her. Kenneth Graham and Barbara Jensen-Osinski seem in essential agreement, though their statements are far less extravagant. Ms. Jensen-Osinski's observation that Tina has given the narrator the chance "to prove his humanity by joining the Venice family" to which she is the "key" seems vaguely reminiscent of the nineteenth-century Shakespeare criticism of Denton J. Snider, and Barbara Currier Bell adds heavy sexual overtones by describing Tina's destruction of the papers as an "act of symbolic emasculation." "The Jamesian extension [of the Eden story] is that, lacking a sense of sexuality, a person can never achieve a true sense of self," and Tina herself, like Eve, has achieved self-knowledge through temptation.[8]

Through all this cloud of sense and nonsense, how

much is clear? If we return to the text of the story itself, there seems no doubt that Juliana does seek to foster a relationship between Tina and the narrator as a means of providing for "the girl" when she should be gone. Surely so shrewd a person must have known from the beginning that the narrator would not, as he pretends, be willing to pay her a thousand francs a month merely to cultivate her garden in the sea. How much of this Tina understood is speculative, but Juliana's character and what we see of the relations between the two women do not suggest that the aunt ever really takes the niece into her confidence on this or any other matter, and in view of Juliana's own frustrated attempt first to hide and then to destroy the papers, she certainly does not intend that Tina should use them as a bribe.[9] My own belief is that Tina is strongly attracted to the narrator and suffers a painfully divided mind between her desire to satisfy him and her unwillingness to betray her aunt. Her offer to give him the papers if he will marry her is a pitiful attempt to reconcile her divided loyalties, and when she realizes that this idea revolts him, she destroys the papers and finds herself whole again. I emphatically reject the idea that her lack of resentment at the end exists only in the narrator's imagination.

The narrator *is* guilty of using Tina to help him gain possession of the papers, and he may well have made insufficient allowance for how a woman of her nature and in her situation would respond to a stranger, like him, who should treat her with decent civility, but he does not make love to her, and he sends her a fair price for the miniature she has given him, pretending that he has sold it for her. No man is under a moral obligation to marry everybody who may happen to fall in love with him, regardless of whether he responds or not, and anybody who believes that a marriage between a man like the narrator and a woman like Tina could possibly have been successful or satisfactory to either party is certainly an optimist. Anna Salne Brylowski is certainly correct when, despite her criticisms of the narrator, she gives him credit for being able to "restrain his monomania for Aspern's letters long enough to spare Tina another deception—a marriage on false pretenses."[10]

"The Liar" (*Century Magazine*, May-June 1888) presents no such problems as either "Louisa Pallant" or "The Aspern Papers." In his preface James ascribes its origin only to a chance dinner-table encounter with the original of the main character, but his notebook entry of June 18, 1884, cites Daudet's *Numa Roumestan*, and two scholars have now shown good reason to suppose that he might have been influenced by "The Prophetic Pictures" in Hawthorne's *Twice-Told Tales*.[11]

Colonel Capadose appears "a fine satisfied soul," and "wherever he rested his friendly eye there fell an influence as pleasant as the September sun—as if he could make grapes and pears and even human affection ripen by looking at them." He "doesn't steal nor cheat nor gamble nor drink; he's very kind—he sticks to his wife, is fond of his children." But he has a "monstrous foible." He "pulls the long bow—the longest that ever was." He "simply can't give you a straight answer." He makes up elaborate stories as he goes along, and it is not safe to believe anything he says.

Oliver Lyon, a gifted portrait painter and the central consciousness in the tale (though it is told in the third person), encounters Capadose at a great English house where Lyon has come to paint a portrait, as the husband of Everina Brant, "the proudest, most reserved of women" and still "the least spoiled beauty he had ever seen," whom, in a manner which recalls the narrator of "Louisa Pallant," Lyon had loved and lost in the long ago. At first the colonel seems a "platonic" or "disinterested," nonmalignant liar, with his romancing only an eccentric form of creativity that does nobody any harm. Yet Lyon is still appalled that Everina Brant could have loved such a man, and it made him "rather sick" to think what she "had done with herself." Granted that the colonel's lying is only a foible, does it cause her pain or has she, in some measure, been contaminated by him? 'Suppose it should someday bring him where he must "sacrifice some innocent person" to cover his tracks: "Could his wife be a party to that final atrocity?" Lyon feels that he must know.

He gets a better chance to resolve the problem than he could reasonably have hoped for. He paints the colonel's portrait, bringing out "the inner man," which Mrs. Capadose had assured him in advance was wholly noble, and the result is "a masterpiece of fine characterization, of recognizable treachery."[12] When Lyon is supposed to be away but is actually present unseen, the Capadoses get into his studio to view the unfinished work, and Mrs. Capadose is grief stricken and overwhelmed, the colonel himself being too dense to see anything except that Lyon has made him very handsome. But when his wife has opened his eyes, he returns to the studio by himself and slashes the canvas to bits.

The test comes later. The Capadoses admit having visited Lyon's studio to view the portrait, by which they both profess to have been altogether delighted, but when they propose to renew the sittings, Lyon tells them that the picture has been destroyed. Without hesitation, the colonel now proceeds to "sacrifice some innocent person," a drunken, superannuated model who had come into the studio one day while he was being painted; though he had never seen her before, he had proceeded to describe her interest in him and how she had been following him about, and he now avers that he had seen her lurking again the day he came to see the picture and blames himself bitterly for having gone away without taking proper precautions. Mrs. Capadose backs him to the hilt: "Truly her husband had trained her well." Lyon has his answer.

On the surface, "The Liar" tests Colonel Capadose and his wife and finds them both wanting; more subtly, it also tests Lyon himself. It is true that as the story stands, the painter's cruelty is severely limited. "He had exposed his friends to his own view, but without wish to expose them to others, and least of all to themselves," and he sends them both away at the end without having lost face. Yet his private probing is not wholly disinterested. He has a score to settle with Everina Brant, and though it would be an exaggeration to say that he wishes to make her suffer, he would relish some sign that she regrets him or recognizes his superiority to the man she has taken instead, and this means enough to him so that he accepts even the loss of the picture as part of the price he is willing to pay for what he has learned. But there remains one other question that cannot be definitely answered. It is quite clear that we are intended to regard the portrait as a great work of art. Suppose Colonel Capadose had not destroyed it. Would Lyon, as Mrs. Capadose believes, have sent it to the Academy? And if he had, would it not have revealed the moral nakedness of his subject to other perceptive persons quite as clearly as it did to Mrs. Capadose?

"A London Life" (*Scribner's Magazine*, June-September 1888), whose thirteen chapters fill more than 150 pages of the New York Edition, is not technically impressive. James himself points out in his preface that Lady Davenant's interview with Mr. Wendover is incompatible with his design of viewing the action from Laura's vantage point, but the hurried ending is equally unimpressive, even if we accept its inconclusiveness as part of his design. He was also aware that the international note is rather forced in this story. There was no necessity for viewing the corruptions of London society through the eyes of an *American* innocent. James did without this quite successfully in both *What Maisie Knew* and *The Awkward Age*, and whatever point he might have had in using this element here is somewhat blunted by making the corrupt Selina quite as American as the idealistic Laura.

The latter is a penniless American girl who lives in London upon the bounty of her sister and brother-in-law, Mr. and Mrs. Lionel Berrington, both of whom lead useless, disreputable lives and are engaged in degrading amours. Laura suffers intensely over the deterioration of the sister she has always loved and admired.

Returning from Paris after a clandestine excursion, Selina Berrington denies she has been there with her lover, Charley Crispin, but after Laura and her American escort, Mr. Wendover, surprised the pair in the Soane Museum, she confesses and hysterically promises amendment. Repentance, if not feigned, is short lived, however, and during a performance of *Les Huguenots* at Covent Garden, she "bolts," leaving Laura alone in a box with Wendover. Almost beside herself, the girl sounds out Wendover's attitude toward her, but he fails to rise to the occasion, and she leaves the theater alone, overwhelmed with shame.

Lady Davenant, Laura's aged, worldly friend, now tries to play the matchmaker, but Wendover can only say that he had no idea of offering marriage. Laura, now sick in both mind and body, forces Lionel to tell her where Selina and her lover have gone and follows them to Antwerp. From here she goes to America, and Wendover, awake at last, follows her. We are not told what happens between the sisters in Antwerp nor whether Wendover is finally successful in his suit.

This story was suggested to James by the French novelist Paul Bourget, who tried to explain the suicide of a French girl on the hypothesis (later rejected as fanciful) that, having been shamed by her mother's immoral life, she offered herself to a young man in the hope of his delivering her from her degrading surroundings and was crushed by his lack of response. James changed the basic situation because he did not believe he could depict "a woman carrying on adulteries under her daughter's eyes" in an American magazine. He rejected the suicide and added Lady Davenant, Selina's neglected, self-sufficient, rather insensitive children, and the scene at the opera house.[13]

The success of James's characterization of Selina is open to question. He himself felt that "on my page," she "doesn't in the least achieve character." Actually we do not get to know her well enough to be sure whether or not she is sincere in the scene in which she hysterically dissolves in tears and vainly promises to amend her ways. In itself this scene does not seem to harmonize with her callousness elsewhere, and though her "bolting" as she does at the opera gives James a brilliant scene, one can find it convincing only on the hypothesis that she is mean enough deliberately to humiliate her sister as much as possible, for she has had abundant opportunity to go off with her lover less spectacularly. Wendover is hardly more than a "nice" young man who needs to have everything explained to him. The dissipated, emotional Lionel Berrington, his children, and their melancholy governess are all satisfactory as far as they go. The unsentimental, rather cynical Lady Davenant, who has lived in the world too long to expect human beings to behave very well yet is penetrating enough to recognize merit when she sees it and sufficiently kindhearted to give herself some trouble to serve it, even if she must be considered a meddlesome old woman for her pains, is more thoroughly "done."

There is no real problem in "A London Life," however, except that connected with the heroine, and this is the child of the critics rather than the author. Ever since it became the fashion to interpret the governess of "The Turn of the Screw" in terms many of which would fail to carry conviction even in Fantasyland, all the rest of

James's seemingly "good" characters have fallen, one after another, under suspicion. A reader who should base his understanding of "A London Life" upon what some critics have written rather than on the story itself might very well come away with the impression that Selina, not Laura, was the character he was intended to admire. It is not Selina's adultery that causes problems in the Berrington household but merely the fact that her self-righteous, meddlesome sister could not take such things in her stride. Such interpretations may show a good deal about the critics and the age they live in, but they tell us nothing about either James or "A London Life."

For there is no character in his books—not even Isabel Archer, not even Fleda Vetch—to whom James commits himself more unreservedly than to Laura Wing, and this commitment is entered in his notebook and his preface as well as in the story itself. He tells us specifically that he placed both "A London Life" and "The Chaperon" in the New York Edition in the same volume with *The Spoils of Poynton* because all three heroines had "acuteness and intensity, reflexion and passion," and "a high lucidity" which gave their doings importance. Laura specifically was "designed to appear" as a "touching creature" and "a rare little person who would have been a rare little person anywhere." She was "a charming and decent young thing" thrust through no fault of her own into "a dreadful crisis." "A year ago she knew nothing, and now she knew pretty well everything." Evil had been thrust upon her in a "beautiful place, where everything spoke of peace and decency, of happy submission to immemorial law," and whoever, in James, may meddle in matters which are none of her concern, she does not. She never reproaches Selina until after reproach has become necessary to protect her from the exposure Lionel threatens, and even then she calls herself "a little presumptuous prig," and "her uppermost feeling" is shame, not for her sister but for herself. Much later she asks herself "Was she cruel by being too rigid?" "Of course I make you angry," she tells her sister, "but how can I see you rush to your ruin—to that of all of us—without holding on to you and dragging you back?"

Does this mean, then, that Laura always does the right thing in the right way? Nobody who knows *The Spoils of Poynton* and *The Portrait of a Lady* need ask that question. Fleda and Isabel and Laura and many more in James are "limited" heroines. They all *mean* to do the right thing but they make mistakes. James was not composing Wagnerian operas nor creating demi-gods. Unlike some of his readers, he did not find fallible human beings to fall outside the range of his sympa-thies, and he must have known that a young girl of Laura Wing's background and situation who would always function with perfect tact and wisdom must be more a phenomenon than a sympathetic human being. He put the voice of worldly wisdom into the story in the person of Lady Davenant. "Let her go," she advises Laura concerning her sister. Or "let her stay then! Only get out of the house." And when she hears that Selina has gone off with her lover, she adds, "Oh my dear, I dare say it will be very comfortable: I'm sorry to say anything in favour of such doings, but it very often is. Don't worry; you take her too hard." "We shouldn't feel more for people than they feel for themselves," she declares, which is the same principle enunciated by those who urge that we owe no duty to society that society will not accept. Undoubtedly this is prudence and common sense. It is also the formula for being comfortable in this world. But it does not make for either moral greatness or social progress.

"The Lesson of the Master" (*Universal Review*, July 15-August 16, 1888) is the earliest of James's stories about writers that really deals with writing as such, and though it is much shorter than "A London Life," it is a masterpiece of irony and ambiguity. The basic idea came out of a conversation with Theodore Child about marriage and the artist. It at once occurred to James, as he recorded in his notebook, that "a very interesting situation would be that of an elder artist or writer, who has been ruined (in his own sight) by his marriage" and who tries to save a younger writer in whose talent he deeply believes from making his mistake "by some act of bold interference—breaking off [the latter's] marriage, annihilating the wife, making trouble between the parties."[14]

In the story the elder artist is Henry St. George, whose work even the admiring young Paul Overt (the author of *Ginistrella*) realizes has fallen off sadly (qualitatively, not quantitatively) during recent years. To Overt, St. George confides that the cause of his decline is that he has gone whoring after false gods, "the idols of the market: money and luxury and 'the world'; placing one's children and dressing one's wife; everything that drives one to the short and easy way." The artist's only concern is with the absolute; the relative does not matter; and since the passion that possesses him is enough to subsume all others, he has no right to be deflected by other interests. Wives are even more dangerous when they think they sympathize and understand than when they do not. A writer who means to do something has no right to have a family. As for St. George himself, he is "a successful charlatan" whose life has become a "hell." Because he has had everything, he has missed everything. Specifically he advises Overt not to marry Marian Fancourt, a charming young girl with whom he has fallen in love and whom St. George also greatly admires. Though Marian seems highly appreciative of the work of both writers, the most St. George will give her credit for is that for about a year she might be an inspiration to his young friend. After that she would only be a millstone around his neck.

Overt takes the "lesson" to heart, goes abroad for

two years, and writes a book. During his absence Mrs. St. George dies, and when he returns to England, he finds the widower engaged to Marian. Naturally he feels betrayed, even tempted to regard St. George as a "mocking fiend," but the latter assures him of his complete sincerity. ("I wanted to save you, rare and precious as you are." "Are you marrying Miss Fancourt to save me?" "Not absolutely, but it adds to the pleasure. I shall be the making of you.") As for himself, he is past saving; he has, in fact, given up writing altogether.

Because James himself led very much the kind of life St. George advocates,[15] it is tempting to accept him uncritically as the author's spokesman, and many have succumbed to this temptation. But James was not an autobiographical writer, and even in his notebook entry about the tale he qualified carefully. The artist he envisaged had, he carefully stipulated, been ruined by marriage "in his own sight." What, then, was the "lesson" of the master? Did the master teach it or only illustrate it? Or did the disciple teach himself through his own experience? Could the "lesson" be that where the heart is concerned, it is not safe to accept advice from others, whether they are wholly disinterested or not?

Ambiguity extends into every phase and aspect of this story. St. George did not know that his wife was soon to die, but she *was* in poor health, and he was, clearly, greatly attracted by Marian Fancourt. On the other hand, there is no suggestion whatever that he planned infidelity or that Marian would have countenanced it if he had, and he could hardly have cold-bloodedly planned to keep the girl from Overt and all other possible suitors on the mere chance that he *might* sometime be free to marry her himself.

The women are ambiguous also. Mrs. St. George, pretty and still young looking, is "an important little woman" in an "aggressively Parisian dress," who declares that she never *made* her husband do anything except when she made him burn a bad book. Paul Overt immediately jumps to the conclusion that the lost work "would have been one of her husband's finest things," but we have no grounds on which we can decide either that he was right or that he was wrong. The working conditions she creates for her husband are of a simplicity so Spartan that it is hard to see how a celibate could have improved upon them, and St. George himself writes Overt after her death that "she took everything off my hands—off my mind. She carried on our life with the greatest art, the rarest devotion, and I was free, as few men can have been, to drive my pen, to shut myself up with my trade." What deleterious influence, then, did she, or did marriage, exert upon his production?[16]

Marian Fancourt is, on the surface, much more sympathetic than her predecessor, though she is notably less so at the end of the tale, as she looks forward to her marriage, than she had been when we first encountered her. There is no evidence that she possesses the first wife's superb organizing ability, and it seems unlikely that she will be better for St. George as a writer as distinct from a lover. One would expect him to be much less satisfied to be shut up in his windowless writing room after his marriage to her, but if he plans, as he says, to give up writing, how will this square with what we (and presumably she) have hitherto seen as her enthusiasm for literature? But here again we have no means to determine how much real understanding of such things she has. Her "aesthetic toggery" is as conventional in its way as the Parisian clothes of the first Mrs. St. George; is James really any more sympathetic to it here than in the case of Gwendolen Ambient in "The Author of Beltraffio"? Marian has spent most of her life in India with her general father. Is her enthusiasm for art of all kinds perhaps merely that of the eager young provincial, and could she perhaps be more interested in writers than she is in writing?[17]

In the very last paragraph of the tale, ambiguity

extends even to Paul Overt, a simple soul if James ever created one, and it produces another of·the author's famous "open" endings. Paul has now published the book he gave up Marian to write, and both she and her husband think it magnificent, but the narrative voice will commit itself only to the extent that "he's doing his best, but it's too soon to say." For that matter, it is even too soon to be sure that St. George's talent will never experience a resurrection. Paul fears this; he "doesn't even yet feel safe," does not think he should "be able to bear it." But the narrative voice adds that, should it occur, he "would really be the very first to appreciate it."[18]

The last story to be considered in this chapter, "The Patagonia," (*English Illustrated Magazine*, August-September 1888), is a simple, straightforward narrative that presents no technical or psychological problems and does not call for extended discussion. Its importance lies in the testimony it bears not to James's subtlety but to his humanity.

Fanny Kemble told James about a woman who sailed from India under the care of the captain of the vessel to rejoin her husband in England. During the voyage her fellow passengers were so "scandalized" by her shipboard flirtation with another man that she jumped overboard.[19] In James's tale the *Patagonia* sails from Boston to Liverpool, and Grace Mavis, a girl from the "nebulous region" of Merrimac Avenue in the South End, travels in the supposed care of Mrs. Nettlepoint of Beacon Street to be married to Mr. Porterfield, to whom she has been engaged since she was eighteen. Mrs. Nettlepoint's son Jasper, who looks intelligent "but also slightly brutal" and who is actually "selfish beyond the limits" and "of the type of those whom other people worry about, not of those who worry about other people" is also on board. The gossip about him and Grace emanates primarily from "a certain little Mrs. Peck, a very short and very round person whose head was enveloped in a . . . cloud of dirty white wool," who seems to have spent most of her time on Merrimac Avenue observing Grace there and whose habitual dislike of her has now been exacerbated by the girl's failure to speak to her. The suicide is, if anything, over-elaborately prepared for, and the story is told in the first person by a male narrator, a somewhat younger friend of Mrs. Nettlepoint.

In the first of the four chapters of "The Patagonia" James achieves an impressive (and oppressive) picture of Beacon Street and its environs on a sweltering August night; the other three cover what happens on shipboard. Mrs. Peck's portrait is etched in venom; she and her friend Mrs. Gotch would be well cast at the head of a coven; the women who snub Daisy Miller in Rome are angels of compassion in comparison. Jasper too seems without a single redeeming quality; he is inconsiderate of his mother, insolent toward the narrator, and completely conscienceless in the way he brings Grace Mavis, for whom he cares nothing, into a compromising position. His mother's is a more mixed character. Grace had been thrust upon her when the girl's pushing mother appeared with an introduction from one of Mrs. Nettlepoint's friends. She does not really like her, and though she wishes her no harm, she is not willing to take any serious trouble to protect her from a son she must certainly know well enough to be sure that nobody could lead him where he did not wish to go. As the narrator tells her, she shows "a fine sense of maternal immorality."

It is all the more of a triumph for James that he should be able to make Grace hold the reader's sympathy as she does in spite not only of her reckless behavior but also of her complete lack of Daisy Miller's charm. No longer in her first youth, she has not seen Mr. Porterfield since he left her to go to Europe and embark upon what must be the longest stretch of architectural studies on record. At long last she is going out to marry him because his mother, who will live with them, has now "come out" and has a little money, but she does not really love him, or perhaps one should say that she does not know whether she loves him or not. If she had not had the bad luck to encounter the flashy Beacon Street flirt on shipboard and to be, momentarily at least, taken in by him, she would surely have gone through with her marriage, which might have turned out as satisfactorily as most marriages do, but the emotional upset she suffers and the consciousness that the whole ship is gossiping about her are more than she could bear. And so it is that she becomes "the admirable little dismal subject" that James scented as soon as Fanny Kemble told him her story.

V

James's novels during the 1890s were five in number: *The Tragic Muse* (1890), *The Other House* (1896), *The Spoils of Poynton* and *What Maisie Knew* (both 1897), and *The Awkward Age* (1899). His tales during the same period numbered thirty-two, of which he thought well enough of twenty-one to include them in the New York Edition. This chapter will deal with the nine of these that first appeared in 1891 and 1892: "The Pupil," "Brooksmith," "The Marriages," "The Chaperon," "Sir Edmund Orme," "The Private Life," "The Real Thing," "Greville Fane," and "Owen Wingrave." For the six stories of these years not reprinted in the New York Edition—"Nona Vincent," "Lord Beaupré," "The Visits," "Sir Dominick Ferrand," "Collaboration," and "The Wheel of Time"—the reader must consult Appendix A.

"The Pupil" (*Longman's Magazine*, March-April 1891), the first tale published in 1891, is one of James's best. In his preface he cites only one source, the story told him by Dr. William Wilberforce Baldwin, an American physician resident in Florence, "one summer day, in a very hot Italian railway-carriage," about "a wonderful American family, an odd, adventurous, extravagant band, of high but rather unauthenticated pretensions, the most interesting member of which was a small boy, acute and precocious, afflicted with a heart of weak action, but beautifully intelligent, who saw their prowling precarious life exactly as it was, and measured and judged it, and measured and judged them all round, ever so quaintly presenting himself in short as an extraordinary little person."[1] The history of the tale that resulted involved a dismaying episode in James's career, the only rejection he had ever had from an editor of *The Atlantic Monthly*. The functionary involved was Horace E. Scudder, whose motives are unknown. Though James behaved with perfect dignity as always, he did not pass up the opportunity to instruct the newly installed editor how to conduct himself in dealing with authors of established reputation.[2]

The story is written in the third person, mainly from the retrospective point of view of the tutor Pemberton, and, as James himself says, we see the characters only in "little Morgan's troubled vision of them as reflected in the vision, also troubled enough, of his devoted friend." Mrs. Shine puts it a little differently when she writes that "Morgan's perceptions are, as it were, filtered through the consciousness of Pemberton, who is, in turn, affected by them," and adds, perceptively, that Morgan is not "a 'realistically' rendered child" but "an essence, the embodiment of an aware and troubled conscience pitted against the blind, corrupt cynicism of parental dereliction."[3]

The Moreens[4] are a somewhat sleazier version of the Brookenhams in *The Awkward Age*. They are "Bohemians who wanted tremendously to be Philistines" and "adventurers not merely because they didn't pay their debts" and "lived on society, but because their whole view of life . . . was speculative and rapacious and mean." As their son perceives, "all they care about is to make an appearance and to pass for something or other," and he cannot understand "who had poisoned their blood with the fifth-rate social ideal, the fixed idea of making smart acquaintances and getting into the *mode chic*, especially when it was foredoomed to failure and exposure?" They "lived on maccaroni and coffee," "overflowed with music and song," have a villa in Nice when they can afford it and live in cheap lodgings in Paris and elsewhere when they cannot and communicate with one another in a private family language Morgan, "who can chatter in colloquial Latin as if he

had been a little prelate," calls "Ultramoreen" and dis-
dains to use. James did not believe he had really "done"
the Moreens, and though Mrs. Moreen is vivid enough,
this is certainly true of the others. We never learn what
Mr. Moreen does nor anything about him save that he is
always "a man of the world" and wears the ribbon of a
never identified foreign order, and the older son, Ulick,
and the two girls, Amy and Paula, for whom their
parents are forever trying and failing to find husbands,
are little more than names. As for Mrs. Moreen, with
whom Pemberton accuses himself of "a fantastic, a
demoralized sympathy," her "elegance was intermit-
tent and her parts didn't always match." She "did
nothing that didn't show," and, like the rest of the family, she "adored Morgan" but does nothing for him and
is eager to shift her responsibility for him to somebody
else. All in all, Pemberton "had never seen a family so
brilliantly equipped for failure." Morgan is, of course,
in the biological sense, a "freak," the one finely bred,
sensitive, honorable person in a family of "dead beats,"
shabby, "scrappy and surprising, deficient in many
properties supposed common to the *genus* and abound-
ing in others that were the portion only of the supernat-
urally clever." He is eleven or twelve when we meet
him and apparently fifteen when he dies.[5]

Pemberton too is an American, Yale- and Oxford-
trained, who has run through his small patrimony and
depends for his livelihood upon what he can earn by
tutoring or some kindred pursuit. This does not work
very well when he comes to the Moreens, who instead
of paying him try to borrow from him, cannily exploit-
ing Morgan's charm and worth to hold him. This
scheme had worked for two years with the nurse Morgan remembers as Zénobie, and when they have got
beyond being polite to each other, Pemberton describes it to Mrs. Moreen as "a kind of organized
blackmail." When he finally breaks away to go to Eng-

land to coach an "opulent" and stupid youth, she lures him back with the plea that the boy is "dreadfully ill."

In days gone by, some readers were given to sniffing out homosexuality in the relations between Pemberton and his charge;[6] this nonsense seems now to have been abandoned, the favorite form subtlety has taken these latter days being to make Pemberton responsible for Morgan's death; in a small way, he has been treated much like the governess in "The Turn of the Screw."[7]

The situation at the end of the story does resemble (though it also differs from) that at the close of "The Turn of the Screw," where Miles dies in the arms of the governess. The possibility of Pemberton and Morgan going off alone together had been mentioned before, and Morgan had made it clear that nothing could please him more. Now, suddenly and without warning, when the two return from a walk, they find that "the storm had come"; facing "public exposure," the Moreens can no longer bluff it out, and they ask Pemberton to do what Morgan had never expected to hear from them— to take their child. The boy's "sense of shame for their common humiliated state" drops at once, and he experiences "a moment of boyish joy." His "rush of gratitude and affection" almost frightens Pemberton, who is himself conscious of the lack of enthusiasm in his "stammered" response: "My dear fellow, what do you say to *that?*" But the child at once "turned quite livid and . . . raised his hand to his left side," and after that nobody's enthusiasm or lack of it could very much matter.

That is all the evidence James gives us as to what killed Morgan Moreen. He had a defective heart; without that, neither the proved shame and neglect of his parents nor Pemberton's hesitation could have done him in. Obviously he is being subjected to a cruel strain, and obviously he and Pemberton are being confronted with a fresh situation that demands considerable readjustment from both. Obviously too the fact that

Pemberton does not have a weak heart does not mean
that he is in a comfortable situation. Could any young
man without resources have been ready instantly to
assume the responsibility for a fifteen-year-old boy
without even a moment for consideration? Could Pemberton's critics have done it? It is an absurd exaggeration to say, as has been said, that Pemberton rejects
Morgan. The most we can say is that, for a split second,
which is all he has, he gropes. His behavior is not heroic,
but the basic difficulty, so far as it involves him at all, is
merely that he is not quick enough to be able to adjust
himself instantaneously to an unanticipated situation.[8]

"Brooksmith" (*Harper's Weekly* and *Black and
White*, May 2, 1891) was originally intended to be called
"The Servant"; it is the only story James ever wrote in
which the central character is such a functionary. The
tale is told as held in memory by a member of Mr.
Offord's circle, and it was suggested by an anecdote
related to James of a lady's maid who had been
deprived in Brooksmith's fashion. He changed the sex
of the protagonist because

> I desired for my poor lost spirit the measured maximum
> of the fatal experience: the thing became, in a word, to
> my imagination, the obscure tragedy of the "intelligent"
> butler present at rare table-talk, rather than that of the
> more effaced tirewoman; with which of course was
> involved a corresponding change from mistress to
> master.

Mr. Offord, "a retired diplomat" and "the most
agreeable, the most attaching of bachelors," has
accomplished a miracle by setting up a salon without
feminine help. There his friends gather, and Brooksmith, who looks after everything, is the artist who
produces the show. Silently and unobtrusively he
drinks in the good talk ("Quite an education, sir, isn't it,
sir?"); though he is outside the circle, nobody is more

completely "in it" than he. This is all very well while it lasts, but the time comes when Mr. Offord is gathered to his fathers and Brooksmith is left adrift. Offord leaves him a pitifully inadequate legacy, but he "couldn't provide society, and society had become a necessity of Brooksmith's nature." He secures other places, but he can no better function there than a fish that had been taken out of its element. Finally he is reduced to going out on "call" to "wait" on special assignments, and at last he disappears; we never learn what had become of him. He is as pitiful a figure as Melville's Bartleby.

"Brooksmith" has been described as a character sketch or essay of the kind that Lamb or Stevenson or Sir Max Beerbohm might have written.[9] It is one of James's simplest and briefest tales, and it is rather surprising that so depressing a piece should have such charm. This it owes not to any psychological or technical subtleties but rather to the humanity and understanding by which it is informed.

There are character problems and to spare, on the other hand, in "The Marriages" (*Atlantic Monthly*, August 1891), in which Adela Chart attempts to prevent her father from marrying an unsuitable woman by telling her that he had been a brutal and impossible husband to his first wife, whose memory her daughter adores (we are not told what the communication consisted of until later). Mrs. Churchley cancels the engagement, but Adela's conscience troubles her so much that she goes to her later and confesses her fault, only to learn that the woman knew all along that she was lying and broke off because she would not consent to live in the same house with such a girl as Adela had shown herself to be. Colonel Chart had refused to accept her terms; in the last analysis, his loyalty was given to his daughter, not his fiancée. There is a subplot involving a disastrous marriage that had been contracted by Adela's brother Godfrey.[10]

Adela gives the critics a capital chance to divide. Obviously she is one of the meddlers in other people's lives that James generally condemns, but Mrs. Churchley is a dreadful person, "public and florid, promiscuous and mannish," as "undomestic as a shopfront and as out of tune as a parrot." Colonel Chart's marriage to her would have been a disaster for him as well as his daughter. Nevertheless not all readers will believe that, being what she is, Adela would have lied as she does, especially since the lie blackens her father's name. Dale and Chris Kramer judge her extravagantly as "a suitable feminine counterpart for John Marcher in 'The Beast in the Jungle' "; Pelham Edgar, on the other hand, compares her loyalty to her mother to Stransom's fidelity to his lost love in "The Altar of the Dead."[11] It is interesting that as the tale was first conceived,[12] the father was to have had second thoughts about the marriage and act in collaboration with his daughter to call it off. At this point James had not made up his mind what the girl was to tell the fiancée, who would draw back because she suspected her lover had been a party to an untruth. When James came to write *The Golden Bowl* he was inclined to regret that he had used up the title "The Marriages" on a short story.

Though "The Chaperon" (*Atlantic Monthly*, November-December 1891) has an affinity with "The Siege of London," its tone is, if anything, more disillusioned. Mrs. Tramore, the "fallen" woman her daughter mounts a campaign to get back into society, "had never appreciated anything" and was "nothing but a tinted and stippled surface"; "the desire to 'go out' was the one passion" the girl had ever been able to find in her. Fifteen years ago she had eloped with a man who was killed before he had a chance to marry her from a husband "who was somehow perverse and disconcerting without detriment to his amiability" and as "charming and vague" as "a clever actor who often didn't come to rehearsal." Now, after her father's death and against his wishes, as expressed in his will, and the disapproval of all her paternal relatives, Rose, the daughter, has gone to live with her mother and take her in hand.

The first four chapters of "The Chaperon" are preliminary; all the action, which follows after a time interval of "lonely months," occurs in the longer Chapter V. During the interval Rose has steadily refused all invitations addressed to herself alone, and she finally wins her fight, partly because society begins to be amused by the comedy involved in "the reversed positions of Mrs. Charles and Mrs. Charles's diplomatic daughter" and partly because of the help she gets from a suitor she has never shown any interest in before, Captain Bertram Jay, who takes "a public interest in the spiritual life of the army" and carries "a sword in one hand and a Bible in the other," with "a Court Guide concealed somewhere about his person," and whom Rose finally marries, perhaps out of gratitude.

The interest of "The Chaperon" is limited by the pettiness of the issues involved, to say nothing of the fact that the person in whose behalf the battle is waged is hardly worth contending for. James cannot be accused of being unaware of this, however, for he leaves Rose and her mother in society, "engaged for a fixed hour, like the American imitator and the Peruvian contralto." As he originally conceived of the tale, which, like so many, had its origin in an oral anecdote, it was to end on the wistful note of the mother being unhappy because her son-in-law does not seem to like her or approve of her, to which her daughter could only reply, "No, mamma, I'm afraid I can't do that too."[13] James's failure to use this, however, keeps the interest firmly centered upon Rose, whose pluck and loyalty are all we can admire in this story. Mrs. Tramore indeed "has now so many places to go that she has almost no time to come to her daughter's."[14]

"Sir Edmund Orme" (*Black and White*, November 25, 1891) was the earliest of James's ghost stories to strike his characteristic note in this field. He himself wrote in his preface to Volume XVII of the New York Edition that he felt himself to show ghosts best "by showing almost exclusively the way they are felt, by recognizing as their main interest, some impression strongly made by them and intensely received." Clanking chains and gibbering in the casement window were not for him, and Sir Edmund Orme manifests with extreme delicacy, in broad daylight, at church or a public assembly, in "the old, the mid-Victorian, the Thackerayan Brighton, where the twinkling sea and the breezy air, the great friendly, fluttered, animated, many-coloured 'front,' would emphasize the note I wanted, that of the strange and sinister, embroidered on the very type of the normal and easy."

Sir Edmund, a jilted lover of Mrs. Marden's, had killed himself in despair and now haunts her for her punishment, "a splendid presence," faultlessly dressed and of perfect bearing, "never when I'm by myself—only with her"—that is, her daughter Charlotte. Charlotte never sees him, though her mother, who is terrified when the girl is accused of having a touch of the coquette, is desperately afraid she may, and neither does anybody else except the narrator. Mrs. Marden asks him whether he loves Charlotte before he has realized that he does, because she believes that the girl's danger and potential salvation are both bound up with her loving; as Martha Banta has expressed it, the idea seems to be that the ghost "can only be exorcised by the young man who loves truly and by the girl's capacity to love him in return."[15] Charlotte never does see Sir Edmund except, it seems, at the very end, as she "got up to give me her hand" in the moment of her mother's death, and "that was mercifully the last of Sir Edmund Orme."

In his preface James professed to remember "absolutely nothing" concerning the origin of the story, but
there is a notebook entry which, without citing any
source, records the basic idea. Here a girl is followed by
the figure of a young man whom she does not see,
though others do, "and there is a theory that the day she
falls in love, she may suddenly perceive him." She does,
and having accepted her lover she never sees the ghost
again, but her husband never learns that her mother had
been involved until after that lady's death he finds the
evidence in her papers.[16]

In occult lore, ghosts can appear to the person or
persons to whom they are commissioned, or to whom
they bear a message, or who are *en rapport* with them,
while remaining invisible to others. There is therefore
no problem about the ghost's behavior during the earlier portion of the tale. It seems clear too that he wishes
to protect the lover from what he himself had suffered.
Why Charlotte should see him at the end is more speculative. Walter F. Wright seems to be the critic who has
attempted the most definite answer. If Charlotte saw
Sir Edmund, says Wright, he "convicted her of coque-
try and so shocked her into penitence that she is never
guilty of it again. But she never confesses, and her
future husband never asks her." This may be correct,
but it goes beyond the range of the story. Actually
neither party had much time either to ask or answer
questions, for we are told in the brief note preceding the
document which makes up the story that the narrator's
wife died in childbirth only a year after her marriage,
and to this the introducer must even add that he is not
sure the paper is either autobiographical or factual.

"The Private Life"(*Atlantic Monthly*, April 1892) is a
fantasy rather than a genuine tale of the supernatural.
Robert Browning during his later years was

> the accomplished, saturated, sane, sound man of the
> London world and the world of "culture," of whom it is

impossible not to believe that he had arrived somehow, for his own deep purposes, at the enjoyment of a double identity. It was not easy to meet him and know him without some resort to the supposition that he had literally mastered the secret of dividing the personal consciousness into a pair of independent compartments. The man of the world—the man who was good enough for the world, such as it was—walked abroad, showed himself, talked, right resonantly, abounded, multiplied the contacts and did his duty; the man of "Dramatic Lyrics," of "Men and Women," of the "Ring and the Book," of "A Blot on the Scutcheon," of "Pippa Passes," of "Colombe's Birthday," of everything, more or less, of the order of these,—this inscrutable personage sat at home and knew as well as he might in what quarters of *that* sphere to look for suitable company. The poet and the "member of society" were, in a word, dissociated in him as they can rarely elsewhere have been . . . .[17]

This is exactly what "The Private Life" postulates of the great Clare Vawdrey, who sits in his room at the Swiss resort where the tale is staged and works in the dark on the play he has promised to a fellow sojourner, the great actress Blanche Adney, while his commonplace social self is quite otherwise engaged. Like Browning, Vawdrey has magnificent health and "never talked about himself" nor is "anything but loud and liberal and cheerful." but, by the same token, he never utters a paradox or expresses "a shade or play[s] with an idea." All "his opinions were sound and second-rate, of his perceptions it was too mystifying to think."

With the characteristic passion for balance, contrast, and parallelism that often served and sometimes overcame him, James conceived the idea of placing over against Vawdrey the "extraordinarily first" Lord Mellifont, who is "almost as much a man of the world as the head-waiter and spoke almost as many languages." His reputation was "a kind of gilded obelisk, as if he had

been buried beneath it," and his is "the opposite complaint from Vawdrey's." Mellifont is "all public and had
no corresponding private life." He "represented" even
to his wife and is a hero to his servants, but "what one
wanted to arrive at was really what became of him
when no eye could see." What becomes of him as the
tale unfolds is that he just isn't under such conditions. All
of him functions centrifugally. He lives only in public
and social relations. "He's there from the moment he
knows somebody else is."[18]

There is no plot to speak of in "The Private Life,"
nor is there anything that requires elucidation. The
unnamed narrator, whose confidante is the actress,
devotes himself almost as assiduously, though much
more briefly, to probing the double mystery that confronts him as the central figure in *The Sacred Fount*
does to solving the more emotionally charged problems
with which he has to deal. One step in the wrong direction, at any point in its development, would have ruined
"The Private Life," but James's hand never falters, and
the tone is just right.

In his famous essay "The Art of Fiction" in his
Partial Portraits, James wrote that the writer needs "the
power to guess the unseen from the seen, to trace the
implications of things, to judge the whole piece by the
pattern." In the story called "The Real Thing" (*Black
and White*, April 16, 1892), except that here his immediate concern is with not a writer but a painter, James
illustrates what he meant. This tale makes clear what
kind of realism he believed in and illuminates his conception of the difference between copyist and creator.

In spite of its simplicity, a considerable critical
to-do has been kicked up about the little fable, with
some writers insisting upon invoking philosophical
considerations than which nothing can have been
farther from James's mind.[19] Perhaps a very simple
illustration may make this point clearer.

Every teacher of creative writing has probably had the experience of telling a student that a story he had submitted carried general conviction, with the exception of one particular unbelievable incident, only to have the student reply, "Oh, that is the one thing in the story that really happened!" With which the instructor is supposed to be crushed.

But he is not, not if he knows his business. On the contrary he knows it was precisely *because* the incident *did* happen that it is unconvincing on the printed page. It has not been created; it has only been reported. Because it possesses actuality (which is a very different thing from truth), the writer has not thought it necessary to pass it through the alembic of imagination. It has ended up as something that is neither fact nor fiction but something in between, hopelessly out of tune with the imagined or created portion of the tale and therefore failing to carry conviction. For art is not life but the distilled essence of life.

George du Maurier told James of an impoverished army officer and his wife who had been sent to him as possible models by W.P. Frith. This is precisely the plight of Major and Mrs. Monarch in "The Real Thing." "It was very odd to see such people apply for such poor pay. She looked as if she had ten thousand a year," and when she and her husband first entered his studio, the artist supposed they had come to order their portraits painted. He likes them and sympathizes with them, and since he is just starting on a series of illustrations for a novel that deals with quite the kind of people they are, who knows but they might come as an answer to prayer? He tries, tries hard enough to bring himself within hailing distance of losing his commission. The Monarchs are "the real thing," but they cannot grasp or project an idea. They have no imagination and no pictorial sense. "They are only clean and stiff and stupid." In the end he replaces them with a freckled cockney,

Miss Churm, and an Italian, Oronte, who cannot speak English, both of whom have "a curious and inexplicable talent for imitation" and can represent what they are not but what the artist wants them to be. It is another case of "the baffled, ineffectual" incompetence of "the everlasting English amateurishness" as against "trained, competitive, intelligent, *qualified* art."[20]

When James found the germ of a story in an anecdote, he never wanted to hear the details; these he had to work out for himself if his picture was to have life. The trouble with the Monarchs as models, says Harold T. McCarthy, is that they leave no room "for the operation of imagination, of the artist's personal sense of things." And Seymour Lainoff adds that the realism of the painter in the story and, by implication, James's own "can be defined as giving the *shape of reality* or the air of reality to that which may not be real."[21] The only question "The Real Thing" leaves unanswered is whether James does not, in this instance, place a heavier responsibility on the imagination of the model than upon the artist himself, and this is a question on which probably only a professional painter's opinion could have much value.

Like "Brooksmith," "Greville Fane" (*Illustrated London News*, September 17, 24, 1892) takes the form of a memoir, and, again like "Brooksmith," it bears testimony to the breadth of James's sympathies, for its protagonist is the last person one might expect so fastidious an artist to sympathize with. Mrs. Storer (Greville Fane) is one of those cheap, prolific lady novelists of whom there has never been any shortage in Britain who "could invent stories by the yard, but couldn't write a page of English." She is "a dull kind of woman" in her private life, but her memoirist likes her because she rests him from literature. She turns out three novels a year and scorns all talk of "difficulty" in connection with writing, and though she thinks she resembled Balzac, her approach to fiction is much more like Ouida's. "Passion in high life was the general formula" of her work. "She was very brave and healthy and cheerful, very abundant and innocent and wicked. She was expert and vulgar and snobbish."

Early widowed, she is no wiser as a mother than as a writer, but there are no limits to her devotion to her worthless children, and in the years of her declining vogue, she practically writes herself to death for them. Believing that a human being can be apprenticed to the novelistic as to any other trade,[22] she wants her son Leolin to "see life" with a view to accumulating material and educates her daughter Ethel expensively to occupy a great position in the world. Ethel marries "a joyless jokeless young man" named Sir Baldwin Luard and becomes Lady Luard (Mrs. Storer had to write three novels to cover the expense of the wedding). The daughter does not attempt to conceal her contempt for Greville Fane, but neither is she averse to having "the inky fingers . . . press an occasional banknote into her palm." For Leolin "seeing life" means primarily acquiring vices and sponging on his mother, but though he takes to cigarettes at the age of ten, he never rises to the liaison with a titled lady that his mother regarded as elegant. He goes through one period of foraging materials for her novels and another of pondering thoughts of his own too deep for expression, but the closest he comes to producing a book is to take counsel with the narrator as to just how "far" in England it might be possible for a writer of fiction to go.

James himself regarded "Greville Fane" as a "developmental" subject presented in "anecdotal form" and "a minor miracle of foreshortening." As Krishna Baldev Vaid has finely observed, he achieves concentration through making virtually the whole story (if it can be called that) a "summary and report" and "a brief critical-biographical essay" that "accomplishes the dif-

ficult task of creating sympathy for an absurd character" in whom the limitations of the bad novelist are
"subtly intertwined" with those of "the deluded mother,"
at the same time achieving "fictional tension" through
"the contrast between the narrator and Greville."[23] In
the preface to the volume of the New York Edition that
includes this tale, the writer who created that narrator in
his own image declares: "had I believed the right effect
missed 'Greville Fane' wouldn't have figured here." His
self-confidence is abundantly justified. The story is
such a trifle as only one of the elect among the masters
could have created.

Like "Sir Edmund Orme," "Owen Wingrave"
(*Atlantic Monthly*, April 1892), the last 1892 tale, is a
ghost story, but it differs from its predecessor in that
instead of being the motivating force, the supernatural
element enters strongly only at the end to resolve the
situation, and since the hero is a conscientious objector
to war, the reader of today is more likely to concentrate
upon this aspect than on the ghost.

When he wrote his preface to Volume XVII of the
New York Edition, James apparently did not remember
anything about the origin of "Owen Wingrave" except
"the suddenly determined absolute of perception" that
occurred one summer afternoon when he was resting in
a penny chair under a tree in Kensington Gardens and "a
tall quiet slim studious young man, of admirable type"
came along and settled himself with a book in a neigh-
boring seat, and the story was there. His notebooks
make it clear, however, that the first suggestion actually
came from the memoirs of one of Napoleon's generals,
Marcellin de Marbot, in the form of the basic idea of the
soldier and the conflict that must occur if the scion of a
military family rejects his destined career. At first the
author thought the scene should be "distanced, rele-
gated into some picturesque little past," perhaps set in a
haunted old country house at the time of the Napoleon-

ic wars. The haunted house survived, as did the girl who was to complicate the hero's problem by "despising him for his renunciation," and his death on his private battlefield, "the haunted room in which the ghost of some grim grandfather . . . is supposed to make himself visible," but the historical setting was dropped, and the scene became English contemporary.[24]

In the finished story, however, the ghost is that of a great-great grandfather, whose terrible portrait over the stairs at Paramore (it "fairly stirs on the canvas, just heaves a little, when I come near it") Owen hates to pass. His living grandfather in the house is quite ferocious enough, as is too his grim, fire-eating Aunt Jane. Both make it clear to him that if he perseveres in his course, he will be rejected as something too low to be spoken of and will inherit nothing they can keep from him. His own father "had received his death-cut, in close quarters, from an Afghan sabre," and since his elder brother is an institutionalized imbecile, he has been until now the hope of the family. The great-great grandfather lived in George II's time. He had killed one of his children by an unhappy blow on the head struck in a moment of passion, and although the matter had been hushed up, he was found one morning, "without a wound, without a mark," dead from unexplained causes, in the room from which his child had been carried to the grave. Nobody had slept in it since.

Owen first announces his decision to his coach, Stephen Coyle, who, appalled though he is, is much too sympathetic by nature to abuse him and far too intelligent to think him a coward, while Mrs. Coyle simply "threw off the mask, and commended with extravagance the stand his pupil had taken." Both are summoned to Paramore, along with Owen's friend Lechmere, another prospective young soldier, who is supposed to convince him that he has made a mistake, and all are present at the end. What is at issue is a direct conflict of first principles. To Owen war is simply "crass barbarism" and overwhelming stupidity. All the great generals ought to have been shot, Napoleon most of all, "a scoundrel, a criminal, a monster for whom language has no adequate name!" He finds it difficult to understand "why nations don't tear to pieces" any ruler or government official who goes to war. "*They'll* arrive soon enough at a substitute, in the particular case, if they're made to understand that they'll be hanged—and also drawn and quartered—if they don't find one. Make it a capital crime; *that* will quicken the wits of ministers!"

There is little action in "Owen Wingrave." The tale is told in the third person, and Owen's interviews with his aunt and grandfather are only summarily reported. Ironically the climax is brought about by Kate Julian, a poor relation of the Wingraves and a silly chit, who loves Owen but is insanely hooked on the army. It is Kate who taunts him with cowardice and dares him to spend a night in the haunted room, where long before the night is over she has the desolating privilege of finding him dead just where his ancestor had died.

That Owen's death is brought about by supernatural agency James makes it impossible in the frame of the story to doubt. The only other possible interpretation would be that he was frightened to death, and this is ruled out not only by the fact that Stephen Coyle, who knows Owen so much better than any of his relatives, vouches without qualification for his courage, but also, even more conclusively, by the fact that he has already upon his own initiative tested himself by spending one night in the haunted room, faced whatever there was to be faced there, and emerged unscathed.[25]

VI

Between 1893 and 1896 James published eight tales, "The Middle Years," "The Death of the Lion," "The Coxon Fund," "The Next Time," "The Altar of the Dead," "The Figure in the Carpet," "Glasses," and "The Friends of the Friends." All except "Glasses" (see Appendix A) were reprinted in the New York Edition.

"The Middle Years" (*Scribner's Magazine*, May 1893) was the first, much the briefest, and by all means the most beautiful of James's stories about writers. The fable is simple almost to banality. There are no problems, and those who must have them at any cost have been largely compelled to create them out of hand. Writing of Christina Rossetti, Sir Walter Raleigh once remarked that "pure poetry" does not make good lectures, "sanded" poetry being much better for this purpose. Christina Rossetti's poetry, he added, made him want to cry, not lecture. There are not many tales to which such a statement might be extended; "The Middle Years" is one of them.[1]

We meet the novelist Dencombe, who has lost both his wife and his only child, at Bournemouth, where, recovering, as he hopes, from a serious illness, he receives the first copy of his new novel, *The Middle Years*. Because of his illness, he has completely forgotten what he wrote, but as he reads it all comes back to him and with it the precious realization that for once he has realized his aspirations. "It came over him that only with 'The Middle Years' had he taken his flight; only on that day, visited by soundless processions, had he recognised his kingdom."

Satisfaction, alas, is short-lived, for Dencombe feels strongly that *The Middle Years* will be his last book. "His development had been abnormally slow,

almost grotesquely gradual . . . . It had taken too much
of his life to produce too little of his art." He has not had
time to do much more than collect his material; now he
needs another lifetime to make use of it. "Ah for another
go, ah for a better chance!"

Life does not give him that, but it does bring him
Doctor Hugh, one of those perfect readers of whom no
writer finds more than a handful, whatever his circulation figures may be. Doctor Hugh is at Bournemouth as
the private physician of a "generous, independent,
eccentric" countess, who travels with him and a somewhat venomous female attendant, Miss Vernham, who,
we are led to gather, is setting her cap for the doctor and
the fortune that the countess, whose days are numbered, may be expected to leave him. But Dencombe
relapses dangerously, and through no effort of his own
he draws Doctor Hugh's attention away from the countess and is himself tended with "all the new learning in
science and all the old reverence in faith."

The countess dies first, resentfully, and the doctor
loses his prospective inheritance, a loss he takes easily in
his stride. "I gave her up for you . . . . I chose to accept,
whatever they may be, the consequences of my infatuation." And Dencombe follows her, but not before he has
realized that "it *is* glory—to have been tested, to have
had our little quality and cast our little spell. The thing is
to have made somebody care. You happen to be crazy
of course, but that doesn't affect the law." Like all the
sons of men, he has been denied his "second chance."
"There never was to be but one. We work in the dark—
we do what we can—we give what we have. Our doubt
is our passion and our passion is our task. The rest is the
madness of art." It is also both the tragedy and the
triumph of a divinely impossible effort and a doomed,
undefeatable race.

"The Death of the Lion," which has much of the
same material as "The Middle Years" but uses it in an

entirely different manner to secure a quite different
effect, opened the first number of *The Yellow Book* in
April 1894. The editor of that perfect organ of the fin de
siècle, Henry Harland, and its leading illustrator, Aubrey
Beardsley, had captured James by offering him complete freedom of choice as to both length and subject,
and "The Death of the Lion" was followed in its pages
by our next two stories of the literary life—"The Coxon
Fund" (July 1894) and "The Next Time" (July 1895).

Like Dencombe in "The Middle Years," Neil Paraday of "The Death of the Lion" is a neglected writer
approaching the end of his life. Paraday is separated
from his wife, not a widower, but like Dencombe he has
recently experienced a critical illness, and as Dencomb
is guarded and protected by Doctor Hugh, Paraday is in
the hands of an admiring young journalist. The story is
the latter's private record of his experience, filled out by
quotations from his letters to Fanny Hurter, who is an
American girl come to England to secure Paraday's
autograph, but who, being the right sort of admirer, is
easily persuaded to show decent consideration for him
by leaving him alone (the narrator married her before
completing his record). Both stories end with the writer's death, yet, instead of being, like "The Middle
Years," profoundly sad and deeply moving. "The
Death of the Lion" is satirical and ironic in tone and at
times even comic.

After an important journal, *The Empire*, has
"boomed" his new book, the weakened Paraday
becomes a "lion." At Prestidge, Mrs. Weeks Wimbush,
wife of a brewer, entertains him royally. "She was a
blind violent force to which I could attach no more idea
of responsibility than to the creaking of a sign in the
wind. It was difficult to see what she conduced to but
circulation. She was constructed of steel and leather,
and all I asked of her for our tractable friend was not to
do him to death." In her salon, Paraday is no more and

no less important than Guy Walsingham, who turns out
to be "a pretty little girl" renowned for her daring on the
printed page, and Dora Forbes, a man in loud knicker-
bockers who sports a moustache (was James perhaps
thinking of "Bertha M. Clay"?). Mr. Morrow, whose
particular interest is in writers who take "the larger
latitude," wishes to write up Paraday for a syndicate
serving thirty-seven newspapers, but Morrow, who
longs for a "delightful peep" at the scene of Paraday's
labors but has no desire to read his books, does not get
far.

Paraday has produced an elaborate plan or pro-
spectus or preview of his next projected work (similar
to those that James himself sometimes prepared) and a
masterpiece in itself. This is passed about from one to
another of the guests at Prestidge, none of whom trouble to read it, and after his death (his dying request to
the narrator was that he should "print it as it stands—
beautifully"), it turns out to have been lost.

The distinguished writer who is exploited but not
read supplies the basic conception in both "The Middle
Years" and "The Death of the Lion," and this was a
subject that James was well qualified to treat. The idea
"would have the merit, at least," he told his notebook,
"of corresponding to an immense reality—a reality that
strikes me every day of my life."[2] But though, like all
writers, he drew upon his own thoughts and experiences and convictions for material, James was never, in
his fiction, an autobiographical writer, and neither
Dencombe nor Paraday is a self-portrait. Though "The
Death of the Lion" is quite successful upon its own
terms, it is inevitably a light piece compared to "The
Middle Years," and some readers feel their sympathy
for Paraday considerably strained by the spineless way
he permits himself to be exploited by selfish, uncomprehending people, who, in his state of health, subject
him to a strain that he proves unable to support.[3] As the
narrator puts it,

When I hint that a violent rupture with our hostess would be the best thing in the world for him he gives me to understand that if his reason assents to the proposition his courage hangs woefully back. He makes no secret of being mortally afraid of her, and when I ask what harm she can do him that she hasn't already done he simply repeats: "I'm afraid, I'm afraid! Don't enquire too closely," he said last night; "only believe that I feel a sort of terror. It's strange, when she's so kind! At any rate, I'd as soon turn over that piece of priceless Sèvres as tell her that I must go before my date." It sounds dreadfully weak, but he has some reason, and he pays for his imagination, which puts him (I should hate it) in the place of others and makes him feel, even against himself, their feelings, their appetites, their motives.

In both his *notebook*[4] and his preface James traces "The Coxon Fund" back to James Dykes Campbell's interpretation of Coleridge, the irresponsible genius. Yet, "for the dramatist at any rate," the "S.T. Coleridge *type*" is even "more interesting than the man"; wherefore Frank Saltram, who is "like a jelly *minus* the mould," gives "no more than a dim reflection and above all a free arrangement" of "his great suggester." "The Coxon Fund" is much the longest of the tales of literary life with which this chapter is concerned, and James was greatly interested in it, aiming at one point at "a little masterpiece of 20,000 words," again thinking his idea might require 100,000, and then deciding to do it impressionistically, like a Sargent painting.

It is hardly the most significant of the group, however, being rather meandering in its development (there is a gap of four years between Chapters II and III), and a little tepid in its interest. Saltram, "middle-aged, fat, featureless, save for his great eyes," seldom appears on the scene, and though his irresponsibility comes through, the reader must take his genius largely on faith. He "leaves all his belongings to other people to take care of. He accepts favours, loans, sacrifices—all with nothing more deterrent than an agony of shame." Since he is too lazy to write very much, it is in his conversation that his genius really expresses itself, when the spirit moves him, but unfortunately we are not able to hear what he says. He even fails to show up for the public lectures for which he has prepared the "magnificent" prospectuses that are apparently all he ever does prepare. His most winning moment by far comes in the penultimate chapter, in which the narrator encounters him on the Wimbledon Common. "He was as mild as contrition and as copious as faith; he was never so fine as on a shy return, and even better at forgiving than at being forgiven." At this point one really understands why the narrator should at last take his part. But one understands too how, when the "magnificent income" of the Coxon Fund is placed at his disposal, Saltram "drew it," as we are told in the furiously rushed ending, "as he had always drawn everything, with a grand abstracted gesture," and "its magnificence, as all the world now knows, quite quenched him; it was the beginning of his decline."

As the tale stands, then, Leon Edel would seem abundantly justified when, in *Henry James: The Middle Years*,[5] he formulates the "ironic message" of the story:

> The artist must be given full freedom; he must be forgiven his sins against the social body. He must be allowed his transgressions—his illegitimate children, his sublime ignorance of daily routine or method, his sexual irregularities—but it must also be recognized that if he is too well endowed, he might cease to struggle altogether.

Yet I doubt that James thought of the matter thus didactically (the concern of the story seems rather the presentation of a "case" than the inculcation of a moral), and when, in the introduction to Volume IX of his edition of the *Collected Tales*, Edel finds the author suggesting "that genius tends to be erratic, egotistical and anti-social; it may be indulged but must not be pampered," the garment he comes bringing in is too large a size for the tale under consideration to feel comfortable in. All in all, the 1947 observation of F.O. Matthiessen and Kenneth B. Murdock, as editors of James's *Notebooks*, still stands: James largely ignored "the tragedy or suffering involved in the waste of genius," kept "his handling . . . on the plane of social comedy," and thus arrived at an "ironic" conclusion.

Moreover, Saltram's is not the only "case" the tale presents. There is the case of the Mulvilles, all of whose geese are swans and who look after Saltram as the Gillmans looked after Coleridge. There is the (undeveloped) case of the unnamed narrator, their friend. There is the case of George Gravener, once an "intellectual power" in a "devastating set" at Cambridge, later a member of Parliament, and finally a peer, who sees the great man as a humbug and a "cultivated cad" and plays the devil's advocate to those who cry him up ("the only thing that really counts for one's estimate of a person is his conduct"). But above all there is the case of Ruth Anvoy, the earnest young heiress from Boston, upon whom the necessity to make the decision concerning the disposition of the Coxon Fund finally devolves.

The reader, like the narrator, meets Miss Anvoy at one of the lectures where Saltram fails to show. She becomes engaged to Gravener, but the engagement founders when her father suffers reverses and dies, leaving her next to nothing. This does not free her from financial responsibilities, however. She has come to England to visit her transcendentalist aunt Lady Coxon, who has been living there for forty years, first as the wife and now as the widow of Sir Geoffrey Coxon. At his death, Sir Geoffrey left £13,000 for the "Endow-

of Research" calculated to further the discovery of "Moral Truth." His will saddled his widow "with a mass of queer obligations complicated with queer loopholes," and when she dies her wide discretionary powers are inherited by her niece. "It's clear that by Lady Coxon's will she may have the money, but it's still clearer to her conscience that the original condition, definite, intensely implied on her uncle's part, is attached to the use of it. She can only take one view of it. It's for the Establishment or it's nothing." Ruth is so sure of this that she can hardly be said to have confronted a temptation or been involved in the kind of ethical dilemma so often presented by James, and by the time she has been sufficiently impressed by Saltram's greatness there can be little or no doubt what she will do with the money. The irony of the story, as has already been indicated, inheres in the fact that, though in a totally different way, Ruth's bounty serves Saltram no better than that of the Touchetts serves Isabel Archer in *The Portrait of a Lady*. One interesting technical feature of this story is James's occasional interjection of a glance ahead: "At a later time, they grew, poor dears, to fear no snatching"; "He had an incomparable gift; I never was blind to it—it dazzles me still." The most interesting such passage occurs at the end: "Ruth Anvoy hasn't married, I hear, and neither have I." James leaves his readers free to make much or little or nothing of this, as they may choose.

Even though the hero, Ray Limbert, dies over an unfinished masterpiece at the end of "The Next Time," the tale seems a less sombre study of the hopelessly unpopular author than "The Middle Years" and a less elaborate one than "The Death of the Lion." "I seem to catch hold of the tail of a glimpse of my own personality," wrote James in the unusually full account of development of the story in his notebook.[6] The distinctive note here is that the writer makes a deliberate attempt to be bad enough to be popular and always fails. "What was the cerebral treachery that defied his own vigilance? There was some obscure interference of taste, some obsession of the exquisite. All one could say was that genius was a fatal disturber or that the unhappy man had no effectual *flair*. When he went abroad to gather garlic, he came home with heliotrope." In the notebook entry, James harked back to his own early experience trying to write for the New York *Tribune*, which ended with his telling Whitelaw Reid, the editor, that his pieces were the worst he could do for the money, and when the narrator brings cold comfort to Limbert by telling him that "you can't make a sow's ear out of a silk purse," he uses the very same figure that James himself employed after having been booed by the gallery on the first night of *Guy Domville*.[7]

Financial need is the exciting force, for Limbert has three children and an ailing wife, besides which his mother-in-law is quartered on him, to say nothing of three maids and a nursery governess, for the ladies are all "extremely waited on." There is considerable domestic background in this story, and the Limbert marriage is delayed by financial considerations. There is also a good deal about the editorial chores poor Limbert tries to perform. As editor of "a high-class monthly," he is embarrassed by the failure of his own writings to please his employers, and he finally loses his place because he cannot persuade himself to admit to his pages the work of Minnie Meadows, a "new lady-humourist every one seems talking about," who produces "screaming sketches." James's well-known passion for balance decrees the appearance in the tale of Limbert's sister-in-law, Jane Highmore, a best-selling novelist who strives as diligently for critical success as he for a best seller and with the same result. "The harmony between [them] rested on the fact that . . . each would have liked so much to be the other."

Mrs. Limbert is as understanding as a wife could be under the circumstances, feeling that "of course if she could have chosen she would have liked him to be Shakespeare or Scott, but that failing this she was glad he wasn't—well, she named the two gentlemen, but I won't."[8] Ray tries to concentrate not upon doing *his* work but on "what somebody else would take for it." He will "cultivate the market—it's a science like another." He will be "obvious" and popular." So he tries, but the result?

> Obvious?—where the deuce was it obvious? Popular—how on earth could it be popular? The thing was charming with all his charm and powerful with all his power; it was an unscrupulous, an unsparing, a shameless merciless masterpiece. It was, no doubt, like the old letters to the *Beacon*, the worst he could do, but the perversity of the effort, even though heroic, had been frustrated by the purity of the gift.

And so he goes on, moving to the country to save expenses, continuing to try, hoping to be bad enough one way or another. They all live on somehow, but there is no change until at last Limbert embraces the great change that solves everything and nothing.

The words I have quoted are those of the narrator. James considered the possibility of assigning this function to the Jane Highmore character and rejected it because "the narrator must be fully and richly, must be ironically *conscient*," which meant that "*I* become the narrator, either impersonally or in my unnamed, unspecified personality," finally settling upon the latter alternative. The passage in question came back to the mind of Forrest Reid when he was writing his chapter on that superb novel of the supernatural, *The Return*, in his study of Walter de la Mare.[9] De la Mare himself was a very good Jamesian who, like James, enjoyed a very high reputation, but had far fewer readers than he deserved. Exactly as if he had been trying to follow in

Limbert's footsteps, he had designed *The Return* "deliberately as a sensational story, a 'shocker,' a thing the public would infallibly rise to, would recognize as its own." It was awarded the Polignac Prize, but it did not make him a rich man.

"The Altar of the Dead" was first published in the collection of James's tales called *Terminations* that Harper & Brothers brought out in 1895. It is a pretty commentary on the taste of the magazine editors of the nineties that James had been unable to secure serial publication for it, and it is even more appalling that there should still be critics who agree with them, so that the sheep and the goats divide themselves between those who consider the piece one of James's great accomplishments and those who can see nothing in it at all.[10] To the present writer "The Altar of the Dead" is as unmistakably James's most beautiful story as *The Wings of the Dove* is unmistakably the last James novel he would give up before removing to the proverbial desert island, and he was much pleased when he learned that Joseph Conrad had singled it out along with "The Middle Years," to show that James wrote "from the heart," with "some real glow to illumine and warm" his "technical perfection."

After what one gathers has been a fairly distinguished career in government service, George Stransom finds his religion in an almost Chinese reverence for the dead. Securing permission to decorate an altar in a Roman Catholic church, he sets up a lighted candle for each of the friends who, as he puts it, has died in possession of him, and here finds increasing comfort in what comes to seem like a mountain of light. In the course of time, he finds his rites shared by an unknown lady in deep mourning with whom, very gradually, he first becomes acquainted and then establishes a deep friendship and to whom he confides the care of his altar after his own candle shall have been added to it.

Two discoveries follow: first, that all her dead are

one, and, second, that her dead is the late, great Acton Hague, the closest friend of Stransom's youth and early manhood, who later betrayed him and for whom no candle can glow on any altar of his. This, of course, spoils both the rites and the friendship, and the ensuing misery endures almost to what seems the end of Stransom's life.

The lady impinges upon the reader's consciousness as gradually as upon Stransom's own. Her singleness and her devotion are the first things he notices about her. She is more constant in her attendance than he is; he envies her her ability to sink, rapt and motionless, into prayer; she convinces him that women have more of the spirit of religion than men. At first she looks "faded and handsome," and he is sure that she has no fortune. When, at a concert, they meet and speak for the first time, he decides that she is prettier and more interesting than he had supposed. Though she is younger than he is, she is no longer in her first youth, and he feels sure that her youth has been "sacrificed." Later he learns that she writes for the popular magazines, but she never speaks of her work, and he never reads anything she has written. Still later he finds that though she has lived apart from public affairs, there has been one great, and in its end result unhappy, experience in her life that has shaped and colored her character.

Their intimacy develops very slowly. It takes him "months and months to learn her name [which is more than the reader ever does], years and years to learn her address." At first it seems to both that "her debt . . . was much greater than his, because while she had only given him a worshipper he had given her a splendid temple." Later, however, this indebtedness is reversed. He never sees her at home until after the death of the old aunt with whom she has been living; then he feels at last "in real possession of her." But this, like many touches in the tale, is deeply ironical. If he had never entered her

home, Stransom would not have seen Acton Hague's
photograph there or learned of his old friend-enemy's
connection with her. When he has done that, "it struck
him that to have come at last into her house had had the
horrid effect of diminishing their intimacy."

Nothing could more interestingly mark the difference between Henry James and the sex-obsessed novelists of today than his failure to tell us just what the lady's
connection with "their terrible friend" had been. Once
Stransom asks her what Hague did to her but she only
replies, "Everything!" He asks himself whether he is in
love with her "that he should care so much what adventures she had had" and even, with a grim laugh, "why
the deuce" she liked Hague "so much better than she
likes me." But the only thing either he or we are ever
sure of is that she had loved Hague deeply and that in
some way he had betrayed her. Stransom knew that "a
woman, when wronged, was always more wronged
than a man, and there were conditions when the least
she could have got off with was more than the most he
could have to bear."

After their rupture, if one can call it that, both
persons are entirely logical in the positions they take up.
Indeed it is not a rupture in the usual sense of the term,
for "she was not vindictive or even resentful. It was not
in anger she had forsaken him; it was in simple submission to hard reality, to the stern logic of life." She continues to see him at her home, but they can no longer
meet at the church and share their worship there,
because by making Acton Hague the only one of Stransom's dead to whom he had deliberately refused a
candle, he had specifically excluded her from all share
in the rites of his altar and thus made her attitude "all
wrong." With Stransom the case was different. "He had
had his great compassions, his indulgences—there were
cases in which they had been immense"; in his own way,
he had even thought he had forgiven Hague. But "to

provide for him on the very ground of having discovered another of his turpitudes was not to pity but to
glorify him." Yet he knows almost from the beginning
that his compassion cannot match hers. "Women aren't
like men," she tells him. "They can love even when
they've suffered," and he can only reply, "Women are
wonderful."

We shall not judge the situation fairly unless we
remember that we are intended to think of Hague as a
rich, gifted, fascinating, evil man. He filled the life of
everyone "who had the wonderful experience of knowing him," but there can be no question that Stransom's
judgment of him is just. This is made abundantly clear
by the woman's unprotesting reception of Stransom's
statement that "he did me—years ago—an unforgetta-
ble wrong." She accepts his words in silence, tears fill
her eyes, and she reaches out her hand to take his.
"Nothing more wonderful had ever appeared to him
than . . . to see her convey with such exquisite mildness
that as from Acton Hague any injury was credible." Yet
all this is oddly irrelevant. The lady loves Hague as God
in the Christian Gospel loves His sinful children, seeing
all their sins clearly, but with no abatement of His love
and willing, if need be, to die for them.

When the ghost of Acton Hague steps between
Stransom and his friend, it does more than disturb their
personal relations; it also destroys Stransom's worship.
Perfect worship can exist only in an atmosphere of
harmony and adjustment; exclusion and irreconcilabil-
ity are wholly incompatible with it. J.A. Ward says it
very well: "Not until he forgives Hague is Stransom's
altar of the dead complete, for he still shares in the
self-destroying egotism of the world he rejects." And
Walter F. Wright adds a comment that shows that, since
life is one, this statement has the same validity for art as
for religion: "The introduction of Hague has revealed a
flaw in Stransom's spiritual world, and it is obvious that,

if the story is to be artistically complete, this flaw must cease to exist."[11]

The problem cannot be addressed, then, until Stransom rises to the spiritual condition of his friend, and it is the woman's great service to him that she shows him the way, not by preaching to him but simply by being what she is. The barrier is in him, not in her, and only he can remove it. He does not achieve this until after his health has broken, weakening, it would seem, his stubborn, divisive will, and he goes at it at first like an artist. She had felt that she could not use Stransom's altar again until he should be willing to add a candle for Acton Hague, and "there came a day when, for simple exhaustion, if symmetry should demand just one he was ready so far to meet symmetry." When he goes to church for the first time after his illness, and before he ought to be out, it seems to him "that he had come for the great surrender," and when he finds her there, it seems that God must have sent her and him too. But she meets him halfway, for she too has grown; through "the sweetest of miracles" she has lost all sense of their difference. Suddenly what had hitherto been impossible had become not only possible but inevitable. If she can no longer come to church "for her own," she can come "for them," and, though she does not say it, for Stransom. Love has superseded logic or subsumed it. The perfect acceptance that the woman had already achieved in her forgiveness of Hague has now been extended to Stransom too, and the circle is whole again.

In his preface James explains his inability to specify the time when the basic idea embodied in "The Altar of the Dead" first came to him on the ground that it had always been there. The earliest notebook entry referring to the tale is dated September 29, 1894; he returned to it on October 2, and on October 24 he recorded having begun work on the story and broken off, being dissatisfied with it as "a 'conceit,' after all, a little fancy which doesn't hold a great deal"; since at this point he had not yet conceived of either Hague or Stransom's fellow worshipper, this is less strange than it might otherwise seem.[12] Surely Clifton Fadiman was right when he wrote eloquently that "the homage the two characters pay to their dead comes out of a sense of the fullness of life, rather than out of any perverse interest in the smell of mortality. The story is crowded, not with terror, but with love."[13] And surely it is, even for James, magnificently written, richly but never uncomfortably crowded with both music and meaning and full of sentences and phrases that open up vistas and linger in the memory.

The experience of reading "The Figure in the Carpet" (*Cosmopolis*, January-February 1896) is compared by Mathhiessen and Murdock to "that of opening a series of ingeniously mystifying Russian boxes in search of an ultimate kernel."[14] It is the least satisfying of the stories about writers considered in this chapter; naturally it is the special darling of those critics who delight in puzzles.

Just after having published a review of Hugh Vereker's new novel, the unnamed narrator meets the novelist, another of James's great but unappreciated writers, at a party. Unaware of its author's presence in the company, Vereker dismisses the review, in response to a question from another guest, as "all right—the usual twaddle." The reviewer, he says, "doesn't see anything," but this is no great matter, since "nobody does."

Having been apprised of his faux pas, Vereker visits the narrator's room to apologize. He calls himself a failure because everybody misses his "little point," that is, "the particular thing I've written my books for." There is an idea in them "without which I wouldn't have given a straw for the whole job." This involves "the order, the form, and the texture" of his books and adds up to "an exquisite scheme." It is indeed "the loveliest thing in the world," and he never dreamed of making a secret of it. But since "every page and line and letter" of his "whole lucid effort" gives the clue, he cannot help the narrator to spot it. "The thing's as concrete there as a bird in a cage, a bait on a hook, a piece of cheese in a mouse-trap. It's stuck into every volume as your foot is stuck into your shoe. It governs every line, it chooses every word, it dots every i, it places every comma." He cannot even tell whether it is "something in the style or something in the thought," for to him the two are one. In his notebook James called it "this interior thought—this special *beauty* (that is mainly the right word) that pervades and animates" all the rest.

The narrator can make nothing of all this, and the exasperation of his search for the novelist's meaning spoils the books for him. He passes on what Vereker had told him to his friend Corvick, who communicates it to his fiancée Gwendolen Erme, herself the author of a novel, and the pair proceed to devote themselves almost frantically to discovering the figure in the carpet.

Corvick, sent abroad on assignment, cables Gwendolen from Bombay that he has unraveled the mystery and again from Italy that he has presented his solution to Vereker, who has confirmed it, but the letter that follows says only that he will tell her the secret after they are married.

The narrator now goes to the continent to tend a sick brother, where he hears from Corvick that the latter is engaged upon a definitive study of Vereker's work and prefers not to reveal his conclusions in advance. Corvick and Gwendolen are married, but Corvick is killed on their honeymoon, leaving "a mere heartbreaking scrap" of the great work, and when the narrator turns to Gwendolen for enlightenment, she will only say, "I heard everything, and I mean to keep it to myself!" The narrator conjectures that this may mean

that "it's nothing!" but to this she replies, "It's my life."
She publishes a second novel which the narrator thinks
superior to her first, and her life too seems different.
Like the narrator of "The Aspern Papers," who was
tempted to marry Tina Bordereau to secure possession
of Jeffrey Aspern's literary remains, the narrator wonders whether he will be obliged to propose to Gwendolen.

Vereker dies, as does his wife. Gwendolen marries
Drayton Deane, another minor scribbler whom the narrator holds in some contempt, and dies with her second
child. As his last hope, the narrator turns to Deane,
thinking that, as Corvick had told Gwendolen the secret
after their marriage, so she may well have passed it on
to her second husband, but when the question is put to
Deane he is well nigh stupefied. He has heard nothing
about any figure in Vereker's carpet and has no reason
to suppose that there was any.

The obvious objection to all this is that since art *is*
communication, a writer who fails to be understood not
only by the stupid and uncomprehending but even by
his most intelligent and earnest devotees has failed as an
artist and succeeded only as a solipsist or mental mas-
turbator. Vereker plays a cat-and-mouse game, Corvick does the same, and Gwendolen continues the farce
after her husband's death. All James says in his preface
to help us see more than this in the tale is that "no truce,
in English-speaking air, had ever seemed to me really
struck, or even approximately strikeable, with our so
marked collective mistrust of anything like close or
analytic appreciation," to which Bruce McElderry, Jr.,
adds that James "may be laughing at critics, or pretentious authors, or both."[15] That not all readers—or at
least all *writing* readers—have been content to stop
here, a host of studies can testify.[16]

These interpretations range all the way from the
view that there is no secret (see Westbrook, Powers,

and, with significant differences, Vaid) to Dorothy Boland's interesting interpretation in terms of Oriental philosophy. Kanzer, Tyler, and Tintner accent the sexual element. Lainoff, Levy, Recchia, and Boland all take a dim view of the narrator, and Lainoff and Recchia exalt Corvick as the hero of the tale.

Vaid, who rejects Westbrook's view that the novelist is "a poseur, a fraud" and that the critics are his dupes, still reads the tale as a Jamesian parody of one kind of criticism. This writer believes that Corvick did not discover the secret or pass it on to his wife and that his claim to have discovered it was "just a clever trick to patch up his relations with Gwendolen and hasten their marriage." After his death Gwendolen prefers to keep silent rather than admit she has been duped. This view would explain the otherwise puzzling contradiction between what Corvick and Gwendolen tell the narrator about their engagement, but it seems to me out of harmony with the spirit of the tale. There is no real support for a sexual interpretaion beyond the fact that both Corvick and the narrator seems to feel that the solution can only be communicated to a wife or husband. As James himself wrote in his notebook, "There is evidently, about it, a strange mystifying uncomfortable delicacy." Recchia contrasts the "broadness and flexibility of Corvick's attitude" to "the rigid superficiality of the narrator's," whose "wrong-headed critical methods" get in the way of his "innate ability to appreciate a work of art." He searches for a "hidden meaning" instead of attempting to savor the quality or power which emanates from the work as a whole and constitutes its dynamic unity." It is hard to see why Levy, having rejected Corvick, must go on to glorify Deane, maintaining that "Deane understands everything," as against the usual view that he understands nothing. But Levy himself admits that his view of the narrator as symbolizing "what is wrong with or missing in the 'ana-

lytic appreciation' of the age" (James's preface postulates the conspicuous and lamentable absence of such
appreciation) is "hard to prove," and I agree with him
that though the story "proposes that the work of art tests
the humanity of its readers" and that "the novelist works
with ideas, feelings, attitudes, symbols that to be mean-
ingful must be shared and understood," yet "the mode
of exaggeration in which 'The Figure in the Carpet' is
cast, with its strong vein of fantasy and humor, may
occasionally suggest that James is merely playing with
the possibilities of his fable."

Perhaps the most interesting interpretation of the
story is that of Dorothy Boland, who takes her point of
departure from Corvick's discovery of the secret *in
India*. The narrator, she argues, cannot be enlightened
because his motives are selfish. Corvick finds "spirit" in
India; enlightenment comes to him in the Temple of
Vishnu. Gwendolen, then, is being quite truthful when
she says that the secret is "my life," and she does not
attempt to communicate what she knows because such
things cannot be communicated but must be experienced. The figure in the carpet "takes all experience in
its many levels and brings it back to a common point."
What Vereker presents is "not a specific 'system,' but
rather an approximation so close to life that it allows
levels of interpretation."

If "The Altar of the Dead" has been called morbid,
which it is not, it would be difficult to deny that there is
a touch of morbidity in "The Friends of the Friends"
(*The Chap-Book*, May 1, 1896, and *Chapman's Magazine of Fiction*, May 1896, as "*The Way It Came*"),
perhaps James's most powerful ghost story after "The
Turn of the Screw" and "The Jolly Corner." And as the
"Altar" was born out of the author's having been "way-
laid or arrested . . . by some imaged appeal of the lost
Dead,"[17] so this tale began, quite as abstractly, with "the
idea of *Too late*—of some friendship or passion or
bond—some affection long desired and waited for."

The woman who tells the tale has two friends, unacquainted with each other, who have this in common, that as she had seen the ghost of her father at the time of his death, so he had seen that of his mother at hers. But this is not the only reason the narrator feels that her friends should know each other: "They had the same ideas and tastes and tricks, the same prejudices and superstitions and heresies; they said the same things and sometimes did them; they liked and disliked the same persons and places, the same books, authors and styles; there were touches of resemblance even in their looks and features." But whenever she plans to bring them together something interferes, so that it almost seems as if they are fated not to meet. The entire second chapter of the seven chapters that comprise the tale is devoted to these frustrations, and this is the only part of the tale that might perhaps justly be called labored.

At last the narrator becomes engaged to marry the man friend, and when her woman friend comes to congratulate her, they make definite plans for the long-contemplated meeting on the following Saturday afternoon at five o'clock. When the friend arrives home, she receives word that her long-estranged husband has died.

At once, for no discernible reason, the narrator begins to feel that it is terribly important to her that her friends should *not* meet, and she sends her fiancé a note telling him not to come on Saturday until dinner time. The two women have their five o'clock meeting without him, and the narrator does not confess her deceit. But after the woman friend has reached home that night, she suddenly dies.

When the narrator confesses to her fiancé, he astonishes her by declaring that the other woman visited him at his rooms at about the time she is supposed to have died. She stayed for what seemed to him about twenty minutes, and they enjoyed a wordless communion. He insists, "I saw her living . . . . I saw her as I see you now."

But the narrator denies this. "I'm, life, you see. What you saw last night was death."

She soon realizes that she has "something very serious to look in the face." The "Medusa mask . . . had lividly survived, and it was fed by suspicions unspeakable." She tells her fiancé that they must reconsider their situation since another person has now come between them. "How *can* you hide it when you're abjectly in love with her, when you're sick almost to death with the joy of what she gives you? . . . I can renounce you, but I can't share you; the best of you is hers, I know what it is and freely give you up to her for ever!"

Neither party ever marries, and six years later the man dies.

> It was sudden, it was never properly accounted for, it was surrounded by consequences in which . . . I distinctly read an intention, the mark of his own hidden hand. It was the result of a long necessity, of an unquenchable desire. To say exactly what I mean, it was a response to an irresistible call.

Leon Edel has compared this story to Defoe. Though he did not name it, he was obviously thinking of "A True Relation of the Apparition of One Mrs. Veal," and the comparison is well taken. He has also pointed out the resemblance between "The Friends of the Friends" and another tale of James's, the much less effective "Maud-Evelyn," and has compared the narrator's jealousy of her dead friend with Kate Croy's of Milly Theale at the close of *The Wings of the Dove*.[18] It is true, as has been pointed out, that we have no independent witness to what is supposed to happen in this story; the entire narrative is a document written by a jealous woman and briefly introduced by an unidentified friend. But is not this inevitable in all first-person narratives? Though David Copperfield begins his narrative by insisting that he was born, we have nobody besides himself to vouch for it. Our narrator is certainly jealous, but there is no indication that she is either irrational or mendacious. If we are willing to accept the story upon its own terms, which is what we must do with all stories but especially with those involving the supernatural, there is no reason not to accept it as a veracious account. To do otherwise would rob it of all meaning and reduce James to the level of a prestidigatator.

VII

No tale by Henry James made its first appearance in 1897, but the last two years of the nineties brought nine: "John Delavoy," *"The Turn of the Screw," *"In the Cage," "Covering End," "The Given Case," "The Great Condition," *"Europe," *"Paste," and *"The Real Right Thing," of which those marked with an asterisk were included in the New York Edition and are considered in this chapter. Since much more has been written about "The Turn of the Screw" than any other tale (one is tempted to say more than has been written about all the others put together), it will inevitably usurp most of my space.[1]

On January 16, 1895, James confided to his notebook a "ghost-story" he had been told by Edward White Benson, Archbishop of Canterbury, who had it at second hand from "a lady who had no art of relation and no clearness." It concerned an unspecified number of children who had been left in the care of "wicked and depraved" servants in an "old country-house." Having passed their own corruption on to their charges, the servants died in some unspecified manner and then returned "to haunt the house *and* children" so that the latter might "destroy themselves, lose themselves, by responding, by getting into their power." This suggestion apparently lay fallow until the autumn of 1897, when James set to work to make a Christmas ghost story out of it. But it grew in his hands until it became the longest of his tales, more than 50,000 words, and consequently missed the Christmas deadlines. *Collier's Weekly* ran it in twelve installments between January 27 and April 16, 1898. In September it was published in book form along with "Covering End" as *The Two Magics* (obviously indicating black and white magic, the latter being love). It was slightly revised for the New York Edition.

In the prologue, Douglas, who had known the unnamed governess of the tale during his college years, when, some time after her stay at Bly, she had been employed to look after his little sister, reads the story from her manuscript to his friends at Christmastime. We then begin with the young lady's account of her arrival at Bly and her reception there by the well-meaning but illiterate housekeeper, Mrs. Grose, and the eight-year-old Flora. Both Flora and her ten-year-old brother, Miles, strike the governess as angelic children, and she finds it difficult to understand why Miles should have been dismissed from his boarding school as a bad influence. She establishes relations of close intimacy and affection with both the children.

She experiences her first real shock when a male figure appears before her. By her description of his appearance, Mrs. Grose conjectures him to be the ghost of the late Peter Quint, valet to the children's uncle, the master of Bly. This is followed by the manifestation of the "infamous" (according to Mrs. Grose) Miss Jessel, the former governess; she and Quint, it is indicated, had been intimate with each other and much too much so with the children.

The governess sees each of these apparitions four times, and though she has no positive evidence, she comes to believe that the children see them and enjoy contacts with them that imperil their souls. She assumes the duty of saving them from this diabolical influence, but not for a long time does she confront them on the issue. This results in her complete estrangement from Flora, who is taken away from Bly, and Miles dies in her arms after having made what seems a partial confession of guilt.

Obviously we have much here that is not accounted for by the archbishop's anecdote. The governess herself invokes the Gothic tradition as well as *Jane Eyre* when she wonders whether there is "a 'secret' at Bly—a mystery of Udolpho or an insane, an unmentionable relative kept in unsuspected confinement." Governesses were familiar figures in nineteenth century English fiction; the heroine of *Jane Eyre* was the best known among them, and E.A. Sheppard makes a very strong case for the influence of Charlotte Brontë's novel on the tale, at the same time rejecting *Villette* and *Wuthering Heights*, whose influence had been urged by others. He also rejects Miriam Allott's nomination of Mrs. Gaskell's "The Old Nurse's Story," but, like May L. Ryburn and Valerie Parton, he sees Fielding's *Amelia* as something more than a book the governess reads at Bly and also brings *David Copperfield* and LeFanu's *The Cock and Anchor* into consideration. Insofar as it involves or approaches an allegory of good and evil, the "Screw" could hardly have avoided being influenced by Hawthorne, as Nathan B. Fagan has ably argued.[2]

Outside of English and American literature, Sheppard himself suggests *L'Orme de mail* by Anatole France, and Ignace Feuerlicht rather labors resemblances between James's tale and Goethe's famous ballad "Erlkönig" without actually asserting indebtedness. Michael Egan, who believes that Miles "dies of pollution from within, his moral rottenness a fever which burns him up," studies the tale's alleged parallelism to "Ibsen's powerful and shocking tragedy of corrupt innocence," *Ghosts*. Sheppard does not make much of *Ghosts*, but, like Egan, he sees influence from *The Lady From the Sea* (where the Stranger is called "Quaen") and adds *Little Eyolf* for good measure.[3]

Yet perhaps general influences from our cultural and religious background are even more important than any specific literary work. One need not go the whole way with Robert B. Heilman, who interprets the story in terms of the Eden myth, or with Donal O'Gorman, who connects the prologue with Childermass or the Feast of the Holy Innocents, to be sure that its whole treatment of good and evil postulates the Jewish-Christian, perhaps even more specifically, the Sweden-borgian tradition, nor need one accept all Mary V. Hallab's specific conclusions to realize that she has clearly demonstrated that "the story line parallels that of the traditional ghost or fairy tale of the mortal enticed by fairies, witches, or revenants."[4]

But there were influences from life also. "The Turn of the Screw" is a product of the late Victorian world, and Elliot Schrero has conclusively demonstrated that many of the criticisms of the governess now being entered fall to the ground when she is considered against her proper background. I am unconvinced by Leon Edel's argument, supported in part by Leo B. Levy, that the tale reflects James's own nervous condition after the failure of *Guy Domville* and at the time of his settling in at Lamb House, and Oscar Cargill's notion that the governess was drawn from the writer's invalid sister Alice will appeal only to those who must have her abnormal at any cost. Edel is interesting, however, when he resurrects one of James's own governesses, Augustine Danse, and so is Sheppard in calling attention once more to Henriette Deluzy-Desportes (later, in America, Mrs. Henry Field), the governess in the famous Praslin murder case, whom Hawthorne also seems to have used in *The Marble Faun*.[5]

Regardless of what one may believe about the governesse's mental and nervous condition, there is little or no evidence to support Cargill's view that James was influenced by the case of "Miss Lucy R" as reported by Freud and Breuer in their *Studien über Hysterie*, nor yet by the *Hallucinations and Illusions* of Edmund Parish which Cranfill and Clark added to the discussion. What *is* certain is that though James says he did not want the kind of ghosts who figure in the reports of the

Society for Psychical Research, because they could not furnish the thrill he sought, he *was* quite familiar with those reports and with the society, of which his brother William served as president.[6]

James discussed "The Turn of the Screw" in his notebooks, his letters, and the preface to Volume XII of the New York Edition, but he never wrote a line anywhere to indicate that he intended it to be regarded as anything but a tale of the supernatural. It was "a bogey-tale," "a fairy-tale pure and simple," "pure romance," "a wanton little tale," "a *jeu d'esprit*," a "full-blown flower of high fancy," a "perfectly independent and irresponsible little fiction," "an exercise of the imagination unassisted, unassociated," "an inferior, a merely *pictorial*, subject and rather a shameless pot-boiler," "a poor little pot-boiling study of nothing at all," "a monument to my fatal technical passion," and "a piece of ingenuity pure and simple, of cold artistic calculation, an *amusette* to catch those not easily caught." His "little tragedy" was the pathos of exposed childhood, and it had meaning only as "any vision prompted by life" has meaning. Contemplating *The Sense of the Past* in 1900, he wanted it to be "something as simple as *The Turn of the Screw*, only different and less grossly apparitional." Eight years later, he devoted eight pages to the tale in his preface, but he still thought it the kind of story "least apt to be baited by earnest criticism." About that at least he could not have been more wrong.[7]

Two of James's statements have been seriously misinterpreted, however. One is that already quoted about the tale being "an *amusette* to catch those not easily caught." It is clear from the context that he means here that he is trying to write a ghost story that will hold even sophisticated readers, not that the tale has a hidden meaning. The other statement that has been misinterpreted is that he has given the governess "authority," which means that she has kept "crystalline her record of so many intense anomalies and obscurities—by which I

don't of course mean her explanation of them, a different matter." This is completely in line with both traditional ghost lore and the activities of modern psychic
researchers, all of whom knew, with Browning, that
you must mix some uncertainty with faith if you would
have faith be. Even traditional tales of the supernatural
often leave a little crack in the door for the comfort of
the sceptic, and the Society for Psychical Research
vouches only for the fact that psychic phenomena do
occur but accepts any possible explanation of cause and
origin only provisionally. This is what William James
did specifically, and the governess does it too.

Though Edna Kenton is generally given the credit
(or blame) for having first suggested that the ghosts in
"The Turn of the Screw" are hallucinations, this is not
strictly accurate. The idea had been advanced before
1924 by a number of writers, some of them distinguished, and though Harold C. Goddard's elaborate
study was published only posthumously in 1957, he had
been presenting it to his classes at Swarthmore at least
as early as 1920. Miss Kenton's article, primarily a long
purr of self-satisfaction at having been clever enough to
perceive something that nobody else could see, contained little or no argument and attracted little attention, but when, ten years later, Edmund Wilson took up
the notion and presented it with elegant Freudian
trimmings, viewing the governess as a "thwarted" and
sex-starved "Anglo-Saxon spinster" (at age twenty?), he
set off one of the most provocative literary controver-
sies of the century. Actually, however, Wilson did not
provide any more evidence than Edna Kenton. Only a
small portion of his article was devoted to the "Screw,"
and he specifically granted that "almost everything
from beginning to end can be read equally in either of
two senses." The vogue of his study, in other words, was
due more to the climate of opinion at the time it
appeared than to any merits of its own.[8]

All the Freudian critics are thrown into ecstasies by

the fact that Quint first appears erect upon a tower and Miss Jessel beside a body of water, but lakes have other uses in fairy lore besides what the critics would have them mean here. For that matter, Freudian imagery would suit the idea that sexual corruption was introduced into Bly by Quint and Miss Jessel during their lifetime quite as well as the notion that it originated in the sexual fantasies of the governess. Much has also been made of the fact that "The Turn of the Screw" is in Volume XII of the New York Edition instead of in Volume XVII with a number of other ghost stories, but several critics have shown that this can be explained without flying in the face of James's oft-repeated statements that the "Screw" is a ghost story.[9]

The length to which some writers can go in arguing the nonapparitionist case is unbelievable. We have been solemnly assured that because the governess has been hoping to encounter the master, who employed her for her post at Bly and with whom she fell in love, she conjures up the image of Quint, who used to wear his clothes. Or Mrs. Grose doubts the governess's sanity, but she and Miles agree together that they must humor her. Or, again, the governess *does* see the "ghosts"; only they are living persons, Miss Jessel being "a mute, demented woman," probably the master's wife or the insane mother of the children, with Quint as her keeper, from whom she sometimes gets away. Perhaps she might even have forged the headmaster's letter about Miles being expelled from school.

Since Cranfill and Clark blandly assure us that, though not all the difficulties can be cleared up, "thought is free," we can go beyond the text whenever convenient, and no matter though this leaves our whole interpretation floating unattached in general space. So we have been asked to believe that the governess describes Quint not from what she saw but from unrecorded inquiries she made in the village and that

when she finds Miles out on the lawn at night, he is not
looking at Quint on the tower, but that having heard
from Mrs. Grose that she thought she had seen Quint
there, Miles went out to look for him himself. When
necessary, we can rewrite the story. Flora did *not*, for
example, take the boat across the lake; it was where it
belonged all the time; only the governess could not see
it, and when she reached the other side, she imagined
that she saw it there. Harold Goddard did not "mean to
imply that Peter Quint and Miss Jessel exist *only* in the
brain of the governess. Perhaps they do and perhaps
they don't." Possibly the insane may have the power "to
perceive objective existences of another order." Donald
F. Costello, who analyzes both the time scheme and the
structure of the tale with reference to the ghostly
appearances, achieves both horror and mystification by
seeing the "predatory creatures" as real while we read
about them, yet not actually present,[10] while Donal
O'Gorman, the only scholar who has studied in detail
the implications of James's calling the ghosts "goblins"
and or "demons" and his reference to the witchcraft
trials, throws all his valuable material out the window
by finally arriving at the weird and wild conclusion that
it is the governess, not the children, upon whom the
demons have designs, and that it is she, not they, who is
demon-possessed.

   It should be understood clearly that the question of
the reality of the ghosts has nothing to do with whether
readers "believe" in ghosts or whether they think James
"believed" in them; it is merely a question of the *donée*
of the story: the element of "given" upon which it is
based.[11] But in general I think it fair to say that writers
who accept the ghosts interpret the "Screw" in terms of
Jamesian technique and practice, whereas nonappari-
tionists and Freudians go at it as if they were analyzing
actual people instead of characters of fiction.[12]

   The ghosts are alike corrupted and corrupting, and

both, clearly, are damned, but they are not undifferentiated. Miss Jessel is never clearly described; instead we get a general impression of ruined beauty and gentility and of terrible suffering and woe; she must certainly have been intended to awaken pity as well as horror. Quint's features, on the other hand, are described in sufficient detail so that Mrs. Grose is able to recognize him from the governess's record of what she saw. The more common view is that his appearance is intended to suggest a snake or a devil, but E.A. Sheppard devotes a whole chapter of his book to arguing that not only his physical attributes but also his character were intended to suggest Bernard Shaw, as Shaw was understood at the time the story was written!

As presented in "The Turn of the Screw," evil is certainly conceived as something larger and more devastating than either normal or perverted sexuality, but sexuality surely cannot be ruled out. Quint, inferior in station to Miss Jessel, was surely the dominating partner, and it seems fairly clear that she was forced to leave Bly because she was pregnant by him and that, unless she died in childbirth, she committed suicide. Quint himself perished by murder or accident, but he was also certainly diseased, for "there had been matters in his life—strange passages and perils, secret disorders, vices more than suspected—that would have accounted for a great deal more." It is also made clear that Miss Jessel's particular intimacy was with Flora and that Quint was "much too free" with Miles. This, then, must have been the initial element in the corruption of the children, though the corruption need not necessarily have stopped here, and this too must have been where Flora learned the bad language that so shocked Mrs. Grose after she had been taken away from the governess. Probably too it was this kind of thing that Miles talked about to "those I liked" before he was expelled from school.

The children, though equally victimized by the

agents of evil, are as clearly differentiated from each other as their assailants. Miles is the more fully characterized of the two, and it is clear that both Mrs. Grose and the governess are more interested in him than in Flora. At the end Miles is dead and Flora has been removed from Bly, but what is their spiritual condition? Have the forces of darkness lost or won?

Alexander Jones is sure that both children are saved, but most critics consider the two fates separately. Stanley Trachtenberg may well speak for those who give Flora up and Mary Doyle Springer for those who would save her.[13] The little girl rather gives herself away when, upon her last appearance in the story, she not only denies seeing Miss Jessel then but adds, "I never have." It is always dangerous to deny something of which you have not been accused. Mrs. Grose's report of Flora's behavior after she has been separated from the governess (and the reader) is not reassuring, but since we do not see her again, how can we dogmatize about her final condition? It is true that the governess, having been repudiated by the girl, now centers all her energies upon saving Miles, but she does not seem to have given up all hope for his sister: "Far from this, far from *them*," she hopes that "she may be different? she may be free?"

But what then of Miles? Sheppard points out that in Swedenborgian terms Miles, dying unconfessed, must have been lost, for "no one's life can by any means be changed after death," and Carl Van Doren, who adhered to no particular theology, seems in agreement when he writes:

Ancient evil has had its way with a mortal soul, at whatever cost to it or the survivors. Poor little Miles is a childish Faust, who has made his compact with evil in helpless innocence, but who is claimed by his Mephistopheles as ruthlessly as if this had been an equal bargain. *The Turn of the Screw* is the blackest of all nursery tales, the most terrifying of all ghost stories, the most pathetic of all chronicles of damnation.

But neither Pelham Edgar nor Charles G. Hoffmann interprets the ambiguous final scene so darkly; both believe that Miles renounces Quint when he calls his name but that the strain is too much for him and costs him his mortal life. This too would seem to be the governess's view, since the last words she writes are that "his little heart, dispossessed, had stopped." "Dispossessed" of what if not of evil?[14]

The governess herself has been weaving in and out of this discussion of all the other features of "The Turn of the Screw" thus far, which is inevitable both because she is closely involved with the other characters and because the controversy about the governess is the other side of the controversy about the ghosts. Those who do not believe that Quint and Miss Jessel haunt Bly are naturally obliged to account for the governess's seeing them on the basis of some abnormality in her. As we have already seen, she was not even mentioned in James's account of the origin of the story, which is *about* two haunted and corrupted children, and she came into being later, as a "device of narration," "a peripheral character, whose function is to record and to project [the] verbal picture."[15]

That she alone sees the ghosts (except of course, if she is right in her interpretation of the events at Bly, the children themselves) is consistent, as I have already pointed out, not only with all occult lore, according to which such manifestations are highly selective, but with James's own preference in dealing with ghosts ("I feel myself to show them best by showing almost exclusively the way they are felt") and, for that matter, a great many other things too.[16] One would expect the governess to be more "sensitive," in both meanings of the term, than the excellent but significantly named Mrs. Grose,[17] and her affection for the children makes it more natural that she should be placed on her guard against whatever endangers them.

James felt that he had kept the governess's "record of so many intense anomalies and obscurities" not only clear but "crystalline," but that he had not exhibited "her relation to her own nature." On this second point, he and H.G. Wells would seem to have been equally obtuse, for when the latter objected that she was not sufficiently characterized, James admitted the soft impeachment but defended himself on the ground that the tale being what it was, he had "to rule out subjective complications of her own—play of tone, etc.; and keep her impersonal save for the most obvious and indispensable little note of neatness, firmness and courage—without which she wouldn't have had her data." The truth of the matter, however, is that the governess is a very interesting character in her own right, equipped with complete adequacy for the role she has to play. Setting the controversial matters aside for the moment, what, then, can be said about her personality?[18]

She is twenty years old and pretty, a Hampshire vicar's daughter who had been reared in a rather pinched environment (she has never seen a play, and her reading, of fiction at least, has been severely restricted).[19] She is impressible, enthusiastic, nervous, and responsive, very affectionate and demonstrative in her affection, and sometimes extravagant in her language. That she is brave is shown both by her accepting the post at Bly under her selfish and indifferent employer's condition that she must settle all problems herself and never trouble him about anything and by her courage in facing what she regards as supernatural evil after she gets there. She stops at nothing to protect the children, even to the extent of presenting herself as a screen to shield them, or even, if need be, to serve as "an expiatory victim." She is extremely conscientious, given to introspection and self-analysis, capable of both self-blame and self-congratulation, and eager to stand well in her own account and that of others. She torments herself over the responsibilities and anxieties that rob her of her sleep but is still capable of deriving pleasure from the thought that she is carrying a burden that few girls of her age would be able to bear. She trusts her intuitions to the extent of believing much that has not yet been demonstrated, but she questions both herself and the situation by which she is confronted as remorse-lessly as did the most famous ghost seer in English literature, Prince Hamlet. Moreover, though she has a "crush" on her employer, she is clear-sighted enough to be aware of all his shortcomings as the children's guard-ian, and since her first thought upon sighting Quint is that he must be a living human intruder at Bly, she can hardly be called superstitious.

The fact that the tale is told by the governess not only limits the reader to what she knows or believes but secures immediacy by compelling him to think her thoughts after her and share her reactions as they develop in response to the changing situation. At the same time, James achieves distance by using the pro-logue to thrust all the happenings back into the past. The principal function of the prologue, however, is to furnish the governess with a "character reference" and guide the reader's judgment of her. To Douglas, who reads her manuscript to the company, "she was the most agreeable woman I've ever known in her position; she would have been worthy of any whatever." Michael Egan goes beyond the text when he states that James has the children's uncle give her a recommendation after she leaves Bly because "he had seen Mr. Wilson coming," but the prologue does prove that the govern-ess is not unnerved by her experience at Bly, that she continues to give satisfaction in her chosen occupation, and that, when she is about thirty, she is still capable of inspiring affection and respect, even in a man a decade younger than herself. The prologue is misused, however, by those who supply their own ending to the story by keeping Miles alive at the end so that he may grow up into Douglas.[20] Thus Louis Rubin, Jr., remarks that since Douglas is Miles, "the whole basis for believing in the governess's narrative is seriously undercut." It would be indeed, should we grant the major premise; in fact James would be left without a story and Rubin without anything to write about. Trachtenberg goes Rubin one better by seeing Douglas reading the story to expiate his guilt, though what guilt and how it could be expiated before a company none of whom were aware of the identification remains obscure.[21]

Some of the arguments, if they can be called that, that have been advanced to prove the governness hysterical or insane or worse seem to me themselves so clearly worthy of such description that I do not propose to discuss them here.[22] To grant her sanity, unselfishness, and nobility is not, however, necessarily to believe that she makes all the right decisions. John Lydenberg, for example, though rejecting the Freudian view, still sees the children as harried to death by an overprotective, authoritarian young woman who, though heroic, is both masochistic and sadistic, and Ernest Tuveson believes that, unknown to herself, she is a medium who ironically and against her intentions makes it possible for the evil spirits to get in touch with the children.[23] One need not accept such views to appreciate her terrible dilemma. Though she believes the children to be in touch with evil spirits, she knows that she has no proof. If they are guilty, she cannot save them without bringing them to confession and renunciation. But if, on the other hand, they are innocent and she herself becomes responsible for making them aware of the evil influence, where does that leave her?

She never does force the issue with the children until the end, where she loses Flora by estrangement and Miles, so far at least as this world is concerned, by death. She blames herself for her handling of Miles. "I ought to have left it there," she says. "But I was infatuated—I was blind with victory." It is on this basis that Dorothea Krook talks about her "spiritual pride," Charles G. Hoffmann compares her to Oedipus in a ruthless quest for knowledge, and even Robert Heilman, who sees her love for Miles as a disinterested pastoral love, grants her ineptitude. She is an inexperienced girl of twenty who has been thrust into a situation that is not only an impossible one humanly speaking but which has had supernatural terrors superimposed upon it; how can she help rejoicing, in spite of herself, in whatever proves to her that she had been right, not wrong, and reestablishes in her own mind the sanity that James, like Shakespeare with Hamlet, had permitted her to doubt, so that we should not? It is no wonder that even such an admirer as James Gargano should grant that "James's central intelligences would be completely unJamesian if they did not launch into passionate pursuit of knowledge inaccessible to obtuse or even ordinarily active minds"[24] or that some critics should even try to have it both ways, like Cranfill and Clark, who find in her "the earmarks of an inquisitor and some of the characteristics of a saint at the same time." But whatever mistakes she may make, it will be well for all of us if we can come through whatever our own ordeals may be with the credit that belongs to her.

At one time I considered at this point awarding a booby prize for the most absurd interpretation of "The Turn of the Screw," but I now fear conferring such a reward would be unfair to many worthy contenders. Yet the long, sometimes entertaining, frequently exasperating controversy about this tale has not been without its rewards. Literary scholars have learned (or ought to have learned) long ago that since only a limited number of basic situations can be treated in fiction, correspondence does not always prove indebtedness, but the "Screw" controversy does more than provide fresh illustration of this. It shows also that no hypothesis can be too absurd or untenable to be argued quite as convincingly as any other, provided only that the critic is sufficiently bold to disregard the text and sufficiently ingenious and persuasive to be able to make the wrong cause appear right.

The telegraphist who is the central figure of "In the Cage," a tale of some 40,000 words (first published as a small book in 1898 by Herbert S. Stone in Chicago and by Duckworth in London, without previous serialization), has more in common with the governess of "The Turn of the Screw" and the narrator of *The Sacred Fount* than that James sent all three down to posterity without proper names. All three are psychic detectives, and all belong to that group of Jamesian characters whose minds work in their own sphere like that of an artist, conducting explorations into what Walter F. Wright calls "the uncharted realm of inference," attempting to conjure up the whole from random, wayward cues, and with their imaginative activity capable apparently of operating "in inverse proportion to experience," sometimes no longer seeking "corroboration from life" or even finding it "an unwelcome distraction." That this temperament is capable of infuriating those who do not share it much that has been written about both the "Screw" and the *Fount* abundantly attest; if the telegraphist has in comparison escaped lightly, the comparative neglect of her story, among the most complex and accomplished tales of James's maturity, is no doubt responsible. E. Duncan Aswell has, however, now gone far to make up for any neglect the telegraphist may have suffered elsewhere, and Charles Thomas Samuels seems to have followed his lead. It is worth noting that, unlike the other two stories, "In the Cage," though centered in the telegraphist's consciousness is written in the third person; the reader is thus put into possession of certain checks upon her inferences that do not exist in the other two works.[25]

All James remembered, or chose to remember, concerning the origin of "In the Cage" when he wrote his preface to it was that "the postal-telegraph office in general, and above all the small local office of one's immediate neighborhood" set his mind to work upon "the question of what it might 'mean,' wherever the admirable service was installed, for confined and cramped and yet considerably tutored young officials of either sex to be made so free, intellectually, of a range of experience otherwise quite closed to them." There may have been some slight influences from literature, however. Because the *Picciola* (1843) of Joseph Xavier Boniface (Saintine) is one of the novels the telegraphist draws out of the circulating library, Jean H. Frantz (later Jean Frantz Blackall) reasonably postulated it as a possible influence. In his introduction to a collection called *In the Cage and Other Tales*, Morton Dauwen Zabel had already suggested, that Flaubert's "Un coeur simple" might have been involved, and more recently William B. Stone, who also shows that James was more familiar with the conditions under which telegraphists worked than he has often been given credit for, called attention to a tale by Quesnay de Beaurépaire, "Postes et Telegraph," published in *Harper's Magazine* in 1896. Albert C. Friend's attempt to read the story in terms of the legend of Danäe seems to me somewhat forced, but his study of the general meaning of the story is one of the best that has been made.[26]

The cage of the title is literally the postal telegraph enclosure in the grocer's shop of the fashionable Mayfair district in which the tale is set; figuratively it signifies the limitations of the world in which the heroine moves. Because of her humble standing, more than one writer has been led to compare her to Hyacinth Robinson of *The Princess Casamassima*. Like her friend Mrs. Jordan, a clergyman's widow who "does" flowers in the homes of the wealthy, she and her mother have seen better days, but she now perceives no escape from the cage save through her engagement to Mr. Mudge, an erstwhile grocer's clerk on his way up, and her romantic imagination finds an outlet through vicarious involvement in the affairs of the well-to-do society people of the Mayfair district who are forever running in and out, spending what to her would be a fortune on wordy, cryptic messages, sometimes in code.

She comes to live, accordingly, in a "world of whiffs and glimpses," in which she sees "all sorts of things and pieces together all sorts of mysteries." "Sometimes she put in too much—too much of her own sense; sometimes she put in too little." But "her eye for types amounted . . . to genius, and there were those she liked and those she hated," so that as time passes memory and attention give her an "extraordinary possession" of the elements of the lives of those who really interest her.

Such a one—*the* one—is Captain Philip Everard, who is involved in an intrigue with Lady Bradeen. This surpassingly beautiful woman the telegraphist glimpses only twice, but she sees much more of the lover, with whom indeed her own infatuation grows to the extent of taking her out of her way home past the building in which he lives in the hope of meeting him. Once she does and crosses the road to sit with him in the park, where they grow amazingly (perhaps more than quite convincingly) confidential, and where it is delicately conveyed to her that he might not be averse to an intrigue. But from this she shies, instantaneously, though even more delicately, and leaves him alone on the bench under strict injunction not to follow her. She can cope with this kind of thing imaginatively, it seems, but is not prepared to face it in actuality.[27]

The details of the involvement between Captain Everard and Lady Bradeen are never made quite clear, nor is what in the telegram that our heroine saved them from exposure by recovering for them, and only one writer has had the courage really to grapple with all this. Leon Edel contents himself by writing that she rescues Everard "from some undefined imbroglio . . . by remembering a telegram he has sent." When James was asked just what it was that the man had done, he replied only that he did not know and did not wish to know.[28] We do learn at the end that Lord Bradeen has unexpectedly died and that, for some reason, Everard no longer has any choice about marrying the lady, even though he has now apparently ceased greatly to desire it.

The process of the heroine's disillusionment and eventual satisfied acceptance of Mr. Mudge is complex and is complexly indicated. She learns the final details about Captain Everard through Mrs. Jordan, whose awakening runs parallel to her own but eventuates less promisingly. Mrs. Jordan had cherished hopes of marrying one of her clients, Lord Rye, but she settles at last for his butler, now transferred to the establishment of Lady Bradeen and her new husband. But for the telegraphist there is more to it than that. The scene in the park and the fuss over the telegram had only confirmed what she had already known, though she may not have known that she knew it, for she had long been aware that the pleasure she found in her services in the cage proceeded quite as much from hate as from love, and she is almost brutal in indicating to the Captain her awareness not only of his faults but of those of his class. By this time too, for all her tyrannizing over her lover and her priding herself upon the superiority of her sensibilities, she knows in her heart that she is perhaps even luckier than she deserves in having found a man of such stability and integrity. Mudge had long ago attested his manhood (in the orthodox Hollywood cowboy tradition) by collaring a drunken man in the shop, but he attests his kindness, his understanding, and his freedom from resentment and false pride far more substantially by the way he receives his love's confidences about Everard when they are at the seashore together and provides for her drunken mother as they look forward to their marriage without even having been asked to do so.[29] If James is here, like Pope, like Scott, like Cabell, the poet of acceptance, he is surely not the poet of defeat. The artist uses the materials life brings him and shapes them to his use, and no matter if they chance to be common clay rather than gold. It is this that we may expect of our flawed heroine—flawed but capable of growth—now that she has turned her back upon romantic dreams and embraced reality, and it is this that makes her story what Albert Friend has described as a "call for compassion and understanding and love."

Of the three remaining 1899 tales to be considered in this chapter, "Europe" (*Scribner's Magazine*, June 1899, as " 'Europe' ") was the first to be published and is probably the best. It has an affinity with "A Passionate Pilgrim" and "Four Meetings," and it took its point of departure from Mrs. John Gorham Palfrey, the widow of the historian, who lived on in Cambridge, Massachusetts, to an advanced age, attended by "3 poor old maid daughters, who have themselves grown old . . . while sitting there waiting, waiting endlessly for her to depart. . . . They have never been anywhere, never done anything—their lives have passed in this long, blank patience." The original idea was that one of the daughters should die and that when the mother asked what she had died of, she should be told "of old age," the shock of which would dispose of her also. The tale developed differently, however. Mrs. Rimmle's age is never stated except as something phenomenal, but though there is no hint of the supernatural anywhere (the scene is the Rimmle interior in a suburb of Boston), James invests the old woman's unmoving figure with a terror and horror that—like her phenomenal selfishness, seems larger than life.[30]

The great experience of Mrs. Rimmle's life was the visit she had made to Europe long, long ago with her husband, when he was a personage and was received as such everywhere. She brought up her daughters on this memory, and it was always understood that they too would go someday that they might store up the same rich memories to feed upon. But they have waited too long, and every time they prepare to leave, the mother has a "spell" and their trip has to be postponed again. Finally Jane rebels, goes off to Europe with the Hathaways, and being enthralled by it, refuses to return with them, her sister Rebecca keeping her secretly supplied with funds. Finally Rebecca dies, and Maria alone is left to look after Mrs. Rimmle, now become an almost mummified figure who insists that Jane is dead and that Rebecca has gone to Europe. James, who was proud of the compression he had achieved in this 7,500-word tale, speaks of it as "that obscure, or at least that muffled, tragedy." So it is, sympathetically regarded, but there is plenty of rather black comedy too in the way he presents it.

"Paste" (*Frank Leslie's Popular Monthly*, December 1899) plays a deliberate reversal upon Guy de Maupassant's famous story "The Necklace,"[31] in which a woman borrows what she supposes to be a valuable necklace, has the misfortune to lose it, and honorably condemns herself and her husband to privation and virtual slavery to replace it, only to learn in the end that it had been paste. In James's tale, the widow of a vicar, who in her younger days had been an undistinguished provincial actress, leaves at her death a boxful of garish stage jewels hidden away in a closet. Her stepson, believing them trash, gives them to his cousin Charlotte, who loved the old lady, but it turns out that in the midst of all the trumpery there is one string of valuable pearls.

Save for her sweetness and sense of honor, Charlotte is hardly characterized at all, but Mrs. Guy, one of James's appalling vulgar, managing women, through whom the discovery is made, is a vivid brief sketch, and the priggish, mean, hypocritical stepson, Arthur Prime, is drawn with a beautiful, devastating economy, no stroke of the brush wasted. That we should be left wondering at the end whence a poor actress should have derived such a treasure and what it shows about her that she should have accepted it and apparently cherished it would, one might think, furnish enough ambiguity for even a James story, but there is another characteristic turn of the screw at the end. Having learned that the pearls are valuable, Arthur takes them back from Charlotte and tells her that he has destroyed them, but she should have sufficiently known that such insane quixotism did not lie within the scope of his grasping nature so that she would have had no need to be greatly surprised when she found Mrs. Guy wearing them. But, did that lady, as she claims, recognize them "in the Bond Street window" to which Arthur had "disposed of them," or had she perhaps "dealt with Arthur directly," whatever that may mean?

The last story, "The Real Right Thing" (*Collier's Weekly*, December 16, 1899), is again a ghost story but a rather pale one in which indeed no ghost appears to the reader. The suggestion came from Augustine Birrell's mentioning to James that when he had tried to write the life of Frank Lockwood, "so soon after his death and amid all his things," he could not help "feeling as if he might come in."[32] That is what George Withermore feels when he tries to write the life of Ashton Doyne, at the invitation of the author's publishers and his widow. The lady "with her big black eyes, her big black wig, her big black fan and gloves, her general gaunt ugly tragic, but striking and, as might have been thought from a certain point of view, 'elegant' presence," is obviously a "character," but she is also a "case." "She hadn't taken Doyne seriously enough in life, but the biography should be a full reply to every imputation on herself"; thus it is clear that though she puts all she has at Withermore's disposal, her motives are not wholly disinterested. In the beginning the sense of the great man's presence comes as a blessing to his admirer and would-be biographer, and he assumes that Doyne is cooperating with him, but soon this changes to the feeling that he is being balked, and at last it becomes clear to both Withermore and the lady in black that Doyne does not desire a "life," that he indeed positively forbids it. "The real right thing," then, is to leave the man's private life alone and make the public content itself with what he chose to give in the books that are the only possible source of justification for interest in him. Thus "The Real Right Thing" has an affinity with "The Aspern Papers" as well as with James's expression of his own views from time to time. The little story is written with taste and grace, but it leaves at least one reader wondering that James should have found a place for it in the New York Edition from which he had excluded "The Third Person."

VIII

During the year 1900 James published ten tales: •"The Great Good Place," "Maud-Evelyn," •"Miss Gunton of Poughkeepsie," •"The Tree of Knowledge," •"The Abasement of the Northmores," "The Third Person," "The Special Type," "The Tone of Time," •"Broken Wings," and •"The Two Faces." The six titles marked with an asterisk were reprinted in the New York Edition and are considered in this chapter.

Of these, "The Great Good Place" (*Scribner's Magazine*, January 1900) was the first to be published and is by all means the most important. The hero is a writer, but since his problem concerns not writers alone but all men who have found that the world is too much with them, it is not essentially a story of the literary life. In his preface to Volume XVI James writes only:

> There remains "The Great Good Place" (1900)—to the spirit of which, however, it strikes me, any gloss or comment would be a tactless challenge. It embodies a calculated effect, and to plunge into it, I find, even for a beguiled glance—a course I indeed recommend—is to have left all else outside. There then these indications must wait.

This is so coy as to suggest that the subject matter of the tale is too close to the writer to be spoken of. Adeline R. Tintner would seem to have established Balzac's *L'Envers de l'Histoire Contemporaine* as a literary source, and Robert E. Whelan, Jr., has related the story to James's whole moral and spiritual outlook as expressed in his work in general and specifically to his essay, "Is There a Life After Death?"[1]

We may, if we like, call "The Great Good Place" James's utopia, as Harry Silverstein does, or we may go

along with Clifton Fadiman, who reads it as a fairy tale
and interprets it as the author's most unsparing con-
demnation of the materialism of the modern world and
a kind of translation of the spirit of Mozart's music into
the form of a short story.[2] What happens in the tale may
be briefly if not meaningfully told; "The Great Good
Place" must be *read*, not read *about*. George Dane, a
successful writer clogged down with all the impedi-
menta of success, wakes up one morning as much out of
tune with his way of life as Faust or Hamlet when we
first encounter them or Dante at the beginning of the
Comedy or Bunyan's Christian setting out on his pilgrim's progress. With the arrival of the admirer he has
invited to breakfast ("a person whose name somehow
failed to reach Dane's ear"), he finds himself drifting
away to the Great Good Place, and the rest of the story
describes his stay there, where nothing happens except
that he gradually achieves his reconciliation with life. At
the end he wakes up, having slept for eight hours, and
finds that his visitor has cleared his desk for him.

Walter F. Wright has acutely observed that "what
happens to Dane is very real, and the convention of
sleep is but a device, as with Chaucer, for the clearer
vision of reality."[3] But is it a dream or is it a mystical
experience in which Dane reaches another plane of
being? or are the two the same? The difference
between actual time and dream time, as it appears in
this story, is of course familiar in dream literature (one
thinks of one of Mark Twain's most beautiful pieces of
writing, "My Platonic Sweetheart"), and it is clear that
Dane's visitor, whoever he may have been or whatever
he may do, is a person whose presence exhales harmony, like the place Sweet Rocket in Mary Johnston's
novel of that name.[4]

But what, then, is the Great Good Place? It suggests
many familiar things without ever actually identifying
itself with any one of them. It is a retreat ("the break

that lucky Catholics have always been able to make"), a cure, a convent, a country house, a hotel, a club. It is all these things and none of them, for (and the resemblance to mystical experience in general is very striking at this point), it is impossible to define. It was near enough to everyone and everything so that it does not need to be named. Call it an escape from time. Call it the dropping of a burden, the cessation of an ache. Call it the achievement of reason, order, and arrangement. Call it "a meeting after long journeys by complicated ways." Call it homecoming, a return to "some great invisible mother." It is open to as many interpretations as a great work of art.

The Great Good Place is not, to be sure, to everybody's taste. Pelham Edgar called it James's Land of Cockayne and a "somewhat lethargic paradise"; Elizabeth Stevenson (valiant spirit!) was troubled by "the essential unhealthiness of perfect peace, segregated from the stew of life"; J.A. Ward wrote a whole essay on its negative aspects, with provocative references to Melville and Henry Adams.[5] All three seem to me to have ignored the fact that the Great Good Place is not a permanent abode but a power house where batteries may be recharged, the tired rest, and the weary recruit their strength before returning to their work. Some readers have been puzzled too by the fact that nothing is free in the Great Good Place; one "pays" for everything. But surely we misunderstand this if we interpret it to mean that James saw the likes of Ayn Rand turning the corner. It was surely no discovery of his that purgation, cleansing, reconditioning, regeneration (by whatever name you may choose to call it) does not come for nothing.

"Miss Gunton of Poughkeepsie" (*Cornhill Magazine*, May 1900; *Truth*, May-June 1900) is one of the slightest and simplest of James's international tales. Lily Gunton, a young American heiress, becomes engaged to a Roman prince, but the marriage never takes place because the girl expects her fiancé's mother, the "Old Princess," to come forward to welcome her into the family as an American mother would do, while the Princess, for her part, believes that decorum and propriety require the untitled youngster to make the first advances. The story was based on an anecdote related to James in which a girl engaged to the scion of an old Florentine family had yielded in a similar situation, which set him to wondering what might have developed if she had not done so, and he at once proceeded to suggest several possibilities in his notebook entry.[6]

In the story, as he wrote it, which is filtered to the reader through the consciousness of the British Lady Champer, the confidante of both the young people, it is the "Old Princess" who, to please her son, at last gives in, but she humiliates herself in vain, for her letter crosses that in which the impatient, somewhat spoiled and purse-proud young American at last calls off the engagement: "Unless he wants me more than anything else in the world I don't want him." Thereupon she returns to America and engages herself to the young American in the care of whose mother and sisters she had made the return voyage. Slight as the narrative is, however, it is not without nice shadings of its own. It becomes clear at the end that the Prince and his mother were not entirely indifferent to American dollars and that though it was their aristocratic standards that upset Miss Gunton's romance, she had actually been more in love with the "great historic position" of her Prince and the "glamour of [his] name" than she was with him. For all that, it is not only her money that the Romans have lost. The Prince's relationship with his mother has been spoiled too, for it is going to be very hard for her to forgive him for the slight she had been drawn into exposing herself to in his behalf.

In his preface James presents "The Tree of Knowledge" and "The Abasement of the Northmores" together as examples of the "almost heroic dissimulation of capital" of which he was capable in presenting material that was "developmental" in character in the form of "good short stories" without betraying the fact that they were actually "novels intensely compressed." The results struck him as a "successful . . . achieved and consummate . . . duplicity," which, however, did him no good commercially, for he failed to place either story in any magazine, thus leaving them to make their first bow in the collection called *The Soft Side* (1900).

The origin of "The Tree of Knowledge" was, as James recorded, "the 'Gordon Greenough' story told me by Mrs. C.—the young modern artist-son opening the eyes of his mother (the sculptor-father's one believer) to the misery and grotesqueness of the Father's work."[7] The story as it developed is more complicated than that, however, being centered in the consciousness of the friend of the family, Peter Brench, who "despised Mallow's statues and adored Mallow's wife, and yet was distinctly fond of Mallow, to whom, in turn, he was equally dear." "The Master" himself, with "the brown velvet, the becoming *beretto*, the 'plastic' presence, the fine fingers, the beautiful accent in Italian and the old Italian factotum," had never doubted his own possession of "the spirit of Phidias," though the unsold "products of his chisel" with which his studio was crowded "stood about on pedestals and brackets, on tables and shelves, a little staring white population, heroic, idyllic, allegoric, mythic, symbolic, in which 'scale' had so strayed and lost itself that the public square and the chimney piece seemed to have changed places, the monumental being diminutive and the diminutive all monumental." The son, Lance, has been brought up to believe in his father's genius and to desire to emulate him, which he does until he himself goes to Paris to study and learns that he is a "duffer," which opens his eyes to the fact that his father is another, the only difference between them being that the father continues to "grovel in mediocrity" by turning out worthless sculpture industriously and reproaching his son for lack of comparable industry. After Lance returns from Paris, he and Peter Brench have their moment of truth together, and Brench begs the boy not to disillusion his mother and disturb her love. But in the end it becomes evident that Mrs. Mallow has known the truth all along and that it has affected her devotion to her husband not at all.[8]

"The Abasement of the Northmores" probes the hollowness of success and reputation. Lord Northmore, a hopeless mediocrity and, in modern slang, a "stuffed shirt" has made his way in public life "on the back" of the brilliant, modest, unappreciated Warren Hope, who, at fifty-seven, when he died of the chill he had caught at Northmore's funeral, had nothing "as the vulgar said, to 'show' for it all but his wasted genius, his ruined health and his paltry pension." (It is the only serious weakness of the story that James does not sufficiently show how Northmore's victimizing of Hope made his own success possible.)[9]

As the basic idea for the story came to James,[10] Mrs. Hope was to be inspired by the announcement of the forthcoming publication of Northmore's letters to conceive the idea of publishing Warren's, but she was to suffer a body blow when she discovered that though everybody seemed to have saved Northmore's letters, nobody to whom she appealed had kept Hope's; there was simply nothing to publish except what he had written to her. The appearance of the Northmore letters in two copiously illustrated volumes is a publishing disaster, revealing on his part "an abyss of inanity"; the letters are "pompous and ponderous and at the same time loose and obscure"; he managed to be "both slipshod and stiff" at the same time. Because she wants to "score," Mrs. Hope now resolves, despite the indelicacy involved, to publish Warren's letters to her. "She publishes—and does." But then James adds, "Or *is there anything* ELSE *in it?—in connection with the letters she eventually publishes????—???—???*"

There was, and in writing the tale James found it. It happened that Lord Northmore had wooed Mrs. Hope in earlier days, and she still possesses his letters to her. Perhaps if she were to publish these inanities she would secure an even more exquisite revenge upon the North-mores than the contrast the publication of Warren's letters could afford. But when she visits the Northmores to explore the matter, she finds them so crushed by the humiliation they have suffered already that she cannot find it in her heart to humiliate them further, a reaction that recalls Christopher Newman's sparing both the Bellegardes and the early business rival whom he could have crushed with ease in *The American*. Mrs. Hope burns Northmore's letters to her without saying anything to his family about them, and she carefully copies her husband's and has one copy printed from which an edition can be set up after her death.

"Broken Wings" (*Century Magazine*, November 1900) is one of James's tenderest tales; in these days, when feeling is out of fashion in literature, it might even, in some quarters, be called sentimental. But even though in his preface, he professed himself unable to "disinter" its "buried gem," he never wrote a piece that more inevitably expressed his own personality and experience.

Stuart Straith, a painter, and Mrs. Harvey, a writer, had both enjoyed a vogue in their youth, but when the story opens, they are "simply the case of having been had enough of." He, who has not sold a picture for three years, has been thankful for a commission to design the dresses for the play *The New Girl*, and she writes a column for a pittance in a small paper.

The irony of the situation is that "these two worn and baffled workers," who had known and cared for each other in the past and who care still, are kept apart because each supposes the other to be still a glittering success, or, as James puts it, "each, ten years before, had miserably misunderstood and then had turned for relief from pain to a perversity of pride." Both, in other words, "had blundered, as sensitive souls of the 'artistic temperanent' blunder, into a conception not only of the other's attitude, but of the other's material situation at the moment, that had thrown them back on stupid secrecy, where their estrangement had grown like an evil plant in the shade."

In the first of the five chapters of "Broken Wings" we meet both Straith and Mrs. Harvey at a great house party ("the air of the place, with the immense house all seated aloft in strength, robed with summer and crowned with success, was such as to contribute something of its own to the poetry of the evening"), to which he has been invited as representing art and she literature by people as ignorant of the real situation of both as they are of each other's. He is balked in his attempts to reach her by the fact that she seems to be monopolized by "the Ambassador," which of course only reinforces his misapprehensions concerning her. The second chapter is a "scene" in Mrs. Harvey's bedroom between her and Lady Claude, who, being in difficulties, wishes to sound her on the rewards to be derived from literature and is told the truth. In the third chapter Straith and Mrs. Harvey meet when they are seated next to each other at a performance of *The New Girl*, and from then on they rapidly clear up their misunderstandings. "Let us at least be beaten together!" he says as he takes her in his arms; "she let[s] herself go," and "when they had recovered themselves," they break out together "in sweetness as well as sadness" with "And now to work!"

It is impossible to read this story without recalling how James himself had taken stock of his resources and

gone back to work on his fiction after the disappoint-
ment of his hopes for success in the theater nor the
heroic letter he wrote Henry Adams, in response to a
"melancholy outpouring" as late as 1914, in which he
described himself as "that queer monster, the artist, an
obstinate finality, an inexhaustible sensibility," to which
he added that "it all takes doing—and I do. I believe I
shall do yet again—it is still an act of life."[11] If he had
never lost reputation, neither had he had such "success"
as "Daisy Miller" had seemed to promise. No magazine
had printed "The Altar of the Dead," no magazine
would print "The Beast in the Jungle," and of the three
great novels he produced during the twentieth century—*The Ambassadors*, *The Wings of the Dove*, and
The Golden Bowl—only the first was serialized at all,
and the Harpers ran that not in the popular *Magazine*
but in the much more esoteric *North American Review*.

Of "The Two Faces" (*Harper's Bazar*, December
15, 1900, as "Two Faces"; *Cornhill Magazine*, January
1901), perhaps James's very shortest story, he wrote in
his preface that the value by which he had included it in
the New York Edition was peculiarly economic. "It
may conceal rather than exhale its intense little principle of calculation; but the neat evolution, as I call it, the
example of the turn of the whole *coach* and pair in the
contracted court, without the 'spill' of a single pas-
senger or the derangement of a single parcel, is only in
three or four cases (where the coach is fuller still) more
appreciable." This self-satisfaction was abundantly justified, for the brevity of the tale is matched by both its
subtlety and its moral sensitivity. There was never a
better illustration of the truth that for James the world
of "high society" was only a theater to be used to test
and to reveal moral values. However little significance
one may attach to the "presentation" of a bride to London society, James makes it clear that even in such an
action a soul may be saved or lost.

Lady Grantham had supposed that Lord Gwyther

was about to offer his hand and fortune to her when he surprised her by taking off without warning to marry a little girl in Germany and bring her back with him to London. Hereupon he waits on Mrs. Grantham, by this time involved with another admirer, Shirley Sutton, and attempts to pull her claws and put her on her honor by asking her to prepare his unsophisticated wife for her first appearance at a grand "affair." Mrs. Grantham accepts the commission with seeming grace and alacrity—"You'll see what I may still be depended upon to do," she tells Sutton—and ruins Lady Gwyther's social career by decking her out "overloaded like a monkey in a show," a sight all the more glaring in contrast to her own magnificent toilette. The bride's entrance at Burbeck is as artfully prepared for as that of a prima donna at the opera, with the guests "assembled . . . very much as the Roman mob at the circus used to be to see the next Christian maiden brought out to the tigers," and "the poor creature's lost."

Only, once more, the devil is an ass. Not, to be sure, with "the house guests, with Mrs. Grantham as strategist and Miss Banker as spokesmen," for these "are a circle of Madame Merles, judging entirely by the outer shell,"[12] but certainly with Shirley Sutton, in whose consciousness the tale is centered and whose opinion is of much greater consequence. Sutton cannot fail to admire Mrs. Grantham's "perfection resplendent" at Burbeck, but "what in the world," he wonders, has this perfection done to her beauty. "It was her beauty doubtless that looked out at him, but it was into something else that, as their eyes met, he strangely found himself looking." Something had "visibly . . . hardened and sharpened her," something for which at last he can find only one word: "Horrible!" Contrariwise the "small face" looking out over her ridiculous furbelows "that struck him as either seared or sick" went "to the heart" as "exquisite . . . for unimaginable pathos." He will be "off tomorrow morning," and the magnificent Mrs. Grantham has lost two suitors in different ways to the same helpless little girl.

I think it was Meredith (whom James found hard reading) of whom it was said that one of his rules in fiction seemed to be that when you had a really "big" scene to deal with, you must leave it out and content yourself by describing its results. But James too was capable of this procedure. When Lord Gwyther comes to Mrs. Grantham in the first chapter, we are not permitted to hear him voice his all-important request to her. Instead we read: "This was in especial after Lord Gwyther not only had announced that he was now married, but had mentioned that he wished to bring his wife to Mrs. Grantham for the benefit so certain to be derived." And when Lady Gwyther enters at Burbeck, we catch only a glimpse of the two faces; the rest is Sutton's talk with Miss Banker later that evening. The whole tale is handled with great subtlety and consummate art. James puts his readers on their moral as well as intellectual mettle. If they choose to see no more than the "circle of Madame Merles" at Burbeck, that is their affair.

IX

During the years 1901-1908 Henry James published ten tales: "Mrs. Medwin," "The Beldonald Holbein," "The Story in It," "Flickerbridge," "The Beast in the Jungle," "The Birthplace," "The Papers," "Fordham Castle," "Julia Bride," and "The Jolly Corner." One of these, "The Papers," which runs to some 36,000 words, was not included in the New York Edition and must therefore be consigned to Appendix A. Three—"The Beast in the Jungle," "Julia Bride," and "The Jolly Corner"— require more extended treatment than the others; I have therefore reserved them for Chapter X. The other tales make up the chapter in hand.

In one of his notebook entries James calls "Mrs. Medwin" (*Punch*, August 28-September 18, 1901) "really a little cynical comedy." So it is; there is no tale in which he cocks a more irreverent eye at English society. His notebooks[1] credit "the Miss Balch and Lady G. incident" as having suggested the story, and Bernard Richards has now identified Miss Balch, the Mamie Cutter of the tale, as Emily Balch, a minor writer, the daughter of the rector of Emmanuel Church in Newport at the time the Jameses lived there, and Lady G., who became Mrs. Medwin, as Katharine Bucker McVickar, a New Yorker who married the fifth Baron Grantley after a terrific divorce scandal.[2] Miss Cutter, though an American, earns her living by helping doubtful "cases" to maneuver their way into what are regarded as exclusive social circles. Her most important (and most difficult) client at the moment is Mrs. Medwin, who, she knows, cannot be received without the sanction of Lady Wantridge. Unfortunately Lady Wantridge says, "No, my dear, not I. *There* I stop," and when she is reminded that she has shown great charity in other cases, she replies, "There *are* no other cases so bad."

Miss Cutter's problem is first complicated, then unexpectedly resolved, by the inopportune appearance of her half-brother, Scott Homer, an irresponsible sponge, whom she tries unsuccessfully to keep under cover for fear he will hopelessly compromise her. He assures her, however, that English people have "quite a weakness" for him because he is so "diabolically American," and when, in spite of all his sister's precautions, Lady Wantridge encounters him, it turns out that he is right. Scott may not have any morals, but he does have charm, and Lady Wantridge can't find anything wrong with him. Moreover "he has such nice eyes," and she wants him desperately as the "feature" for her "Sundays in the country." Since the young man has no objection to making himself agreeable for a consideration, Miss Cutter has little difficulty in arranging for him to be received at Lady Wantridge's—provided that Mrs. Medwin shall be invited too. The whole transaction is arranged with extreme gentility and without any of the considerations most important to both parties being frankly or openly discussed.[3] Standards can easily be dispensed with when society wishes to be amused.

"The Beldonald Holbein" (*Harper's Magazine*, October 1901), though not much more complimentary to society, has considerably more "heart." In May 1899, when James visited Maud Howe Elliott "at her charming place near St. Peter's," she told him of the "*succès de beauté*" that her mother, Julia Ward Howe, the famous author of "The Battle Hymn of the Republic," had enjoyed in Rome the previous winter, "her coming out (*après*) at the end of her long, arduous life and having a wonderful unexpected final moment—at 78!—of being thought the most picturesque, striking, lovely old (wrinkled and marked) 'Holbein,' etc., that ever was. 'All the artists raving about her.' "[4]

In the tale, which is narrated by an artist whose name we never learn, we meet Lady Beldonald, a vain creature of American origin, "no longer even a little young; only preserved . . . like bottle fruit, in syrup," through a vanity which put her "years ago in a plate-glass case and [closed] up the receptacle against every breath of air." Except for the pitiful heroine of "Glasses," she is probably the vainest woman James ever created, and her life has "its centre in her own idea of her appearance." To accentuate her charms, she makes a practice of keeping plain or ugly women near her to "serve as foils, as accents serve on syllables, as terms of comparison." Only "they must be safe" and "never have moments of rising . . . superior to themselves."

One of these retainers, Miss Dadd, dies at the beginning of the story, to be replaced by a fifty-seven-year-old American relative whom Lady Beldonald has not seen for years. Mrs. Brash is "a small old lady in a black dress and a black bonnet, both relieved with a little white" and "a little old white face, in which every wrinkle was the touch of a master." Both the narrator and his French painter-friend Paul Outreau hail her as "the greatest of all the great Holbeins." She had been "a harmless and sensitive creature hitherto practically dis-inherited," but now she is the hit of the season, and though she refuses to "sit" to anybody, she clearly rel-ishes "the pure joy of deep draught of the very pride of life, of an acclaimed personal triumph in our superior sophisticated world."[5]

Though Lady Beldonald never understands what the artists are chattering about, their talk about Mrs. Brash causes her face to be "invaded" for the first time by anything the narrator can describe as an expression, and it is not long before she ships her relative home. The disappearance of the Beldonald Holbein from London occurs without warning, "producing a consternation . . . as great as if the Venus of Milo had suddenly vanished from the Louvre." The difficulty is that "she had been 'had over' on an understanding, and she wasn't playing fair. She had broken the law of her ugliness and had turned beautiful on the hands of her employer."

After returning to her original condition, Mrs. Brash survives for less than a year: "the taste of the tree ... had been fatal to her; what she had contentedly lived without before for half a century she couldn't now live without for a day." Lady Beldonald sets a new date to begin the sittings for her own much-postponed portrait, and the narrator's last words in the story are: "Since she *will* have the real thing—well, hang it, she shall!" Evidently we may expect no more flattering a likeness than another painter made of Colonel Capadose in "The Liar."

"The Story in It" (*Anglo-American Magazine*, January 1902) is one of the briefest of James's tales. It is also one of the subtlest and most implicational. Read carelessly, it might be taken as belonging in a class with the early and undistinguished "Collaboration" as merely a discussion of aesthetic theory with hardly any story in it. Careful reading, however, makes it clear that the characters are being described *in terms of* what they believe about literature. As James Gargano puts it, the colonel and Mrs. Dyott, who are "essentially characters in the kind of novel they caution respectable people to stay out of" (the burning of the incriminating letter in the first chapter is straight out of French melodrama), defend themselves as "fascinating fictional material," while Maud Blessingbourne "acts out her idealistic conception of life with the same completeness that the colonel and his mistress act out theirs."[6]

Not, however, that they are ever frank and open about it. There are even times when the author's signals to the reader seem deliberately crossed in the interest of subtlety. It is the idealistic widow Mrs. Blessingbourne who is devoted to French novels and D'Annunzio,[7] while Colonel Voyt, whose adulterous relationship with Mrs. Dyott is never obviously spelled out, professes a high respect for the decent woman in life, her difficulty as stuff for literature being due simply to the fact that "the high privilege of virtue is precisely to avoid drama" and that "the honest lady hasn't, can't possibly have, adventures." As James first conceived the story after a discussion with "a distinguished friend, a novelist not to our manner either born or bred" (probably Paul Bourget), he planned to have Maud confess her love for Colonel Voyt,[8] but as the story stands, this is only guessed at by Mrs. Dyott, whose finally passing it on to Voyt is really the only direct thing in the tale.

Maud and the colonel (Mrs. Dyott takes a very minor part in their debate) agree that English and American fiction is innocuous and also that the French are monotonous in their everlasting harping upon the same string, but Maud obviously cherishes the hope of herself writing a different kind of novel upon "a lovely subject," though she admits that "it would take an amount of treatment" and that it might well be "unmarketable." Never laying all his cards on the table, the colonel sticks to it that a romance *is* a relationship, and it is obvious that, being what he is, he can conceive of only one relationship in this area of experience. "The adventure's a relation; the relation's an achievement," and the novel and the drama "are the picture of one." Where the relationship does not exist, the artist is therefore necessarily deprived of material. But Maud comes back at him with "Doesn't it depend a little upon what you call adventures?" and when she talks the matter over afterwards with Mrs. Dyott, whose own relationship to Colonel Voyt she never suspects, she admits that she too has her "little drama," an "attachment," a "passion," which ("thank goodness") is not "shared," and of which the object is "utterly" unaware. When, after shrewdly guessing despite Maud's barefaced declaration to the contrary ("it's not any one you've ever seen") that the colonel is himself the object of this innocent adoration, Mrs. Dyott tells him, he is forced to admit at last that Maud's consciousness "*was*, in the last analysis, a kind of shy romance," though "not a romance like their own, . . . but a small scared starved subjective satisfaction that would do her no harm and nobody else any good," but he still maintains that "only a duffer . . . would see the shadow of a 'story' in it."

Ellen Tremper, who reads the story as a reply to Paul Bourget and, taking her cue from Mrs. Blessingbourne's mention of D'Annunzio, interprets it in the light of James's essay on that writer ("What James attempts to do in 'The Story in It' is to improve on D'Annunzio"), calls Maud "James's spokesman" in this tale. Whether or not one would put it in quite that way, there can be no question that the writer was more interested in subjective adventure than in the moving accident by field and flood. As I have written elsewhere,[9] James is, above all else, the novelist of experience imaginatively apprehended. He wanted to understand life, not merely to fling himself into it, and for understanding a certain detachment is requisite. He embodies therefore the principle that experience in itself is worthless until it has been adequately interpreted by the mind and its significance assessed. And with him, as with Jane Austen and the Brontës, to take two very different examples before him, a very little of what the field and flood people would call experience might produce not only a great deal of feeling but also a great deal of that art which, as he once told the incredulous H.G. Wells, "*makes* life, makes interest, makes importance," adding that "for myself I live, live intensely and am fed by life, and my value, whatever it is, is in my own kind of expression of that."[10]

In its horror of journalism, with all its assaults on privacy, "Flickerbridge" (*Scribner's Magazine*, February 1902) has an affinity with the much more unwieldy contemporarous tale "The Papers" (see Appendix A); in the "sense of the past" it exhales, it suggests the fine unfinished late novel of that title and much of James's work besides. In his New York Edition preface, he declared that the "highly-finished little anecdote" had covered its tracks so completely that it refused to answer any questions concerning its origin; the notebooks, however, make it clear that the original suggestion came from Sarah Orne Jewett's story "A Lost Lover" (in her *Tales of New England*), whose plot however is entirely different.[11] Since James mentions Guy de Maupassant's "Miss Harriet," in Chapter V, he also obviously had it in mind, and that appalling horror story might perhaps have contributed to the grotesquerie of Miss Wenham's appearance.

Flickerbridge is the name of the secluded English village where Miss Wenham, the aged, newly discovered English relative of the enterprising young American writer and journalist Addie Wenham, lives. They have never met, but when Addie, who is in Paris, learns that her artist-fiancé Frank Granger has had a bout with flu in London, she makes arrangements by post for him to go to Flickerbridge to recuperate. "Fiancé" is actually something of an overstatement, for though Addie tells Miss Wenham that Frank is engaged to her, this has, as a matter of fact, been "publicly both affirmed and denied," and what Frank "mainly felt on the whole" as if he were "going to find out" at Flickerbridge was whether he was engaged or not. What he does find there at once, however, is something he had not been prepared for, "one of the sweetest fairest coolest impressions of his life," for the place is an island of peace and quiet almost comparable to the Great Good Place, and Miss Wenham herself scores as marked a success with him as did Mrs. Brash with the artists of "The Beldonald Holbein." This is not, however, because he discovers in her a hidden beauty, for hers is, on the contrary, "an almost Gothic grotesqueness . . . . Her eyes protruded, her chin receded and her nose carried on in conversation a queer little independent motion. She wore on the top of her head an upright circular cap that made her resemble a caryatid disburdened, and on other parts of her person strange combinations of colours, stuffs, shapes, of metal, mineral and plant." Yet "the final effect of one's sense of it was an amenity that accompanied one's steps like wafted gratitude." As he tells her, she is "*all* type. It has taken delicious long years of security and monotony to produce you. You fit your frame with a perfection only equalled by the perfection with which your frame fits you . . . . You're the Sleeping Beauty in the Wood."

The really important thing that Frank Granger finally learns through his experience at Flickerbridge, however, is that he is *not* engaged to Addie Wenham. He first writes her a letter extolling the charms of the place and of her relative in it, then decides not to send it. Should Addie come there and discover her kinswoman, the latter's fate would be like that of Niagara after the explorers had come upon it. As he tells the old lady, "All Addie's editors and contributors and readers will cross the Atlantic and flock to Flickerbridge . . . . You'll be in the magazines with illustrations; you'll be in the papers with headings; you'll be everywhere and everything."

As James originally conceived the story, the young man was not an artist but a barrister and journalist (but at the last, like the young lovers in "The Papers," a journalist awakened), the crowds did come, and "the old woman becomes a show old woman" and "likes it," as in a measure Mrs. Brash seems to have liked what happened to her in "The Beldonald Holbein." But as the story was written, Granger flees before Addie arrives, not being able to bear the thought of witnessing what he fears may ensue or even of seeing her. "We're not engaged. Goodbye."

While it would be harder to find a more Jamesian

story than "Flickerbridge," it is hardly one of his most technically expert narratives. He makes no use of all the background information he gives us concerning the Wenham family on both sides of the Atlantic, and I know nothing anywhere in his work more methodologically naive than his statement about the unsent letter to Addie, "which, if space allowed us to embody it in our text, would usefully perform the office of a 'plate.' It would enable us to present ourselves as profusely illustrated." Mrs. Brash's *succès de beauté* with a small circle of sophisticated people who have had personal contact with her may be believable, but it is much harder, in this story, to envisage the transatlantic horror that Frank looks forward to. Nor is the young man himself a character whom we can easily conceive of as existing in anything but a Jamesian world. His response to both Miss Wenham's personality and her setting reaches a pitch of intensity that hardly seems reasonable under the circumstances, and it is even more difficult to believe that any young man would break with a girl not for anything she had done but for something he had made up his mind she would do in a hypothetical situation. But though not all readers seem yet fully to have recognized it, it ought surely to be clear by this time that James is by no means wholly a realistic writer.

Some of these considerations also apply, in a measure, to the much more ambitious story, "The Birthplace" (first published, without previous serialization, in *The Better Sort*, 1903). It is nowhere stated that the literary shrine of which Morris and Isabel Gedge are placed in charge is the Shakespeare House at Stratford, but it is perfectly clear that this is what it is. It is "the supreme Mecca of the English-speaking race," and the great poet who lived there is called "Him," as if he were the Deity. The Gedges are as poor as they are civilized, and the job comes just in time to rescue them from a very uncongenial berth in a fifth-rate library, stocked mainly with the kind of romances we used to think of as being read mainly by servant girls. They ought, therefore, to feel that they are in paradise, and for a time they do; they read and study industriously, and Morris even takes to prowling through the house in the darkness, seeking a mystical communion with "Him."

What they soon discover, however, is that the distinguished gentlemen who administer the trust by which the Birthplace is operated regard "the supreme Mecca of the English-speaking race" as a "Show" that is expected to return dividends and in which they have a vested interest, while the gaping tourists who tramp through the place during its busy seasons have no desire whatever to read "His" works but do wish to have the exact spot where "He" was born pointed out to them, with a host of other such "human interest" details, all entirely without reference to whether they are being fed fact or fiction.

With a woman's practicality and a keen appreciation of what "He" is doing for them and the bread "He" is putting into their mouths, Isabel adjusts herself easily, but Morris finds himself "splitting into halves, unmistakeably" and quite clearly "on his way to becoming two quite different persons, the public and the private." For a time he tries to achieve a more scholarly presentation, offering tentatively what is not certainly known, but word comes back to his employers, and Mr. Grant-Jackson arrives to deliver a stern warning. Badly frightened, Gedge thereupon assures his wife that he has killed his conscience, after which he learns romancing supremely well. In the last chapter James treats us to a superb parody version of what all custodians aspire to:

"Across that threshold He habitually passed; through those low windows, in childhood, He peered out into the world that He was to make much happier by the gift to it of His genius; over the boards of this floor . . . His

> little feet often pattered; and the beams of this ceiling . . .
> he endeavoured, in boyish strife, to jump up and
> touch."

And much more to the same effect. Isabel is not yet
entirely at her ease: "There would be more than one
fashion of giving away the Show, and wasn't this perhaps a question of giving it away by excess?" But she
need not have been concerned. Receipts soar, and the
fame of the gifted custodian even reaches America. At
his next visitation, Mr. Grant-Jackson brings the glad
tidings that the stipend of the Gedges has been doubled.

Two sharply opposed interpretations of the meaning of Gedge's experience have been entered. The first
may best be stated in the words of Quentin Anderson:
"We know that in Shakespeare's supposed birthplace an
artist has in fact been born—but we know not how any
more than in the case of Shakespeare." The other view
is that of such writers as Joseph Holleran and Morton L.
Ross, who take the custodian's conscientious scruples
very seriously indeed. As Holleran reads it, "The Birthplace" deals not with the evolution of an artist but the
prostitution of an honest man. Gedge "sacrifices his
conscience" and becomes a fraud, and "only James's
masterful irony saves 'The Birthplace' from being a
tragedy," while Ross bluntly calls our hero "both a liar
and a hypocrite" and the story "a double-edged commentary on both the mechanics and the morality of
literary idolatry."[12]

Warrant can be found in the text for these very
earnest and highly moral interpretations, but it seems to
me that the tone of the whole tale is against them.
Though James got his idea for the story from an anecdote of Lady Trevelyan's about a couple who actually
did give up their work at Stratford because, after six
months, they could no longer tolerate the "humbug, full
of lies and superstition imposed upon them by the great

body of visitors,"[13] the reference to Gedge in James's
preface as "another poor gentleman—of interest mainly
in being yet again too fine for his rough fate" hardly
suggests that we are to think of ourselves as face to face
with the loss of a human soul. Moreover, in a world full
of lies that wreak such havoc as we see all around us,
making a great moral issue out of Gedge's performance
has, one must admit, its comic side.

In any case, the story is told delightfully. Both the
Gedges are likable and believable; Miss Putchin, the
retiring caretaker who instructs them in their duties and
to whom it has never occurred to do anything but give
the public what the public wants, is a vivid brief sketch;
and Mr. Grant-Jackson looms portentously, like Mrs.
Newsome across the Atlantic in *The Ambassadors*. It is
hard to believe, however, that Gedge, lost soul or
accomplished showman as the reader may elect, would
put himself through all the tricks of his parody lecture
for the benefit of the admirably intelligent and sympathetic Mr. and Mrs. D.B. Hayes of New York, the only
visitors with whom, on their previous visit to the Birthplace, he had frankly discussed his problem.

"Fordham Castle" (*Harper's Magazine*, December
1904) is as sympathetic a story as "Broken Wings," but
there is far more astringency in the mingled "pathos and
drollery" of its development. It is also, in its way, one of
James's international tales, and in the comparisons it
affords between the situations of the two leading characters it illustrates once more his well-known passion
for symmetry and parallelism.[14]

James had long known that socially ambitious
wives and socially or professionally ambitious children
have often felt the need of keeping unfashionable husbands and parents out of sight. He had written of one
such young lady in "Pandora," but she would have been
quite incapable of the kind of inhumanity manifested
by either Mrs. Magaw's daughter Mattie or Abel F.

Taker's wife Sue. We meet Taker and Mrs. Magaw
(both Americans) at a Swiss pension in view of the Lake
of Geneva, where they have not only been kept out of
sight but their very identities erased ("You think it isn't
so much to do—," the man asks the woman, "to lie down
and die for them?"), while Mattie and Mrs. Taker (now
the mythical Mrs. Sheerrington Reeve) both gravitate
to the festivities at Fordham Castle, where they soon
recognize each other as kindred spirits and from which
they address their letters to "Mrs. Verplanck" and "Mr.
C.P. Addard," respectively.

Taker is forty-five and Mrs. Magaw is past fifty,
and at first they keep up their respective fictions with
each other: he has been to Constantinople to visit Mrs.
Addard's grave and she has a daughter buried in Rome.
As they become more intimate, however, they tell each
other the truth, and though "he wondered what she
could see in him in whom Sue now at last saw really less
than nothing," he is finally able to tell her frankly that
"I'd give Mrs. Taker up, definitely, just to remain C.P.
Addard with you." She, however, is a "large simple
scared foolish fond woman," whose unreclaimed coun-
tenance was "uninhabited" except for "vague anxiety,"
and since she is "neither fair nor slim nor 'bright' nor
truly, nor even falsely, elegant," she resents her situation
much less than he resents his. It finally develops that
Mattie has achieved her goal by bagging Lord Dunder-
ton at Fordham Castle, and when she telegraphs her
mother that she can come now, that agreeable lady
accepts with alacrity. Taker, for his part, expects no
such summons; neither does he any longer greatly
desire it. Indeed, since he is "dead," he does not see how
he could well appear at Fordham or elsewhere, except
as a ghost.

X

As was stated at the beginning of Chapter IX, the three most significant tales of the 1901-1908 period have been reserved in this chapter for more extensive treatment than the others. The first of these is "The Beast in the Jungle" (first published, without previous serialization, in *The Better Sort*, 1903). James recognized its affinity with "The Altar of the Dead" by making it the second item in Volume XVII of the New York Edition, where "The Altar of the Dead" stands first, and it has been well nigh universally regarded as one of his very greatest stories, a view I have no inclination to challenge.

Both the editors of the *Notebooks* and Charles G. Hoffmann cite Hawthorne, and specifically "Ethan Brand," as a possible influence upon this story, and Jessie L. Lucke saw Hollingsworth in *The Blithedale Romance* as Marcher's original. Leon Edel was reminded of Guy de Maupassant's "Promenade," and William Nance harked back to the Oedipus story. He also notes that James had been reading his brother's book, *The Varieties of Religious Experience*, and I am inclined to add hypothetically that the Grimms' story "The Youth Who Could Not Shudder" might also have contributed. But Edel is primarily concerned with what he considers a reflection of James's experience with Constance Fenimore Woolson, and this is accepted by Ellen Tremper, who interprets not only "The Beast in the Jungle" but also "The Aspern Papers" and "The Jolly Corner" on this basis, while Milton M. Mays thinks he finds varied indications of James's life experience in the two late tales.[1]

John Marcher, who enjoys "a modest patrimony," a library, and "a little office under Government," had met May Bartram a decade before the story begins, when she was twenty and he five years older, and had then confided in her his "sense of being kept for something rare and strange, possibly prodigious and terrible." Sooner or later the Beast would leap upon him out of the Jungle, perhaps to overwhelm him, and there is nothing he can do about it save to wait and endure. One of the first striking manifestations we encounter of his self-centeredness is that when he meets May again at Weatherbee, at the beginning of the tale—handsome, but "ever so much older" than before and, like the lady in "The Altar of the Dead," marked by her life experience—he has only a vague memory of their former interchange but with all the details wrong and with the confidence he had reposed in her having completely escaped him. May, on the other hand, has forgotten nothing. Instead of laughing at him, she had accepted his communication with perfect sympathy and understanding. She believes in him and agrees to "watch" with him, and this gives him a wonderful sense of no longer being "so abominably alone." But both irony and the hint of future developments are involved in the realization of both characters that they have already missed something and in Marcher's rejection of the suggestion that perhaps what he expects may be simply the experience of falling in love.

It must be clearly understood that Marcher is not a "bad" man. It is true that in effect May is sacrificed to him, but this is not his intention; he never deliberately exploits or victimizes anybody. He is "tremendously mindful" of all she does for him and worried over whether he is not receiving more than he gives. He escorts the lady to the opera and observes her birthday with more expensive gifts than he can really afford. He even thinks of asking her to marry him, and in a way it is only his consideration for her that prevents this: he is a man marked by destiny, but he is also a man of feeling, and he cannot believe that a man of feeling would ask a

lady to accompany him on a tiger hunt. His egotism
coexists with a naiveté that almost makes it seem innocent; when she praises his attitude toward his ordeal, he
asks, "It's heroic?" and again, "I *am* then a man of
courage?" Nevertheless, his egotism is appalling. When
May is stricken at last by mortal illness, he wonders
momentarily whether her death might be the leap of the
Beast for which he has been waiting, but he rejects this
idea as he had previously rejected the love experience
(it would be, for him, a "drop of dignity") and even
goes the length of pitying the "sphinx," the "lily" that
May has become, because she may have to die without
finding out what is going to happen to him!

While we must never forget in dealing with Marcher
that his is a failure in understanding rather than good
intentions, it is equally important to remember that this
does not completely exonerate him. The consciousness
of being set apart, even for misfortune, can easily
become a force for distortion, especially when, as in
Marcher's case, one does not see it as requiring any
action or entailing any obligation. Gamaliel Bradford
remarked of the poet Cowper, who thought he had
committed the unpardonable sin, that he preferred
being damned to being convinced that he had been
mistaken, and theologians have always realized that the
sinner who supposes his sins to have been so uniquely
great as to carry him beyond the bounds of God's mercy
is guilty of monstrous presumption as well as of the sin
of despair.

May Bartram achieves the near miracle of knowing
Marcher thoroughly, loving him, and yet viewing him
almost objectively; at the same time she protects him by
trying to help him "to pass for a man like another." As
for him, he realizes nothing except through her (he has
not even grasped his own aging until he sees with the
eyes of his flesh that she is visibly growing older), and it
is a tragedy for both of them that she cannot communi-

cate to him the most important piece of knowledge she has about him, for the simple reason that this is one of the things a man must learn for himself or die without knowing. For the Beast in Marcher's jungle is not imaginary; it is only different from any beast Marcher had conceived. Marcher is the empty man with whom literature since James's time has become so tiresomely preoccupied, the embodiment of what Hemingway called "Nada," the man "to whom nothing on earth was to have happened," and this he becomes through his inability to love. Life offers its best to him, and he passes it by, not because he does not value or desire it but simply because he does not recognize it. As children get "warm" from time to time when searching for a companion in a game of hide-and-seek and then veer off again, he experiences flashes of prescience that give us moments of hope for him: the fear of being too late; the thought that not to be anything would be worse than to be bankrupt, hanged, or dishonored. But he fails to follow up these clues because he cannot believe that such things could happen to so marked and exceptional a being as himself.

May, on the other hand, learns the truth as early as the end of the second of the six divisions of the tale, where Marcher accuses her of knowing what is to happen to him and of withholding her knowledge from him because it is too terrible to tell. She will only say that he will never know and never suffer. During her final illness she adds that it has already happened and that he has not recognized it. Why should he seek to know that which he need not know? It is enough that *she* knows and that she can be grateful for having lived to learn what it is not. He continues to experience flashes of perception. He feels that she has more to give him than he has yet received. Once he even asks her if she is dying for him, and in a sense she is, as Milly Theale dies for her friends (or enemies) in *The Wings of the*

Dove. But since he also accuses her of deserting him and leaving him alone to meet his fate, it is suitable that he should be left stranded on the periphery as he is at her funeral.

For if he is sometimes perceptive, he is more often blind. He can charge her with withholding information from him and, almost in the same breath, tell himself that, except for her feminine intuitions, she has no more knowledge than he has. Yet her own love and understanding never falter, and some hope remains to the end. "The door's open," she tells him. "It's never too late." She is right when she says, "I've shown you, my dear, nothing," but this is merely because he has no eyes, and she is right again when she says, "I haven't forsaken you" and "I'm with you—don't you see?"

But she is mistaken about one thing. Ultimately Marcher does "know" and suffer too, though this is not until after her death, when everything has become "vulgar and vain" without her, through a chance encounter near her grave, which has become to him something like Stransom's altar of the dead, with a desperately bereaved, "deeply stricken" young widower, visiting the grave of his young wife nearby. This man is one of those who, as Henry Adams, glancing obliquely at his own never-healing wound, once expressed it, "suffer beyond the formulas of expression—who are crushed into silence and beyond pain," and Marcher envies him! "What had the man had to make him by the loss of it so bleed and yet live?" And, by the same token, what had Marcher himself missed? "No passion had ever touched him, for this was what passion meant; he had survived and maundered and pined, but what had been *his* deep ravage? . . . He had seen *outside* of his life, not learned it within, the way a woman was mourned when she had been loved for herself." This man had lived, and May had lived, but Marcher had escaped living, and "*she* was what he had missed." The Beast

had sprung at last, and we leave Marcher, in his awakened anguish, flung face downward, upon May's grave.
Knowledge has come at last.[2]

"Julia Bride" is one of the most amazingly neglected of all James's tales; except for Peter Buitenhuis
and Adeline R. Tintner, nobody seems to have given it
more than a passing glance. Even the general survey
books manage to slight it. F.W. Dupee merely regrets
that James should have found space for it in the New
York Edition, and Bruce R. McElderry, Jr., who says
something about nearly everything, gives it two brief
sentences that inadequately summarize the action and
indicate that the scene is New York City. Charles G.
Hoffmann awards it a page, but though he grants that it
is "well-written and well-constructed" and "characterized by a lucid, smoothly rhythmic style," he finds it
"slight in theme and not indicative of any particular
growth or development in James's art" and explains the
neglect it has suffered on the ground that it has attracted
attention neither as a success nor a failure. As for Pelham Edgar, he merely entered the amazing judgment
that its "development . . . is so slight as to make comment unnecessary."[3]

Buitenhuis groups Julia Bride with Daisy Miller
and Pandora Day as picturing "the evolution of characteristic American girlhood," which from James's point
of view obviously spelled deterioration, "over three
decades," and documents his findings by reference to
the articles the novelist contributed to *Harper's Bazar* in
1906-1907. I find it difficult to understand why this
critic should feel that Daisy fails to "arouse deep feelings of sympathy" simply because "she dies wronged
and innocent" with "little comprehension of the causes
of her fate," but it is certainly true that as "the victim of a
mistaken upbringing," Julia sees "more and more as the
story progresses," achieves self-knowledge, and enters
a judgment upon herself and her society. That society

has been corrupted by wealth as desperately as the
society we are to encounter in *The Ivory Tower*. Julia,
her generally admirable ex-stepfather, Mr. Pitman, and
her much less admirable ex-suitor, Murray Brash, are all
engaged in negotiating rich marriages, and it cannot be
without significance that though we learn much about
her desire—and her need—to be united to the wealthy,
high-minded Basil French, we are never told that she is
deeply in love with him. Buitenhuis stresses the use
James makes in the rich imagery that runs all through
this story of materials drawn from financial transactions
and animals (as from those kept in the Central Park
zoo), and Adeline Tintner adds much on architecture,
but even the new Metropolitan Museum (1902), which
James first saw on his 1904-1905 visit, and which is the
scene of the first two of the three chapters in the story,
seems to have impressed him principally as a monument of "acquisition," and though Julia's excessive
prettiness makes an art museum an eminently suitable
background for her, it is interesting in view of the
impressive use James makes of works of art and the
interaction between works of art and their viewers
elsewhere in his writings that we never see her admiring
any particular picture or statue. Instead, she merely
"saw the great shining room, with its mockery of art and
'style' and security, all the things she was vainly after."

If Buitenhuis groups Julia with Daisy and Pandora,
she has a different kind of affinity with Maisie Farange
(*What Maisie Knew*) and Nanda Brookenham (*The
Awkward Age*). Her mother has been divorced twice
and is now separated from her third husband, and Julia
herself has six broken engagements on her record (she
kept all the rings: "three diamonds, two pearls, and a
rather bad sapphire"). Her present connection, Basil
French, who is out of the bluest page in the blue book,
"a man of intelligence, a real shy beautiful man of the
world," dry but distinguished, is obviously much "gone"

on her, but his ideas of propriety are strict and those of his family, if possible, even stricter. "He's dying to find out" whether what he has heard whispered about Julia is true, "and yet he'd die if he did!" Moreover, there is Mrs. George Maule in the background. Doubtless there is more than one Mrs. Maule, but this one is a cat with kittens, "four little spotlessly white ones, among whom she'd give her head that Mr. French should make his pick."

What Julia needs then is a character witness for herself and her mother, and her best hope is her mother's second husband Pitman, an eccentric but worthy gentleman who has the habit of twirling his pince-nez at the end of a very long string (once, years ago, he hit her in the eye with them rather badly), with whom she lived between twelve and seventeen. "Julia Bride" is narrated from Julia's point of view (she is understanding enough so that, unlike Daisy, she does not need an observer), and the first chapter is taken up with her inward preparation for meeting Pitman at the Metropolitan and the second mainly with what they say to each other there. What she wants him to do is to clear her mother by taking the blame for their divorce upon himself, though she knows that the opposite is true, but unfortunately Pitman is on the verge of arranging a marriage with Mrs. David E. Drack, who is quite as squeamish about divorce as the Frenches, and what he wants of Julia is precisely that *she* should give *him* a clean bill of health! Here is the familiar Jamesian irony and parallelism of situation again, with the interesting variation that while Julia wants him to lie for her, he only wants her to tell the truth for him. Mrs. Drack "wasn't refined, not the least little bit." She has "a huge hideous pleasant face" and is clearly "not shy," but she is "bland and good," and it is suitable that she should come upon Julia and Pitman in the Metropolitan Museum, for hers is a "suspended weight and arrested mass," and she would dwarf any smaller building. Julia's finest moment comes at the end of Chapter II, for though she has told Pitman she will not go to see Mrs. Drack, when she is confronted by her she tells the truth, thus making it impossible for him to serve her need. "She gave him away, in short, up to the hilt, for any use of her own." As she has said, she cannot lie, though she seems to have no objection to other people lying for her.

We are not told whether Julia has been guilty of anything worse than recklessness and bad taste in connection with those six broken engagements. Murray Brash seems to have been the man with whom she "had been *most* vulgar, most everything she had better not have been," and if we may accept his testimony, they only exchanged their "young vows with the best faith in the world" and would have married except for the lack of means on both sides. "What harm in the sight of God or man, Julia, did we ever do?" But Murray is obviously not a man of the finest sensibilities, nor, since as Julia herself says, "I should have taken the precaution to have about a dozen fewer lovers," did the six young men to whom she had been engaged exhaust the list of her amatory connections. Describing her "younger romps" in terms of architectural imagery, probably derived, as Ms. Tintner suggests, from the Villard Houses, James does say that she had been "dishonoured" by them. "She had tumbled over the wall with this, that and the other raw playmate, and had played 'tag' and leap-frog, as she might say, from corner to corner," and she herself is well aware that she has ignorantly and pitifully groped and floundered in "wretched frivolity" and "preposterous policy . . . from the very dawn of her consciousness." Apportion the responsibility between her society, her mother, and herself as you like; what is clear is that she has not escaped unscathed. That is all we know about it and all we need to know.

The third and last chapter of "Julia Bride" concerns

the girl's conference in Central Park with Murray Brash, to whom she turns as her last hope after Pitman has failed her. Murray is "charming coarse heartless," and he is amiability itself; if it will help Julia, he will lie for her until he is black in the face. But his complaisance has a price tag attached. For at this point James indulges himself in more parallelism. Murray too is contemplating marriage, with one Mary Lindeck, who has money but not the social position she covets, and what he expects of Julia is that if he lies for her, she shall return the favor by introducing him and Mary into the circles in which, as Mrs. Basil French, she would be expected to move. Julia, in no position to refuse, avoids a definite answer, and technically the ending of the tale is "open." Practically, however, it is closed, for the girl clearly has no hope, and we leave her, imprisoned in her own foolish, ignorant past, in the same position that Marcher occupies at the end of "The Beast in the Jungle," flung upon her face on the bed in her unfashionable room and yielding "to the full taste of the bitterness of missing a connexion, missing the man himself, with power to create such a social appetite, such a grab at what might be gained by them."

In his New York Edition preface (Volume XVII) James tells us how "poor re-invoked Julia" came to him crying "Here we are again!" and placing herself "for this positively final appearance" at his disposal. He didn't think her "particularly important in herself," but her "reference" seemed to him "multitudinous," and he tried to use her as a "silver key, tiny in itself, that would unlock . . . the treasure of a whole view of American manners and morals." This is exactly what is accomplished in a tale technically foreshortened and rich in its implications. Buitenhuis is certainly correct in finding that "the freedom of relations between the sexes that James had accepted as a desirable American norm . . . in 'Daisy Miller' came in for a critical reappraisal in 'Julia

Bride,'" and it is the more remarkable therefore that the author should have managed to write as both an impeccable moralist and a warmly sympathetic human being. The means he employs in his first two chapters to endear both Julia and Mr. Pitman to the reader, culminating in her unselfish act at the end of Chapter II, would make an interesting study in themselves.

"The Jolly Corner" (*English Review*, December 1908) was James's last ghost story, and except for "The Turn of the Screw" by all means his greatest. The idea came to him on August 3-4, 1906, and kept him awake all night. He seems to have written the tale shortly thereafter, and at the time at least it seemed to him "a miraculous masterpiece."[4]

Various sources have been inconclusively suggested: the Dionysos myth, the twenty-fifth chapter of Matthew, Hawthorne's "Egotism," and Benjamin Franklin's glass armonica.[5] However all this may be, there were certainly influences from life. James's own pursuit of "the awful agent, creature or presence, whatever he was" whom he chased through the Galerie d'Apollon in the nightmare he recorded in *A Small Boy and Others* bears a marked resemblance to Spencer Brydon's involvement at "the jolly corner," and some of Brydon's reactions to the changes he sees in New York upon returning there after an absence of a generation were certainly based upon James's own when he came back after a twenty-two-year absence in 1904, even though one may totally reject the efforts of some critics[6] to read deep autobiographical and psychological interpretations into the story. As for method, though the tale is centered in Brydon's consciousness, James does not wholly exclude comment by the author or a hypothetical unnamed observer.

It hardly needs saying that in most ghost stories, the ghost encountered is the spirit of a dead person; "The Jolly Corner" exemplifies the much rarer type in which we have to deal with the ghost of a person who is still alive, in this case the ghost of the ghost-hunter himself or, if one wishes to express the matter more "psychologically," his potential self or what he might have been had he lived his life in a different milieu or under different circumstances. I have no desire to desupernaturalize the story nor to explain away the *frisson* James obviously intended the reader to experience, but I gladly grant that it *is* a study of character and personality as well as a thriller. Moreover, there are *two* characters—Spencer Brydon and Alice Staverton—and though we see much more of him than we do of her, her importance is not to be minimized, for if he does, as the dominant interpretation would have it, achieve any species of redemption or salvation at the end, it is through her that it comes, which gives her an obvious affinity with both May Bartram in "The Beast in the Jungle" and the unnamed friend of George Stransom in "The Altar of the Dead."

In her devotion and understanding, Alice is comparable to the other two women; she listens without chattering and knows how to encourage without scattering abroad "a cloud of words." But, as befits the heroine of a ghost story, she is more "psychic" in her divinations; thus she knows what the ghost will be like before Spencer Brydon encounters it, for she has seen it in her dreams. She is also, I think, more sophisticated than the other women, and one suspects her of greater executive competence. One can hardly imagine either of the others speaking ironically of Spencer's "ill-gotten gains" or his sentimentality or telling him frankly at the end that she intends to "keep" him. She is the only one of the three women who does "keep" her man, and she may very well have planned this from the beginning, for she tells him at the outset that the old house would make a very different impression "if it were only furnished and lived in."

He is fifty-six years old when the story opens and

has just returned from Europe to his native New York and the deserted house on "the jolly corner" where he lived as a child. Alice is in the "afternoon of noon," "the delicately frugal possessor and tenant of the small house in Irving Place to which she had managed to cling through her almost unbroken New York career." As "a pale pressed flower (a rarity to begin with)," she confronts the strain and stress of the "awful modern crush" and all its "public concussions and ordeals" without fear and with such "a slim mystifying grace" that it is difficult to tell whether she is "a fair young woman who looked older through trouble, or a fine smooth older one who looked young through successful indifference," but her heart is clearly with those "memories and histories" of an older New York that she shares with Brydon. Her impregnable stability is one of the things about her that he admires most. Nothing, he thinks, could have altered her fundamentally; she would have been what she is anywhere or under any circumstances; hers was a "perfection" that nothing could have "blighted."

His own options had been much more varied; if he had remained in New York, he might have developed into something altogether different from what he is, might, for example, have manifested executive powers "quite splendid, quite huge and monstrous." She feels this quite as strongly as he does (the phrase indeed is hers), but when he asks her if she would have liked him thus, she simply replies, "How should I not have liked you?" Yet here again, as with the other women, James makes it quite clear that Alice does not "idealize" Brydon, for when he asks her whether she thinks him "as good as I might ever have been," she replies, "Oh no! Far from it! But I don't care." True, clear-sighted understanding coupled with generous acceptance— once again this appears to be the only love worth having, and the only kind that can survive the shocks of life.

Alice Staverton is no less important to Brydon than

the other women are to their men, but in a sense she is less involved in his ordeal, for she is absent from the scene through the whole long second chapter of "The Jolly Corner" (there are only three, and the last is very short), while Brydon prowls through the midnight hours at the "jolly corner," first stalking and then being stalked by the Spencer Brydon that he might have been. For this is Brydon's obsession: "He found all things come back to the question of what his personality might have been, how he might have led his life and 'turned out,' if he had not so, at the outset, given it up." James's description of the double stalking is a brilliant tour de force, but when Brydon is confronted at last by the hideous maimed monster he thinks he has been seeking, the shock nearly kills him (indeed he afterwards believes that he had died and come to life again), and he knows no more until morning, when he finds himself lying in the hall with his head in Alice's Madonnalike lap.[7]

The last chapter of "The Jolly Corner" is as profound as it is brief, and the critics have been considerably stimulated by it. Thus Dorothea Krook tells us that Brydon is saved because he learns just in time the lesson Marcher fails to learn until it is too late. In *The Ambassadors*, she believes, James entered a claim for "the redeeming power of consciousness alone," while "The Jolly Corner" "points directly toward James's . . . perhaps most poignant story, 'The Bench of Desolation,' in which the redeeming power of the mere capacity to receive love shows us the last flickering pin-point of light in the dark night of a world sunk in helpless, hopeless suffering."[8] There is indeed a religious element in these late stories; this encourages William A. Freedman[9] to compare Brydon's symbolic death and resurrection with what seem to him relevant passages in Dante, Plato (the allegory of the cave), and especially the New Testament story of the raising of Lazarus. But when we speak of what Brydon learns in this chapter, we need to tread warily. As has already been remarked, the usual view is that Brydon does at the end find some kind of redemption.

Allen F. Stein, on the other hand, denies that he undergoes any radical change as the result of his encounter with the monster: "His much vaunted awakening love for Alice is simply a shift from a bare acknowledgement of her existence as a friend who will tirelessly listen to his talk of himself to a complete dependence on her as a buffer to shield him from having to face the harsh facts of life." He remains what he has always been and simply "perverts Alice's potentially redeeming love."[10] I think we must grant that Brydon does not seem at the end to have arrived at any settled conviction about the ghost, for the very violence with which he protests that the thing is not himself shows that he is not sure. Peter Buitenhuis thinks that when Alice tells him, "No, thank heaven, it's not you!" she does not really mean it but is merely comforting him as one might comfort a frightened child. Such at the moment she might indeed do, but for the long haul she is certainly more interested in removing his blinders than in fastening them more firmly upon him. Is it not much more likely that what she is saying is more like what we mean when we tell somebody who must be rebuked for an unworthy action that this is not "like him" or that he is "not himself"?

A careful reading of the last few pages of the story seem to make it clear that Alice, who has seen the monster in her dreams, is not actually denying the monster element in Brydon; as we have seen, she has already specifically told him that she does not think him as good as he might be. But because she knows and cherishes his best potentialities, she knows too that he cannot be *identified* with the monster, and because she loves him she can accept even the "unhappy" and "ravaged" horror that has so terrified and revolted him along with the other constituent elements of his personality. For of course we must not think of the Spencer Brydon who might have lived out his life in New York as "bad" or of the Brydon who had returned from Europe as "good." He himself has told Alice that his life has not been "edifying," that in some quarters at least it has been considered "selfish frivolous scandalous" and "barely decent," while even Alice tells him bluntly that "you don't care for anything but yourself." He might have some difficulty in accepting this as the whole truth, but he does know that his experience has been defective and incomplete and admit the need of cultivating "his whole perception" and bringing it "to perfection, by practice." His search for his other self is a search for integration or wholeness, or, in more conventionally religious terms, a search for salvation, and at the end of the story we are at least permitted to hope that he may finally achieve this through a woman's unselfish, all-comprehending love.[11]

XI

During 1909 and 1910 James published his last five tales: "The Velvet Glove" (*English Review*, March 1909), "Mora Montravers" (*English Review*, August-September 1909), "Crapy Cornelia" (*Harper's Magazine*, October 1909), "The Bench of Desolation" (*Putnam's Magazine*, October 1909-January 1910), and "A Round of Visits" (*English Review*, April-May 1910). Since the publication of the New York Edition was completed in 1909, it was not possible to include any of them in that collection; they made their first appearance in book form in *The Finer Grain* (Scribners, New York, and Methuen, London, 1910).

James could not therefore discuss any of these tales in one of his prefaces, but he attempted to supply the lack in a measure by writing the following for the jacket of *The Finer Grain*:[1]

The Finer Grain consists of a series of five tales representing in each case a central figure (by which Mr. Henry James is apt to mean a central and lively *consciousness*) involved in one of those greater or less tangles of circumstance of which the measure and from which the issue is in the vivacity and the active play of the victim's or the victor's sensibility. Each situation is thereby more particularly a moral drama, an exposure of the special soul and intelligence presented (the sentient, perceptive, reflective part of the protagonist, in short), but with high emphasis clearly intended as its wearing for the hero or the heroine the quality of the agitating, the challenging, the personal *adventure*. In point of fact, indeed, it happens in each case to be the hero who exhibits the finer grain of accessibility to suspense or curiosity, to mystification or attraction—in other words, to moving experience; it is by his connection with and interest in the "grain" woman that his predicament, with its difficult solution, is incurred. And the series of illustrations of how such predicaments *may* spring up, and even be really characteristic, considerably ranges from Paris to London and New York, and then back again, to ambiguous yet at the same time unmistakable English, and ultra-English ground.

Though very few things are quite certain in this world, it still seems safe to say that a reader who failed to understand the stories in *The Finer Grain* would not understand the "blurb" much better, and I may even add that the tales themselves would furnish a new reader as infelicitous an introduction to James's short pieces as would *The Sacred Fount* to his novels. For they all deal with fairly strained or advanced "cases" even for him, and though the two New York tales are "documented" far beyond his wont, the collection may still be said to demand as much allowance for improbabilities or impossibilities as, say, *The Merchant of Venice* or *The Winter's Tale* (to which latter one critic has aptly compared the story whose central situation seems farthest "out," "The Bench of Desolation").[2] As Adeline Tintner observes, they are all "fairy tales or nightmares written for adults" and each "illustrates the ironical consequences of some transformation."

Ms. Tintner also quotes James's amanuensis Theodora Bosanquet to the effect that it is "almost literally true to say of the sheaf of tales collected in *The Finer Grain* that they were all written in response to a single request for a short story for *Harper's Monthly Magazine*" and that he wrote them all by hand at a time when he had generally given up writing for dictation. "The Velvet Glove" seems to have been turned out in the spring or early summer of 1908 and the other four during the ensuing winter. "Mora Montravers," the longest and the last to be written, was not finished until April 13, 1909.

The title "The Velvet Glove" has a double meaning, referring as it does to both the title of Amy Evans's latest novel and to the pressure she tries to put upon John Berridge to write "a lovely, friendly, irresistible log-rolling Preface" for it. Ms. Tintner thinks the story may have been influenced by Balzac's *"La Paix du Menage,"*[3] but her real stress falls upon the idea that not only the "Glove" but the whole *"Finer Grain* suite of stories seems to be an Edith Wharton suite."[4] This she develops most elaborately in connection with the "Glove," where she sees "a meticulously worked out classical mythology understructuring the imagery, language and characterization, all mounted to launch an elaborate literary joke," with Edith as both "the heroine of the mock-epic and the butt of the joke" in "the dual role of Artemis and the Scribbling Princess." Two things at least seem beyond dispute. The nighttime ride John Berridge has with the Princess in Paris was certainly based on James's own 1907 excursion with Mrs. Wharton, as she described it in her autobiography, *A Backward Glance,*[5] and he did suspect her of having been involved in asking him to write an article about her which he finally declined to do.

"The Velvet Glove" is by all means the "lightest" of the five tales. In the Paris studio of the sculptor Gloriani, whom readers of James had already met in *Roderick Hudson* and *The Ambassadors,* John Berridge, a literary lion currently triumphant both in the bookstores and on the stage, encounters a young English lord who seeks to interest him in a Princess who is also Amy Evans, a writer of what seem to be rather trashy novels. Berridge has no more than agreed to look at one of her books when she swoops down upon him, a dazzling vision, and offers to take him away from the party to ride through Paris in her motor car and wind up with supper at her house. Her flattery enroute proceeds to the shameless length of kissing his hand. "He had all but made the biggest of all fools of himself, almost as big a one as she was still," in permitting himself to entertain the pleasant delusion that she was attracted to him personally, but his awakening is swift and sudden.

Upon arrival at their destination, he leaves her, refusing to come in for supper ("I seem to have supped my fill, Princess"). He will not write her preface, he tells her, nor will he ever see her again. "Nothing would induce me to say a word in print about you. I'm in fact not sure I shall ever mention you in any manner at all as long as ever I live." This, he explains, is not because he does not "like" her, for, on the contrary, he adores her. But he is ashamed for her. She has mistaken her role in life. Because she *is* Romance, she should live it, not try to write it. "Don't attempt such base things. Leave them to us. Only live. Only be. *We'll* do the rest."[6] Then he kisses her passionately upon the lips and goes his way.

His refusal seems to me equally convincing, though very differently motivated, whether we see him as a dedicated artist who will not prostitute himself by praising trash or take Allen F. Stein's less flattering view of him,[7] but one reader at least does not find the kiss believable, not in a writer so chary of osculation that he managed only one example in all the multitudinous pages of *The Portrait of a Lady*.

With "Mora Montravers" we had better have the story line before us at the outset. Mora is twenty-one, an orphan, and extremely pretty. For six years she has lived with Mr. and Mrs. Sidney Traffle, Mrs. Traffle being her mother's half-sister. The Traffles have done their duty by her but never really liked her (when Mr. Traffle asks his wife, Jane, whether she is "at all attached" to Mora, she only replies, "Why she's my sister's child"). Mora has always manifested artistic talent, and she has now left the Traffles and is presumably living in

Walter Puddick's studio, her aunt is sure as his mistress, though both she and Puddick deny it. Traffle, who has considerably more imagination than his wife in her "damp severity" (she has never stopped crying) thinks Mora and Walter such a "rum pair" that they may well be telling the truth, and James gives us no reason to suppose that they are not.

Puddick clearly adores and idealizes Mora ("she's the very cleverest and most original and most endowed, and in every way most wonderful person I've known in all my life"). When the Traffles confront him on the issue, he is naturally quite willing to marry her, but he warns them that if he does, he will probably lose all control over her, "which won't be best, you know, for any one concerned."

Mrs. Traffle, who can see nothing beyond the conventions, offers to settle £450 on Mora once she becomes a respectable married woman, and when these tidings are conveyed to the girl, she embraces the condition, though the Traffles are not immediately made aware of it. But her motive is merely to secure the money for Puddick. She does not love him, and once they are married, she sets all her sights on being "free," though not for long, one gathers, since Sir Bruce Bagley, Bart. is seen hovering just around the corner. But when Traffle gets back home, after having learned all this through accidentally encountering Mora in a museum, it is only to become aware that Puddick has spent two hours with Mora's aunt, who has so completely capitulated to him that she is now quite determined that *he* shall have the money: "I mustn't abandon him." She even speaks of "Walter" as her nephew and plans to visit his studio to see his work, and one gathers that she will be less "damp" from here on.

Obviously we have here a young lady who is as much of an individualist and as capable of unconventional behavior as the heroine of *Wuthering Heights* when she marries Linton to help Heathcliff, but James makes it easier for us to accept her by keeping her in the background. She does not enter at all until the third chapter, and her appearances thereafter are brief. Though she precipitates the situation, our attention is concentrated not on what she does but on how the Traffles react to it; consequently we do not get to know her well enough to be sure either that she would do what she is described as doing or that she would not.

Jane Traffle, as we have seen, plays the game quite according to the rules, with no inclination to examine them critically or inquire whether they serve any useful purpose, while her husband, perhaps significantly an amateur painter, inclines rather toward "the impartial, the detached, in fact—hang it!—even the amused view." Though not unaware of the scandalous aspects of Mora's behavior, he still feels that "if any 'fun' . . . was to come of the matter, he'd be blamed if he'd be wholly deprived of it." Mora's bolt brings spice into his existence and makes him feel "happier than for a long time" because he thinks it will be "so interesting" to see what becomes of her. Through most of the tale the reader uses his eyes, for there is much more of him than there is of Jane, and in a modest and much less dignified way than Lambert Strether in *The Ambassadors*, he leads a secret life of imaginative sensibility. But Jane has her innings at the end, when she moves over into Puddick's corner, and we see a new dimension of her, the existence of which she had until now no more suspected than we had ourselves.

Ms. Tintner suggests that in "Mora Montravers" James may have been doing over Edith Wharton's story "The Mission of Jane" along lines suggested by Bernard Shaw's criticism of *The Saloon*, the dramatic version of "Owen Wingrave." According to the *Notebooks*, however, the original idea, recorded as early as 1901, came from what was said to Sir J.S. by the man with whom his niece had bolted and was living: "If I marry her I lose all control of her. ("I will if you insist, etc.—but—etc.") They *did* insist, and what he foretold happened—he lost all control. But imagine the case in which (*given the nature of the girl*) one of the parties interested or connected *doesn't* insist, while the other does, for the appearance, and the situation springing from that—the opposition, the little drama for short thing.[8]

"Crapy Cornelia" is the first of the two New York stories in *The Finer Grain*. The name of the hero, White-Mason, another Jamesian middle-aged, sensitive gentleman, reminded Buitenhuis of the Mason in "A Most Extraordinary Case," who dies after it becomes clear to him that he is not going to win his girl. What is far more inescapable, however, is that White-Mason's reaction to the new, glittering, garish, arrogant, luxurious, overwhelming, and overweening New York, whose glare resembles that of primitive cinematography[9] as contrasted with the soft, caressing tones of the photographs that he has known, is that of James himself, except, of course, that James did not come back to New York in 1904 in search of a wife. White-Mason does, and we find him at the beginning on a bench in Central Park, preparing to call upon Mrs. Worthingham in her ultrafashionable, luxurious apartment, where everything is shiningly new. He has been refused in his time by three women (fortunately in each case, as he now sees it), and it appears that this might well be his last chance.

When he makes his call, he also finds another lady, whose contrast to his contemplated wife is emphasized by the "frumpy, crapy, curiously exotic hat" under which he notes her "good little nearsighted insinuating glare," in possession, and since Mrs. Worthingham does not bother to introduce them, it takes him a little time to realize that she is Cornelia Rasch, the friend of his

youth, who, like himself, has recently returned to New
York. She readily consents to his calling upon her,
where she is surrounded by her old family possessions
from Twelfth Street, and the renewed contact with the
things of the past is enough to block White-Mason's
intended proposal, at least to the extent of leaving him
hesitating "like an ass erect on absurd hind legs between
two bundles of hay."

Mrs. Worthingham is surrounded by every beauty
that money can buy, and James uses all her possessions
to illuminate her personality; like Madame Merle in *The
Portrait of a Lady*, she can hardly be thought of as
existing outside her setting. White-Mason notes at once
that her smile twinkles

> not only with the gleam of her lovely teeth, but with that
> of all her rings and brooches and bangles and other
> gewgaws, to curl and spasmodically cluster as in emula-
> tion of her charming complicated yellow tresses, to
> surround this most animated of pink-and-white, of
> ruffled and ribboned, of frilled and festooned Dresden
> china shepherdesses with exactly the right system of
> rococo curves and convolutions and other flourishes, a
> perfect bower of painted and gilded and moulded
> conceits.

She is " 'up' to everything, aware of everything—if one
counted from a short enough time back (from week
before last, say, and as if quantities of history had burst
upon the world within the fortnight)." She is indeed like
"a great square sunny window that hung in assured
fashion over the immensity of life," and her "rabid
modern note" proclaims not only her "bright pampered
confidence" but her "innocent egotism" and "gilded
and overflowing anarchism" as well. In her White-
Mason sees with a shudder what to expect from

> the music of the future—that if people were rich
> enough and furnished enough, exercised and sanitated

and manicured and generally advised and advertised and made "knowing" enough, *avertis* enough, as the term appeared to be nowadays in Paris, all they had to do for civility was to take the amused ironic view of those who might be less initiated.

Whether all this is good or bad in itself is in a sense irrelevant; it is wrong for White-Mason, since

the high pitch of interest, to his taste, was the pitch of history, the pitch of acquired and earnest suggestion, the pitch of association, in a word; so that he lived by preference, incontestably, if not in a rich gloom, which would have been beyond his means and spirits, at least amid objects and interests that confessed to the tone of time.

In his day "the best manners had been the best kindness," not flaunting how intensely, how fiercely one might be "in the know." And of all this, of everything indeed "that really and intimately and fundamentally concerned him," Mrs. Worthingham is obviously "as ignorant as a fish."

Nothing much happens after this save that White-Mason visits Cornelia and feels at home in her plain, lived-in, comfortable apartment, where the tone of time is as much in evidence as it was absent from Mrs. Worthingham's, and they talk over the past and their future, and he sinks comfortably into the chair by her fireside that he hopes to occupy often. Whether or not "Crapy Cornelia" is, as Strother Purdy[10] judges it, "a major work of the major phase," it is certainly a tale of considerable art in which two kinds of women and two ways of life are masterfully contrasted. Beyond that, one can only record one's own impression. One reader at least, though completely convinced that his re-encounter with Cornelia Rasch would "spike" White-Mason's contemplated proposal to Mrs. Worthingham, is doubtful that, being what he is, he would ever have considered the latter as seriously as he does, more doubtful that he would talk her over with Cornelia so frankly, and quite unconvinced that Cornelia would ask him, "Do you mean you want to marry *me*?" to which he would reply, "No, Cornelia—not to marry you." All this, to be sure, might well be understood between them, but to have it spelled out so bluntly suggests Mrs. Worthingham's world rather than that of Cornelia and White-Mason.

"The Bench of Desolation" is the *Finer Grain* tale that has been most admired; it is also the one in which the "fairy tale" or "nightmare" quality is strongest, or, to put it differently, in which we are asked to swallow the greatest number of improbabilities. The only source James cites is an anecdote mentioned to him by "Mrs. F.F." at a Christmas house party in 1908,[11] but he himself, at one point in the tale, compares Kate Cookham to Meg Merrilies in Scott's *Guy Mannering*. As we have already seen,[12] Joseph Milicia has labeled the piece James's *Winter's Tale*, and Dorothea Krook invokes a greater work of Shakespeare's when she comments upon the surrender of the old lovers (and haters) to each other at the end:

> This is King Lear, in the guise of a shabby broken little bookseller, saying "I am a very foolish, fond old man . . . . Pray you now, forget and forgive"; and Kate Cookham, who once looked like a "vindictive bar-maid," responds with the only form of Cornelia's tenderness that the situation admits of.

But this critic also writes that "if 'Mora Montravers' has a little touch or taint of Ibsen, 'The Bench of Desolation' . . . is Hardyesque" and especially suggestive of *Jude the Obscure*. As to the method, both Krishna Baldev Vaid and Mary Doyle Springer have shown in some detail that though we are often confined to what Dodd sees or believes, it is also made clear that there is an element of interpretation in what he gives us; the omniscient author does not quite abdicate.[13]

At the beginning Herbert Dodd has broken his engagement to Kate Cookham, and we "come in" on the viragolike scene in which she threatens suit for breach of promise. Each party has suspected the other of infidelity, which suspicion was certainly groundless on his part and in large measure at least on hers also. We also learn later that Kate is bluffing and knows she has no case. But Dodd, a secondhand bookseller and a comparatively weak man who likes to think of himself as a gentleman, does not even ask legal advice, and they settle for £400, of which he never pays more than £270.

This is quite enough, however, to break him. He mortgages his house, his shop, and his stock, loses his business, and becomes a clerk at a dirty desk in the gasworks. He marries "beautiful, gentle, tender-souled" Nan Drury, who has fascinated him partly through her addiction to "pretty, dotty, transparent veils," but she turns into a chronic though gentle complainer (heaven knows she has enough trouble to make her something much worse), and by the time they are married, Herbert is thinking of her as "red-nosed and dowdy." She bears him two little girls, neither of whom lives to grow up, and then dies herself.

Though the bench on the marina looking out to sea has had happier associations for Dodd in the past, it now becomes his bench of desolation. There one Saturday afternoon he encounters a handsome, refined, well-dressed woman—"spare, fine, worn, almost wasted—who, it gradually dawns upon him, is Kate. "She was simply another and a totally different person." He can see that she is "strangely older, . . . marked by experience and as if many things had happened to her; her face had suffered, to its improvement, contraction and concentration," and she whose "outrageous vulgarity . . . had kept him shuddering so long as a shudder was in

him" is now a "grave, authoritative, but refined and, as
it were, physically rearranged person." Later, when he
asks her where it all came from, she will answer, "The
wonder of poor me? It comes from *you*."

She invites him to tea the next day in the sumptuous
quarters in which she is staying at the hotel, but it
requires two more meetings at the bench to get him to
accept the twelve hundred and sixty pounds into which
she has turned his two hundred and seventy. She has
never ceased loving him, nor has her knowledge of his
weakness made any difference to her. "I'd have loved
you and helped you and guarded you, and you'd have
had no trouble, no bad blighting ruin, in all your easy,
yes, just your quite jolly and comfortable life." She had
known she had to take care of him even though he
would have none of her. He was quite incapable of
looking after investments himself, and since she had no
money of her own, there was no place she could get the
capital she needed except from him. She had done
everything for his sake and brought his money back to
him fivefold.

> He leaned forward, dropping his elbows to his knees
> and pressing his head on his hands. So he stayed, saying
> nothing; only, with the sense of her own sustained,
> renewed, and wonderful action, knowing that an arm
> had passed round him and that he was held. She was
> beside him on the bench of desolation.

Whether or not all this is believeable is something
each reader must decide for himself, but there can be
no question about the fine art with which James tells the
tale or the charm of the atmosphere of forgiveness and
reconcilation (his own addition to the anecdote he
heard) that he creates. Objectors may of course be
reminded that Shakespeare "gets away" with much
more in *The Winter's Tale* and the other pieces commonly called his "reconciliation plays," but much can

be done in a post-Elizabethan poetic drama that will not quite "go over" in a modern prose tale. Suppose we are willing to grant that the law of compensation does operate in a fashion for Dodd and Kate, what compensation has there been for Nan and her two children in their graves? "The end of the story, then," writes Joseph Milicia, "is largely one of magnificent forgiving, though the ambiguities remain . . . . But the stress is certainly on weariness as well as on reconciliation . . . . Clearly the reconciliation is a positive act, but at a dreadful cost of youth and wasted energy." So Kate herself cries, "Oh, the blind, the pitiful folly!" and even Ora Segal, who is perhaps the most emphatic of all the critics in accepting what Kate says about her motives at face value and seeing her as "one of the Jamesian devoted women," grants that the tale presents "two weary middle-aged people [who] are conscious of the dreadful waste and suffering of the past" and that, although like *The Golden Bowl* and unlike most of James, it ends in reconciliation rather than renunciation, it is still "profoundly sad."[14]

It is not only because it ends with a fatal pistol shot, an uncommonly violent termination for James, that his last published story, the innocuously entitled "A Round of Visits," makes such a painful impression. Egotism, selfishness, vanity, vulgarity, shameless indulgence in luxury and heartless indifference toward those who have it not, epidemic sickness, infidelity, adultery, divorce, embezzlement, and suicide—these are the materials of which it is compounded, and the tale is set in an atmosphere of freezing cold outside and intense heat inside the great hotels, where "the luxuriance, the extravagance, the quantity, the colour, gave the impression of some wondrous tropical forest, where vociferous, bright-eyed, and feathered creatures, of every variety of size and hue, were half smothered between undergrowths of velvet and tapestry and ramifications of marble and bronze." Martin and Ober have noted a whole series of resemblances to the "Inferno" section of *The Divine Comedy*, while Ms. Tintner, taking her clue from James's use of the Miltonic words "Pandemonium" and "labyrinth," reminds us that in *The American Scene* James had compared the old Waldorf-Astoria, which becomes the Pocahontas in the tale, with Satan's palace in *Paradise Lost* and that Milton had had Mammon and Mulciber invent the skyscraper James so detested in hell before it came into being in Chicago! Mrs. Folliott, the city, the weather, and the flu are all called "terrible"; the word "horror" is employed ten times, and "loss," "pain," "ache," "blow," "dismay," "misery," "monstrous," and "anguished" all occur twice or more. All in all, "the violence of the images prepares us for the violent suicide at the end."[15]

The original idea for "A Round of Visits," running clear back to 1894, merely concerned a man who could find nobody to listen to his trouble. James kept it in mind through the years, but it took him a long time to find the particular line of development he finally employed.[16] Martin and Ober have been reminded of the double suicide in Zola's *Thérèse Raquin* and Ms. Tintner of Edith Wharton's story, "A Cup of Cold Water," where the resemblance is much closer. But whatever literary influences may have entered, James's own observation of New York was all important, and in these pages New York is virtually indistinguishable from hell. If James needed overtones from Dante and Milton to add dignity and grandeur to this conception, its horror was all its own.

Mark Monteith returns to New York at the beginning of this tale in far less comfortable circumstances than does White-Mason in "Crapy Cornelia," for his old friend Phil Bloodgood has absconded with much of his fortune. Recovering from a siege of flu, he ventures out on his round of visits (there are no homes in this story, only hotels and "studio apartments") seeking not pity, not even sympathy so much as

> to give some easier turn to the mere ugliness of the main facts; to work off his obsession from them by mixing with it some other blame, some other pity, it scarce mattered what—if it might be some other experience; as an effect of which larger ventilation it would have, after a fashion and for a man of free sensibility, a diluted and less poisonous taste.

But Mrs. Folliott, who has also been swindled by Bloodgood, though less seriously than Monteith, is too much absorbed in her own misfortune to think of another's, and Mrs. Ash can think only of her separation from her husband, one of whose paramours is Mrs. Folliott. Fortunately, or unfortunately, as the reader may choose, an extremely pretty girl whom Mark encounters by chance, and who is humane and perceptive in unpropitious surroundings, suggests that he visit her brother-in-law, Newton Winch, a widower who has been suffering from his own complaint and who is terribly "down" ("Well then, feel for others. Fit him in. Tell him why!").[17]

Mark remembers Newton Winch from his college and law school days, but not with pleasure. He was common and vulgar then. To his amazement he now finds him refined, perceptive, sympathetic, mindful of others, nervous enough to fly out of his skin, and sharpened to a point. Evidently some very painful experience has been at work upon him, perhaps to his physical destruction but certainly to his spiritual profit.[18] As a matter of fact, Winch, like Bloodgood, is an embezzler who is expecting the arrival of the police, and though Monteith does not know this at the beginning, it comes out as they talk and reach out toward each other, acknowledging their common human kinship and need of sympathy. For it is this doomed man alone, among those he has visited this afternoon, who understands Monteith's problem and cares about it. "He knew within the minute that the tears stood in his eyes; he stared through them at his friend with a sharp 'Why how do you know? How *can* you?' "

But Monteith gives as well as takes in this encounter, for without being a healer he could not himself be healed. Instead of being absorbed in his own trouble, he now expresses sympathy for, of all people, the man who had robbed him. "It was as if a far-borne sound of the hue and cry, a vision of his old friend hunted and at bay, had suddenly broken in," and he says, "I mean I don't take any interest in *my* case—what one wonders about, you see, is what can be done for him." If he had the chance, "I'd go to him. Hanged if I wouldn't— anywhere!" if not "in kindness, " at least "to understand." And Newton, his defenses now dropped, says, "You save my life."

Not, however, for this world. For when the police arrive, and Monteith, at his request, answers the door, Winch seizes the opportunity to possess himself of the revolver whose sinister gleam Monteith had observed where his friend had, in his haste, only partially concealed it when his guest arrived. "Don't you think, sir, you might have prevented it?" the "emissary of the law" asks Monteith, to which he replies, "I really think I must practically have caused it."

James gives us no indication of the spirit in which this is said, and it remains one of the most ambiguous endings he ever achieved. It has been interpreted in various ways. "The sight of Monteith, the very absence of a quarrel strained Winch's spirit to the breaking point." "It is Monteith's pain that makes living unendurable for Winch." Or he had tried to kill himself before Mark arrived but then lacked the courage which he has now found through Monteith's sympathy.[19] We lack the data to determine authoritatively which of these meanings, if any, was in the author's mind.

"A Round of Visits," with its "terrible" milieu and its grim conclusion, was not, it must be admitted, the most cheerful piece with which James could have signed off as a teller of tales, and autobiographically and psychologically oriented critics have been tempted to interpret this and his other last tales as reflecting his condition at the time he wrote them. That he had personal problems, especially health problems, at the time there can be no doubt. That he saw New York in 1904-1905 as he has portrayed it is likewise not in doubt. But you may be as psychological as you like and you will on that account discover no failing in his sense of values or human sympathies. Moreover, it should be remembered that though "A Round of Visits" was the last story James published, it was not the last he wrote. That was "Mora Montravers," and whatever else may be said of that tale, it is certainly not grim. However Winch's final act is interpreted, an aging writer who could conceive of Monteith rising above his own woes as he does at the end or of Herbert Dodd and Kate Cookham turning away from the past to embrace love in terms of salvation can hardly be called a pessimist.

Appendix A: *Stories by Henry James Not Included in the New York Edition*

ADINA (*Scribner's Monthly*, May-June 1874) has been called a companion piece to "The Last of the Valerii," but this is not correct. "The Last of the Valerii" ends with the reinterment of the Juno by which Count Valerio has been enthralled, while in "Adina" Sam Scrope casts the beautiful topaz intaglio that had once belonged to the Emperor Tiberius into the Tiber after his fiancée has run off with the young shepherd Angelo Beati. But the motivation in "Adina" is entirely human and realistic, and though the tale is fairly successful upon its own terms, it is a much less substantial piece than "The Last of the Valerii." Sam Scrope, a classical scholar, is still a very nasty man. He cheats the shepherd who had dug up the gem in ignorance of its value and haughtily refuses to make restitution after Angelo's eyes have been opened. If the Italian's vengeance had been violent, the reader would have condemned him, but since he merely woos Adina at the garden window, one cannot but feel that Scrope is well served. The Roman background embraces a midnight mass at the Sistine Chapel.

AT ISELLA (*Galaxy*, August 1871) is merely an anecdote. An American meets at Isella, where James once spent a night, a beautiful Italian woman who is fleeing from a brutal husband to the man she had loved before a European-style arranged marriage had handed her over to the other man and gives her the money she needs to hire a private carriage and escape before her pursuer arrives. The rest is all European scenery and atmosphere, some dozen pages of it before there is any suggestion of story. The historical and literary associations that cluster about the lady in the narrator's mind become faintly absurd when she reminds him of Lucrezia Borgia, Bianca Capello, and the heroines of Stendhal, and it is hardly believable that, being what she is, she would confide so quickly and completely in a total stranger.

BENVOLIO (*Galaxy*, August 1879) is a unique item in James's oeuvre, a rambling, unlocalized, old-fashioned narrative with very little dialogue, which adds up to a kind of apologue reflecting influences from Milton, Hawthorne ("Rappaccini's Daughter"), George Eliot (*Romola*), and others. Benvolio is a young poet whose unreconciled needs for both society and solitude are manifested in everything from the character and furnishings of his dwelling to the attraction he feels to two women—the Countess and Scholastica. His art dries up during his sojourn with the Countess, and he becomes productive again after his (presumably) final return to Scholastica; "only many people said, his poetry had become dismally dull." See Adeline R. Tintner, "The Countess and Scholastica: Henry James's 'L'Allegro' and 'Il Penseroso,' " *Studies in Short Fiction*, 11 (1974), 267-76, and Mary Doyle Springer, *A Rhetoric of Literary Character: Some Women of Henry James*, pp. 139-59.

COLLABORATION (*English Illustrated Magazine*, September 1892) is mostly talk, mainly about art and nationality and the relationship or lack of it between them, in a painter's Paris studio. The closest approach to a story comes when the attempted collaboration on an opera between a young German composer and a French poet breaks up the composer's engagement to a French girl whose mother still nurses the wounds inflicted by the Franco-Prussian War. See Adeline R. Tintner, "Rudyard Kipling and Wolcott Balestier's Literary Collaboration: A Possible Source for James's 'Collaboration,' " *Henry James Review*, 4 (1982-83), 140-43.

COUSIN MARIA. See MRS. TEMPERLEY.

COVERING END appeared without previous magazine publication in *The Two Magics* (1898). One of James's potboilers, it has an interesting history. It was commissioned as a one-act play, *Summersoft*, for Ellen Terry, and when it became clear that she was not going to produce it, James turned it into a long short story whose narrative passages sound much like transformed stage directions and published it in a volume with "The Turn of the Screw." Later, at the request of Johnston Forbes-Robertson, he expanded *Summersoft* into a three-act play, *The Higher Bid*, which Forbes-Robertson and his wife, Gertrude Elliott, performed briefly in Edinburgh and London in 1908-1909. In the story, Clement Yule owns a beautiful but heavily encumbered old English estate, called Covering End. Prodmore, who holds the mortgage, is prepared to relinquish his claim if Yule will abjure his radical opinions, stand for Parliament as a conservative, and marry Prodmore's daughter, Cora. But Mrs. Gracedew, a wealthy and enchanting young American widow from Missoura Top who has been led to Covering End by her passion for British antiquities and who virtually takes charge of the place as soon as she arrives there, sends Cora off with the man she loves, buys the estate from Prodmore at an exorbitant price, and presents it to Yule, along with herself. This opus shows how close James could come to the kind of farce comedy popular in the Edwardian theater. The initial idea was recorded in James's *Notebook* (pp. 184-89). Leon Edel publishes both dramatic versions with valuable introductions in *The Complete Plays of Henry James*. He cites Osterly House, near Reston, Middlesex, as the original of Covering End and compares aspects of the story with *The Portrait of a Lady*, *The Spoils of Poynton*, and *The Princess Casamassima*; in his edition of James's *Collected Tales*, he also invokes *The Tragic Muse*, "Owen Wingrave," and the play *Guy Domville*. As a converted play, "Covering End" suggests both *The Other House* and *The Outcry* (the latter is also preoccupied with British antiquities), and Mrs. Gracedew's piety toward the past, especially in Chapter IV, has some affinity with "The Altar of the Dead."

CRAWFORD'S CONSISTENCY (*Scribner's Monthly*, August 1876) is a rather melodramatic, sensational tale, not very characteristic of James. Crawford, a young man of independent means, devoted to reading and scientific experimentation, becomes engaged to Elizabeth Ingram, a beautiful but vapid girl, like "a blushing rose that had no odor." Three weeks before the wedding, the engagement is called off, and Crawford is given no reason save that Elizabeth had "mistaken the nature of her affection for him." On the rebound, he offers himself to a vulgar woman whose manners appall society. After he has lost his money in a bank failure and been compelled to earn his living as a clerk, his wife turns into a virago and at last succeeds in drinking herself to death. Through it all, Crawford, feeling that because he did her "a great wrong by marrying her," he has no reason to complain, remains at all times "the embodiment of deference and attentive civility," and her death cannot be said to restore his equlibrium "for the excellent reason that . . . he had never lost it." The brilliant second match that had been arranged for Elizabeth Ingram falls through after she has been made hideous by smallpox. Since, like the narrator, the reader has never been permitted to "walk all round" Crawford, the story leaves him feeling merely that human character and behavior are indeed inscrutable and that even the best of human beings can be capable of both incredible folly and incredible self-control.

A DAY OF DAYS   (*Galaxy*, June 15, 1866) is a slight but rather charming tale. If it has a theme, it must be that our destinies can be determined not only by our temperaments but also by our moods and impulses. A well-to-do unmarried young lady, keeping house for her scholar-brother in rural New England, entertains a young scholar who has called to see him on a day he chances to be away. The two are obviously attracted to each other and feel that this meeting might be important in their lives, but both shy off from pursuing the acquaintance, and the stranger takes his leave. The insight into character revealed in this tale rings true, but the conversation is at times unbelievable, most notably in the visitor's almost formal analysis of his own character.

DE GREY: A ROMANCE   (*Atlantic Monthly*, July 1868) is a sinister tale of the supernatural, skirting the vampire theme that James also suggests in "Longstaff's Marriage" and *The Sacred Fount*. A curse upon the house of De Grey decrees death to the wife of the heir. After Paul has returned from Europe and fallen in love with her, his mother's companion, Margaret Aldis, defies the curse and refuses to die, but all she achieves is to transfer its operation: Paul is killed by a fall from his horse, and she is found beside him on the road, holding him in her arms but with her mind gone. Balzac (*Le Peau de Chagrin*) and George Sand have been conjectured as influences upon "De Grey," and surely the idea of the curse must be indebted to Hawthorne's *The House of the Seven Gables*; there may also have been some influence from "Rappaccini's Daughter." The scene is New York State, but the atmosphere seems European: Mrs. De Grey even has a Catholic priest in residence, who lives on her bounty and advises the lovers like Friar Laurence in *Romeo and Juliet*. Strictly speaking the curse is not believable, and the ending is sensational in the extreme, but both are in harmony with the eerie atmosphere James created; if these things could happen to anybody, the reader is made to feel, it must be to just such tense, passionate people as we meet here.

The Diary of a Man of Fifty (*Harper's Magazine* and *Macmillan's Magazine*, July 1879) is that of an English general who, in 1874, returns to Florence, where, twenty-seven years ago, he had loved the Countess Salvi and left her because he did not trust her. Her daughter, the widowed Countess Scarabelli, is now being courted by Stanmer, a young Englishman in whom the general sees a replica of his younger self, and because the widow seems to him to have inherited both her mother's charm and her volatility, he tries to warn Stanmer against making the mistake he himself so narrowly escaped. The young man disregards the warning, and we learn in the final diary entry that he married the Countess and that the marriage is happy. This leaves the general wondering whether he had been wrong nearly a generation before and needlessly robbed himself of his life's happiness. Peter Buitenhuis has suggested that the tale was inspired by Turgenev's *Diary of a Superfluous Man*, and since Edward Sheldon had some contact with James, one cannot but wonder whether he had "The Diary of a Man of Fifty" in mind when he gave his most famous play, *Romance*, a frame in which a bishop tries vainly to dissuade his grandson from marrying an actress by telling him the story of his own involvement with a famous opera singer many years before.

Eugene Pickering (*Atlantic Monthly*, November-December 1874) is set in Homburg, "several years ago before the gambling was suppressed," but the title character and the narrator, an old schoolmate encountered there, are both Americans. Eugene has been psychically crippled by a father, now dead, who was perhaps suggested by Meredith's Austin Feverel. He is "out" now, on his way to Smyrna of all places to marry a girl he does not know because, like everything else in his life, his marriage has been "arranged" for him by his father. Inevitably he develops a bad case of puppy love for Madame Blumenthal, "a faded, crumpled, vaporous beauty," an aspiring novelist, dramatist, and pseudo-intellectual, and above all an adventuress with "something sinister about her." For the thrill of a fresh experience, she engages herself to Eugene, then abruptly and cruelly dismisses him. Despite his disastrous rearing, Eugene does not follow the best traditions of nineteenth-century Romanticism by blowing his brains out but proceeds to Smyrna, even though he has just had word that his prospective bride is as little attracted by an "arranged" marriage as he is. Parenthetically we are informed that the young people do finally make a match of it. At one point, all the principals attend an operatic performance by Adelina Patti, whose singing Madame Blumenthal characteristically finds too fine-spun and refined. See Patricia Marks, "Culture and Rhetoric in Henry James's 'Poor Richard' and 'Eugene Pickering,' " *South Atlantic Bulletin*, 44, January 1979, pp. 61-72, and Adeline R. Tintner, "Henry James's Shakespearian Burlesque," *AB Bookman's Weekly*, March 29, 1982, pp. 2430 ff., who sees James combining suggestions from *Romeo and Juliet* and *Antony and Cleopatra* to produce his only burlesque.

GABRIELLE DE BERGERAC (*Atlantic Monthly*, July-September 1868) is the story of a romance between an aristocratic girl of prerevolutionary France and her little nephew's tutor. Love triumphs over great obstacles, and we are told that both Gabrielle and her husband perish as Girondists under the Terror. "Gabrielle de Bergerac" has charm beyond any other of James's uncharacteristic experiments during his early career, and it proves conclusively that he could have produced successful period romances had he chosen to turn his talents in that direction. George Sand and Sir Walter Scott (the latter very probably as filtered through Balzac) were important influences, and at least one scene has the flavor of *Henry*

Esmond. The story is told by the nephew, now grown old, to a friend who has shown interest in his aunt's portrait, and its only weakness is that one can hardly believe the child would have been able to overhear and understand so much or that he could have remembered it in such detail after so many years. See Percy G. Adams, "Young Henry James and the Lesson of his Master Balzac," *Revue de Littérature Comparée*, 35 (1961), 458-87.

GEORGINA'S REASONS (New York *Sun*, July 20, 27, August 3, 1884) was regarded by James as one of his poorest stories, though he said the *Sun* paid him thousands for it. Its origin was a true-life anecdote related to him by Fanny Kemble that he thought "incredible and almost silly," but he was never the man to shrink from a difficult subject. The scene is New York "in the ancient days when Twelfth Street had but lately ceased to be suburban." Georgina Gressie, whose parents oppose her romance with the naval officer Raymond Benyon, weds him secretly but swears him never to claim her without her concurrence. She returns to her father's house and Benyon is sent abroad. When she becomes aware that she is pregnant, she persuades Mrs. Portico to take her to Italy, where her child is born, put out to nurse, and finally disappears, and where Mrs. Portico dies. Much later, Benyon learns by chance that Georgina has married again. He returns to New York and demands that she permit him to divorce her so that he may wed Kate Theory, but she refuses to release him from his vow. The "reasons" for Georgina's strange behavior are hardly set forth adequately, and many find it incredible that Benyon should consider himself bound by his vow after Georgina has deserted him and committed bigamy besides. Yet the woman remains a baleful, living character, and the story exerts a weird, not quite Jamesian fascination. Readers of *The Wings of the Dove* find an interesting anticipation of that masterpiece in Kate's being occupied in Italy in nursing a consumptive sister, Mildred Theory, who dies. The only significant study is Adeline R. Tintner, "Henry James and Miss Braddon: 'Georgina's Reasons' and the Victorian Sensation Novel," *Essays in Literature*, 10, Spring 1983, 119-124.

THE GHOSTLY RENTAL (*Scribner's Monthly*, September 1876),

James's second bonafide ghost story, has the supernatural atmosphere that the first, "The Romance of Certain Old Clothes," had conspicuously lacked, but the narrative is not handled well. The reader is asked to believe that Captain Diamond has been receiving rent for years from what he believes to be the ghost of the daughter he had wronged, and just after the masquerader has been unmasked as a living woman, it is suggested that the father has manifested to her in the moment of his death. Naturally the juxtaposition of true and false supernaturalism does not come off successfully. The best general commentary on the tale is Martha Banta's in her *Henry James and the Occult* (Indiana University Press, 1972), pp. 106-110; see also Robert J. Andreach, "Literary Allusion as a Clue to Meaning: James's 'The Ghostly Rental' and Pascal's *Pensées*," *Comparative Literature Studies*, 4 (1967), 299-306.

THE GIVEN CASE (*Collier's Weekly*, December 31, 1898-January 7, 1899) was suggested by a *Fortnightly* article (see *Notebooks*, pp. 163, 234-35) contrasting French and English views of the obligation a woman assumes by permitting herself to engage in a flirtation when the man has been made to care deeply. Mrs. Despard has a brute of a husband who, for some reason best known to himself, does not wish to relinquish her, and Margaret Hamer is engaged to a man about to return from India for whom she no longer cares. Both Barton Reeve and Philip Mackern are free. The women are close friends, and Margaret becomes Reeves's confidante while Mrs. Despard warns Mackern off. From the "given case" the two women reach opposing conclusions. Margaret surrenders to Mackern but Mrs. Despard sends Reeve away. The balance is developed, mainly through a series of confrontations, in terms of dramatic scene, and the reader is perhaps kept busier figuring out relationships than the slight narrative adequately rewards him for.

GLASSES (*Atlantic Monthly*, February 1896) is a longish story of middling quality whose principal interest is that as "Brook-smith" demonstrates James's capacity to sympathize with a servant and "Greville Fane" with a cheap and vulgar novelist, so "Glasses" demonstrates that he could also embrace a very silly woman who at the end can "charm with her pathos more even than she had charmed with her pleasure" and, for good measure, take in her ugly, awkward, rather foolish lover (later husband) as well. Flora Saunt is a fantastically beautiful girl, besotted with her own loveliness, whose weak eyes she refuses to protect by wearing disfiguring spectacles: "She couldn't submit to the imputation of a flaw." Her blindness costs her Lord Iffield, but Geoffrey Dawling, whom she has spurned, remains faithful. "I would take her with leather blinders, like a shying mare." The story is told by a painter who has often transferred Flora's beauty to canvas and who reencounters her in a box at *Lohengrin*, now blind, guarded by her devoted husband and radiant as ever, pretending to survey the stage and the house through opera glasses. The tale began for James "by my seeing a very pretty woman in spectacles... on the top of an omnibus," and in his *Notebooks* (pp. 205-206) he indicates that he might have called it "The Spectacles" if Guy de Maupassant had not used that title. Adeline R. Tintner, "Poe's 'The Spectacles' and James's 'Glasses,'" *Poe Studies*, 9 (1976-77), 53-54, makes a case for the Poe story as influence. Though the plots of the two tales are entirely different, in both "excessive vanity literally and figuratively destroys beauty." See also the same writer's "Why James Quoted Gibbon in 'Glasses,' " *Studies in Short Fiction*, 14 (1977), 287-88, and Sharon Dean, "The Myopic Narrator in Henry James's 'Glasses,' " *Henry James Review*, 4 (1983), 191-96.

THE GREAT CONDITION (*Anglo-Saxon Review*, June 1899), which was based on an anecdote told to James by George Meredith (see *Notebooks*, pp. 269-73) is an international tale only in the sense that Mrs. Demerel is an American and both her lovers English. Since her background is wholly undocumented, Braddle is unwilling to marry her without assurances that she has nothing to hide. She refuses either to affirm or deny anything but promises that if he still wishes to ask his question after they have been married for six months, she will answer it. Instead he goes off to search for her traces in both the United States and the Hawaiian Islands, where he finds nothing, and Mrs. Demerel marries his friend and confidant Henry Chilver, who had always regarded Braddle's conduct as that of a self-tormentor. More than a year later, Braddle, still miserable and inwardly divided, encounters the others again, and now Mrs. Chilver tells him frankly that she had nothing to confess but had made the condition she did because she knew that a man incapable of trusting her was not the man to spend her life with. In his *Collected Tales* Leon Edel suggests that both "The Great Condition" and "The Given Case" show that James's feelings about women were still ambiguous in the nineties. It would seem to me more to the point to find in it an effective contrast between quixotic, priggish, suspicious men like Braddle and those who, like Chilver, know that love, no less than religion, demands commitment and a leap into the dark. Mrs. Demeral's test works as unerringly as the caskets set up by Portia's father in *The Merchant of Venice*. The tale contains a high proportion of dialogue for James. I have been privileged to read an article by Adeline R. Tintner, " 'The Great Condition': Henry James and Bergsonian Time," which will probably be in print in *Studies in Short Fiction* before my book. Taking her cue from the extraordinary number of references to time in this story, she argues that though "Henry James was no philosopher, not even a literary philosopher like Bergson, yet he seems to have intuited the Bergsonian distinction between time as duration concretely experienced and time abstractly recorded, in 'The Great Condition.' "

GUEST'S CONFESSION (*Atlantic Monthly*, October-November 1872) relates how John Guest mismanages the financial affairs of Edgar Musgrave, "a shrivelled, evil-tempered, tight-fisted hypochondriac," and saves himself from prosecution only by signing a humiliating confession and promising restitution, which he effects. Edgar dies, and his brother, the narrator, falls in love with Guest's daughter, Laura. Guest, who hates David Musgrave because the latter has witnessed his humiliation, refuses to consent to the marriage. David first threatens to show Laura Guest's confession, which is now in his possession, but soon suffers a change of heart rather like Newman's in *The American*; he burns the paper and Guest gives in. "Guest's Confession" has generally been dismissed as one of James's most unpleasant and unsuccessful stories, but of late it has come in for more respectful treatment by Krishna Baldev Vaid, Peter Buitenhuis, and Adeline R. Tintner, who com-

pares it to *The Merchant of Venice* in " 'Guest's Confession'
and Shakespeare: Henry James's Merchant of New York,"
Studies in Short Fiction, 19 (1982), 65-69.

THE IMPRESSIONS OF A COUSIN (*Century Magazine*, November-December 1883), which was suggested by an incident related by Thackeray's daughter Lady Anne Ritchie in
her book on Madame de Sévigné, was regarded by James
himself as "rather thin" and "wanting in actuality." The scene
is mainly New York City and "Centerville," the heroine's
"seat" on the Hudson, but the characters are familiar with
Europe, and the exotic Mr. Caliph, Eunice's trustee, who
embezzles her money and reflects James's mistrust of finan-
ciers, exhales the atmosphere of Haroun-al-Raschid and *The
Arabian Nights*. Caliph schemes to cover his tracks by having
Eunice marry his wealthy half-brother, Adrian Frank, but the
plan founders on her secret passion for Caliph himself, which
survives even her knowledge of his pilfering. Apparently
Adrian makes good his brother's defalcation, but Eunice does
not marry him, and he turns for consolation to Catherine
Condit, in whose diary the story is told. Taking her cue from
Catherine's statement about Adrian—"He is a charming
creature—a kind of Yankee Doodle Donatello. If I could only
be his Miriam, the situation would be almost complete, for
Eunice is an excellent Hilda"—Adeline R. Tintner, in " 'The
Impressions of a Cousin': Henry James's Transformation of
The Marble Faun," *Nathaniel Hawthorne Journal*, 1976, pp.
205-14, interprets the story as her title indicates. See also
Raymond D. Havens, "Henry James's 'The Impressions of a
Cousin," *Modern Language Notes*, 65 (1950), 317-19.

JERSEY VILLAS. See SIR DOMINICK FERRAND.

JOHN DELAVOY (*Cosmopolis*, January—February 1898) was
suggested by the *Century*'s rejection of James's memorial
article on Alexandre Dumas *fils*, on the ground that that
author's subject matter could not be discussed or even mentioned in a "family magazine." Robert Underwood Johnson
had added that the article would have been acceptable if
James had made it merely personal. In the story the narrator
achieves what the sister of the recently deceased novelist John

Delavoy regards as the definitive description and evaluation of his work, but the editor of *The Cynosure*, who has had it set up in type without reading it, reneges on his promise to publish on exactly these grounds, thus leaving its puzzled writer no recourse save to cry, "I simply try to express my author, and if your public won't stand his being expressed, mention to me kindly the sources of its interest in him." The puzzle, however, is not difficult to solve. At the moment John Delavoy is news. He is being talked about by people who would not dream of reading his books; the editor is therefore immensely interested in pictures, chit-chat, and personal gossip, but he will not touch serious criticism or anything that faces the fundamental questions involved in a serious consideration of the writer's work. The situation is complicated by the editor's personal interest in Miss Delavoy, and his refusal to budge costs him the girl, to the narrator's gain. The length to which James goes in permitting his three principals to thrash out the issues shows how deeply he felt on the subject, and his merciless exposure of the big magazines as interested only in circulation figures makes one wonder how he was ever able to place this tale.

A Landscape Painter (*Atlantic Monthly*, February 1866) deals with a wealthy amateur painter who, recovering from an engagement broken off because of the girl's mercenary spirit, falls in love with a twenty-seven-year-old school and music teacher on the Maine coast, proposes marriage, and is promptly accepted. Because he does not wish to repeat his earlier experience but to be loved for himself alone, he does not tell her that his income is $100,000 a year. But when, after their marriage, he attempts to make a clean breast of the matter, he finds that she already knows everything, having surreptitiously read his diary while he was sick. She admits that she would not have married him without his money but insists that she has played fair: "I never said I loved you . . . . I said I would be your wife. So I will, faithfully." When he tells her that hers was the act of a false woman, she replies that it was merely that of a woman and urges him to be a man. The diary entries in which the story is told end there, but from the introduction we learn that Locksley died at thirty-five, apparently not long after his marriage, and that his wife has since followed him. The surprise ending is not a trick, as in "A Tragedy of Error," but is grounded in character, not accident, and involves a revelation of character. James lulls his readers into believing that they are reading a sweet country love story and then jolts them, as if he were Bernard Shaw, yet in looking the tale over, one perceives that the woman's conduct throughout has been consistent with the final revelation. Miriam Allott, " 'The Lord of Burleigh' and Henry James's 'A Landscape Painter,' " *Notes and Queries*, N.S. 2 (1955), 220-21, shows that James was virtually burlesquing Tennyson's sentimental poem. See also Leo B. Levy, "Consciousness in Three Early Tales of Henry James," *Studies in Short Fiction*, 18 (1981), 407-12. (The other two tales discussed are "My Friend Bingham" and "Osborne's Revenge.")

THE LAST OF THE VALERII (*Atlantic Monthly*, January 1874) is based upon Prosper Mérimée's *La Vénus d'Ille*, which James had translated, and shows the influence of James's own interest in Roman excavations and perhaps, in the character of Valerio, of Hawthorne's Donatello in *The Marble Faun*. The Mérimée story is out-and-out supernaturalism, but James's tale can be interpreted as either supernaturalism or a study in abnormal psychology. The young Count Valerio, whose Catholicism has never been more than nominal, is seized by a kind of spiritual atavism when a statue of Juno is excavated upon his estate; he installs the goddess in a private chapel where she finally demands libations and blood sacrifice. His American wife, whose artist-godfather tells the story, breaks the spell and rewins her husband's love by having the statue reinterred, though Valerio surreptitiously retains one broken hand.

A LIGHT MAN (*Galaxy*, July 1869) has two young men, Theodore and Max, living with an eccentric, partly pitiful, partly sinister aged dilettante, Mr. Sloane, one as his secretary (Sloane is supposed to be writing his memoirs), the other as a guest. The story, told in extracts from Max's diary, concerns their relations with Sloane and with each other as affected by their relations with him. By the time Sloane dies at the end, it is clear that Max is a scoundrel (his diary reveals him as one able "to name, but not to feel his depravity") and that both young men failed to become Sloane's heir. There may be some difference of opinion as to whether Sloane or Max is the central character and who is the light man. One wonders whether Sloane was intended to suggest William Beckford and whether James had Swinburne in mind in portraying him as "a curious blend of sensuality and impotence." See Charles K. Fish, "Description in Henry James's 'A Light Man,'" *English Literary History,* 2 (1965), 211-15.

LONGSTAFF'S MARRIAGE (*Scribner's Monthly,* August 1878) is one of James's oddest, most abnormal, and least convincing tales. It opens on what seems to be comedy but ends as something close to tragedy, and it illustrates James's passion for symmetry carried to a fantastic extent. The narrative is that of the omniscient author, and the scene is Nice and Rome "forty years ago." The American Diana Belford, virginal as her name, attracts the attention of Reginald Longstaff, a young Englishman who believes himself to be dying, but when he begs her to marry him at his bedside, accepting his distinguished name and fortune, she repels him so coldly that he is crushed. Diana, repenting what now seems to her her cruelty, returns to America, and during the two years that pass before the story is resumed it becomes clear that she has taken on both Longstaff's passion and his malady. In the wild hope of meeting him again, she returns to Europe and runs into him in Rome, recovered in both health and spirits. It is now her turn to summon him to *her* bedside and beg him to marry *her.* He complies, but though he implores her to live, she refuses, because "it would be wrong of me."

LORD BEAUPRÉ (as "Lord Beauprey," *Macmillan's Magazine,* April-June 1892) is a lengthy but very light social comedy, easy to read and entertaining. To protect himself from a horde of designing women, the new Lord Beaupré, an immensely rich and desirable *parti,* permits it to be given out that he is engaged to Mary Gosselin, an old friend who, with some misgivings, agrees to the ruse to accommodate him. The plan has been engineered by Mary's mother, who has two motives: she would like, if possible, to capture the lord for her daughter, and she also wishes to keep Mary away from the American, Bolton-Brown. But by the time his lordship has become aware that he would like to turn his make-believe engagement into a real one, Mary is ready to put an end to the comedy and engage herself to this same Bolton-Brown. Her disappointed mother, who fancies herself omniscient in her understanding of human motives, believes that if the noble lord had not been so delicate that he did not wish "to make [Mary] feel as if she had lent herself to an artifice only on purpose to get hold of him," the outcome might have been different, but the reader is not necessarily obliged to take this at face value. For James's original idea for this story and the modifications he introduced into it, see his *Notebooks*, pp. 114-16.

THE MARRIED SON was James's contribution to the Harper composite novel, *The Whole Family*, which ran in *Harper's Bazar* from December 1906 to November 1907 and was published as a book in 1908. Each chapter was written by a different author from the point of view of a different character, and since the whole was intended to add up to a coherent story, each contributor read and continued the work of his predecessors. The action centers around the engagement of the daughter of the family, and the basic idea was that of Howells: "A marriage cannot possibly concern the married pair alone; but it is in the notion that it can that most of our marriages are made." Peggy's engagement is broken, and at the end she elopes with another man. James was not impressed by all of his collaborators, and his contribution, not surprisingly, is the longest of the twelve and contains some pretty dense prose. Like the New York stories in *The Finer Grain*, it is full of New York City references. The married son is an aspiring artist, unsympathetic toward the family business, best known for its ice pitchers. He is not the most engaging of James's many sensitive young gentlemen, and he is obviously living what Thoreau called a life of quiet desperation. That James should have been willing to participate in so undistinguished an enterprise for a fee of $400 suggests that he was more the professional writer and less the aloof artist than many readers suppose. See Bruce R. McElderry, Jr., "Henry James and *The Whole Family*," *Pacific Spectator*, 4 (1950), 352-60, and Earl F. Walbridge, "*The Whole Family* and Henry James," *Papers of the Bibliographical Society of America*, 52 (1958), 142-45, where further references are given.

MASTER EUSTACE (*Galaxy*, November 1871) deals with a spoiled brat of the aesthetic variety who has been pampered by an indulgent mother. During his absence in Europe, she marries one Cope, a former suitor, and when Eustace returns home he repudiates her brutally and makes such a scene that Cope tells him the truth: he is his father. In his fury Eustace tries to shoot himself but succeeds only in breaking a mirror. His mother, however, dies of the shock and strain she has been put through. The story is told retrospectively in the first person by an old maid who was the mother's companion. Eustace is well characterized, but there is no real "scene" until nearly the end, which has not been adequately prepared for. The rest is mainly straightforward exposition and analysis of character. Cornelia P. Kelley many years ago pronounced the tale a frustrated attempt to present George Sand materials in an American setting. For an ingenious commentary on the Shakespearian echoes in this tale, see Adeline R. Tintner, "Henry James's Hamlet: 'A Free Rearrangement,' " *Colby Library Quarterly*, 18 (1982), 168-82.

MAUD-EVELYN (*Atlantic Monthly*, April 1900) has its affinities with "The Friends of the Friends" and *The Sense of the Past*, both stories involving the supernatural, as well as with "The Altar of the Dead" and Densher's devotion to the memory of Milly Theale in *The Wings of the Dove* and therefore inevitably with James's own feeling for Minny Temple, by whom Milly was partly inspired. Unfortunately, however, though the story of Maud-Evelyn is related with much art and, at the outset at least, considerable charm, it pushes its situation beyond the bounds of absurdity and comes up with what most readers find morbid and unhealthy. That the Dedricks should have made a religion of the worship of their dead daughter, preserving her relics and imagining for her the life she never had, is touching and believable, but that even such a fatuous and, one suspects, lazy and self-serving youth as Marmaduke should have been drawn into their orbit to the extent of imagining himself first the girl's lover, then husband, then widower proves that there were turns of the screw that even James could not manage. The suggestion for the tale came from a story Paul Bourget told James as having reached him through the Italian fictionist Luigi Gualdo. James had the whole story in mind almost immediately, even developing a variation that later became "The Tone of Time" (see *Notebooks*, pp. 213, 265, and cf. Edel, *The Ghostly Tales of Henry James*, p. 598). Neil B. Houston's admiring article, "Henry James's 'Maud-Evelyn': Classic *Folie à Deux*," *Research Studies of Washington State University*, 41 (1973), 28-41, has more interest for psychologists and psychoanalysts than for readers of James.

THE MODERN WARNING (*Harper's Magazine*, June 1888, as "Two Countries") is one of James's least successful stories. The heroine, Agatha Grice, is crushed between her brother, Macarthy, an American businessman, "thin, dry, fine," ill-tempered, prejudiced, and fanatically anti-English, and Sir Rufus Chasemore, a brilliant Tory in government service, her marriage to whom Macarthy regards as "an abjuration, an apostasy, a kind of moral treachery." Compared to Macarthy, Sir Rufus, despite his extreme conservatism, seems "easy and genial," but after an extended visit to America, he writes a book that amounts to "a vivid warning, a consummate illustration of the horrors of democracy." To please his wife he voluntarily promises not to publish it. After a time, Agatha, recognizing its quality and feeling their marriage spoiled by her having been the occasion of her husband's drawing back from what he had thought it right to do, withdraws her objection but takes poison when she finds herself unable to face the strain of her brother's impending visit. Since her suicide is quite unprepared for, it seems melodramatic rather than tragic. Sir Rufus is, for once with James, a highly intelligent Englishman, but the horrors of English poverty are not glossed over. The method is very lax for James in the late eighties: "I find it difficult to explain"; "the three Grices—I had almost written the three Graces," etc.

A MOST EXTRAORDINARY CASE (*Atlantic Monthly*, April 1868) is that of Colonel Mason, a "war-wasted" young officer who is taken from his dingy hotel room in New York by an almost forgotten aunt at the close of the Civil War and moved to her country house on the Hudson, where he is to be nursed back to health by her; her niece, Caroline Hoffman; and young Dr. Knight. The doctor and the two women perform their functions triumphantly, but Mason falls in love with Caroline, and when he learns that she has engaged herself to Dr. Knight, he loses his will to live and dies. Dr. Knight regards his as "a most extraordinary case." The characters are well drawn, and though the method is easy and relaxed, there are incidental, though sometimes awkward, indications that the young author is already becoming sensitive to the technical problems involved in story telling. The great weakness of the story is the passive role assigned to the hero, who has nothing to do but die. In her article "In the Footsteps of Stendhal: James's 'A Most Extraordinary Case' and *La Chartreuse de Parme*," *Revue de Littérature Comparée*, 55 (1981), 232-38, Adeline R. Tintner shows how James "adapted important structural relationships in Stendhal's masterpiece for his own tale" and also suggests literary influences, models, and/or possible relationships for a number of other stories.

MRS. TEMPERLEY (*Harper's Weekly*, April 6, 13, 20, 1887, as "Cousin Maria") presents a tiny woman with a gentle, loving exterior, much given to "the friendly apostrophe and even the caressing hand." There is "no hint of the bully in her," yet "the masculine element was [sufficiently] included in her nature" so that in her widowhood she has no difficulty in keeping her three daughters completely under her control. The tale opens in New York, where she rejects the proposal of "Cousin Raymond," a distant relative and an artist, for the eldest Dora, because the girl is still too young and is continued five years later in Paris, where Mrs. Temperley has established herself in style and has her eye on arranging great marriages for her children. She has pretty much given up on Dora, knowing that though she will not marry against her mother's will, neither will she accept a man she does not love, but she still puts Raymond off on the ground that Dora, "wants to stay" with Effie and Tishy. The mother is appalling. Dora, "original and generous and uncalculating, besides being full of perception and taste," has, in her lover's eyes, and in the reader's, "but one defect—her admiration for her mother was too undiscriminating." Perhaps it is not wholly convincing either. The tale is a minor expression of James's well-known horror of parents who attempt to control their children's lives.

MY FRIEND BINGHAM (*Atlantic Monthly*, March 1867) presents George Bingham, who, on the Maine coast, accidentally, occasions the death of a little boy and then falls in love with the child's mother and marries her. The mature James might have made something moving out of this difficult material, but at this stage the young writer was not yet ready, especially in a story told in the first person by "a cordial observer," to enable the reader to understand the mother's grief or to judge whether the passion of the lovers had been conceived and presented as powerful enough to overcome the barrier between them. A good deal in this story is told rather than shown, and it is at best a question whether all the material about Bingham's background, as sketched in at the beginning, is sufficiently relevant to the author's purpose or made use of.

A NEW ENGLAND WINTER (*Century Magazine*, August-September 1884) delighted Howells with its vivid pictures of Boston and environs, an interest that must surely be shared by all who know this region. The tale, however, though grace-fully done, hardly matches the setting. Mrs. Daintry's son Florimond, a painter of obviously little talent, prefers Paris to Boston, and when she learns he is coming home for a visit, his mother engineers an invitation, though not to her house ("it would be too marked"), to Rachel Torrence, a distant but impoverished connection from Brooklyn and an intelligent, cultivated, talented girl. Mrs. Daintry does not wish to have Florimond fall in love with Rachel (though she does not mind exposing her to *his* charms) but merely hopes that she will make Boston sufficiently attractive to him so that he will make a good long stay. Unfortunately it is not Rachel but her rather silly hostess, Mrs. Mesh, who attracts the son, and though their connection remains innocent, Mrs. Daintry becomes suffi-ciently alarmed so that she develops a sudden, burning desire to visit Europe and takes her son with her.

NONA VINCENT (*English Illustrated Magazine*, February-March 1892) is an unimportant offshoot of James's own expe-riences as an aspiring playwright (Leon Edel has made a case for Mrs. Alsager having been studied from Mrs. Hugh Bell and the actress Violet Gray from Elizabeth Robins, who had been unsatisfactory as Claire in the dramatized version of *The American*). Allan Wayworth, a painfully earnest young writer and a kind of protegé of Mrs. Alsager, whose husband is "a massive personality in the City and a heavy one at home," gets his play produced in London after many disappointments. The play itself, whose name we never learn, gets good reviews, but Violet Gray, who plays the heroine, Nona Vincent, is judged not to have either understood or projected the character. Before the second performance, Mrs. Alsager, upon whom Nona had been modeled, pays a kindly visit to the actress; this gives Violet the clue she had been seeking, and she goes on to triumph. At the same time, Nona herself "manifests" to Waymarsh. During the rehearsal period Violet and Mrs. Alsager had each told the playwright that the other is in love with him, but in the last paragraph we are hurriedly informed that he finally marries Violet. She is an admirable, honest, hard-working young woman, who, like Miriam Rooth in James's great theater novel, *The Tragic Muse*, testifies to his ability to avoid all the clichés that commonly appear in the portrayal of actresses in fiction, but he does not succeed in making her passage from failure to success convincing; neither is the supernormal element involved in Nona Vincent's appearance to the playwright satisfactorily handled.

OSBORNE'S REVENGE   (*Galaxy*, July 1868) relates how Philip Osborne, believing that his friend Robert Graham has committed suicide because he had been jilted by a heartless girl, Henrietta Cosgrove, goes to Newport to teach her a lesson. He finds her accomplished, charming, and of spotless reputation, nearly falls in love with her himself, and is only saved from making a fool of himself through learning that she was already engaged to another man before meeting Graham, who had made her life a burden with his unwelcome attentions and whose romance with her existed only in his own warped mind. Though Osborne is the central character, the reader's interest is centered upon discovering the truth about Henrietta (James would soon do something similar upon a larger scale with Angela Vivian in the novel *Confidence*). The surprise ending is a piece of ironic comedy as well as a study in morbid psychology. The only weakness of the story inheres in the difficulty of believing that a man like Osborne could be so attached to such a poor creature as Graham turns out to have been.

THE PAPERS (published, without previous serialization, in *The Better Sort*, 1903) is one of the least rewarding stories of James's maturity. It is not so much that it is a poor story as that he should have let it run on to 36,000 words without ever developing more than a tepid interest. It began (see *Notebooks*, pp. 313-14) with the simple idea of contrasting the successful and the unsuccessful journalist, Howard Bight and Maud Blandy, who, at the end, after they have both been so shocked by the conscienceless excesses of journalism as to forswear any future connection with it, are to marry. Their counterparts as the tale develops are A.B.C. Beadel-Muffet, K.C.B., M.P., the most successful publicity seeker and press manipulator of his time, and Mortimer Marshal, an aspiring playwright who cannot get publicity for love nor money. At one point, Bight schemes to help Marshal by feighing his involvement in the Beadel-Muffet story, but the plan founders when the latter, now in hiding, is reported a suicide in Germany. Maud first, then Howard, is appalled by the report, fearing the man a victim of a publicity campaign run out of control, but the predominantly comic tone of the tale is saved by his return, now more of a press sensation than ever. Adeline R. Tintner, " 'The Papers': Henry James Rewrites *As You Like It*," *Studies in Short Fiction*, 17 (1980), 165-70, reads the tale as an attempt to transpose "the theme of one of Shakespeare's most enchanting fantasies to the world of London journalism." Maud is Rosalind, but Jacques has the Orlando role.

THE PATH OF DUTY (*English Illustrated Magazine*, December 1884) was based upon a real life situation that had been related to James. Ambrose Tester, M.P., loves Lady Vandeleur, but their association is innocent, and since there is no reasonable prospect of her gaining her freedom, he yields to family pressure and engages himself to a charming young girl named Joscelind Bernardstone. Then Lord Vandeleur unexpectedly dies, which gives everybody a nice little Jamesian problem of conscience to wrestle with. Tester honors his obligation to Joscelind, but the result is far from satisfactory. Having learned "how sweet it is to renounce hand in hand with one we love," both he and Lady Vandeleur now find themselves in love not only with each other but, more dangerously, with their own nobility, while the unloved wife and mother "meets everywhere the implication that if two people in our time have distinguished themselves for their virtue, it is her husband and Landy Vandeleur."

POOR RICHARD (*Atlantic Monthly*, June-August 1867), the second of James's stories with a Civil War background, was the longest tale he had yet written, the first to be published in installments, and the first that came to the editorial attention of W.D. Howells. Gertrude Whittaker, a plain, well-to-do country girl, is courted by Richard Clare, a somewhat dissipated, loutish young farmer, and by two soldiers, the high-minded Captain Severn and the treacherous Captain Luttrel. This is one of the early James stories that shows most clearly the influence of George Sand. It also involves the same kind of ethical problems he was to deal with in his greatest work, but though there are individual scenes of power, he was not yet ready to handle the whole convincingly. Too much is expounded instead of being revealed in the development of the narrative, much of the talk seems academic and formal, and Richard's redemption and development are not traced in sufficient detail to be convincing.

A PROBLEM (*Galaxy*, June 1868) is not a story of the supernatural but a psychological study somewhat akin to Howells's 1890 novel *The Shadow of a Dream*. A young honeymoon couple are told by an Indian fortune teller that they will have one child, a girl, and that she will die young, whereupon both remember having been told by other purported psychics to look forward to two marriages. They make themselves sick worrying over how all these prophecies can possibly be fulfilled and if they are not which, if any, will be, and the result is dissatisfaction and unhappiness, which finally lead to a break. After the wife's return to her mother, their child does die, and their shared grief brings the couple together again. "A Problem" is a very short tale for James, and considering the limited space at his disposal, he handled both narrative and characterization satisfactorily though without distinction.

PROFESSOR FARGO (*Galaxy*, August 1872) is an undistinguished tale told by a narrator who invokes Don Quixote and Goethe's

Mignon, but more likely influences emanate from Turgenev
(*A Strange Story*) and Hawthorne (*The Blithedale Romance*).
The tale also has affinities with James's own novel *The Bostonians* and with *The Undiscovered Country* by Howells, while
Fargo himself, a fake spiritualistic medium who gives a show
with Colonel Gifford, a poverty-stricken mathematical genius
and frustrated inventor, and his deaf-mute daughter, a light-
ning calculator, suggests Melville's *Confidence Man* and
Mark Twain's backwoods fourflushers and scoundrels. The
narrator, a commercial traveler, encounters the trio first in the
little town of P—— and later in New York City, which is as
grubby here as in the final pages of James's first novel, *Watch
and Ward*, and where Fargo punishes Gifford for his failure to
support his deceptions by seducing his daughter, after which
Gifford suffers a mental collapse.

THE ROMANCE OF CERTAIN OLD CLOTHES (*Atlantic Monthly*,
February 1868), James's first ghost story, is set in mid-
eighteenth-century Massachusetts province and shows the
influence of Hawthorne. Unless we choose to take an exception for "De Gray," which opens in 1820, this tale, "Gabrielle
de Bergerac," and *The Sense of the Past* are James's only
"historicals." Two sisters fall in love with the same man, who
weds the younger, making the elder very jealous. The wife
dies after the birth of a child but first makes her husband
promise to keep her clothes for her daughter (compare the
deathbed vow in *The Other House*). The husband then marries the older sister, who, after financial reverses, torments
him into letting her get into her sister's trunk. He finds her
dead beside it, "and on her blanched brow and cheeks there
glowed the marks of ten hideous wounds from vengeful
ghostly hands." As Cornelia P. Kelley long ago observed, this
tale is developed impressionistically in a series of pictures, but
it makes less use of its New England background than some of
James's other early stories, and it has little historical coloring
and even less ghostly atmosphere. James has the avenging
spirit function for a rather petty reason in quite conventional,
traditional fashion, and there is no sign of the innovations that
would enable him to bring back some masterpieces in kind
from his later excursions into ghostly territory.

ROSE-AGATHE (*Lippincott's Magazine*, May 1878, as "Théo-dolinde") is the *jeu d'esprit* par excellence about James's *jeux d'esprit*. Sanguinetti, an American long resident in Europe, a collector of "pretty things," is so fascinated by a beautiful mannequin in a coiffeur's shop that he negotiates for its pur-chase, describing it so affectionately meanwhile to his friend, the narrator of the tale, who has only seen it from afar, that the latter believes Sanguinetti is shamelessly negotiating for the proprietor's wife. The richly atmospheric Parisian scene, unusually rich in sense impressions for James, especially those of taste and smell, with which the story opens is by all means the best thing in it.

SIR DOMINICK FERRAND (*Cosmopolitan Magazine*, July-August 1892, as "Jersey Villas") involves the ethics of publish-ing materials that reveal the secrets of the dead. In a hidden compartment discovered in a curious secondhand desk he has purchased, Peter Baron, an impecunious writer, discovers letters that impeach both the public and private character of an English politician and statesman. At about the same time, he finds himself falling in love with a young widow, an aspir-ing composer and a "sensitive" who lives in the same board-inghouse as himself. Mrs. Ryves knows nothing about what the papers contain, but she feels that they are evil and begs Baron not to publish them. After a harrowing struggle with his conscience, he turns down the editor who has offered him a substantial sum for them and promised to publish his own stories besides; then, like Tina in "The Aspern Papers," he burns them one by one. Later he learns that Sir Dominick Ferrand was the natural father of Mrs. Ryves and a consider-ably better man than the letters had indicated. Baron and Mrs. Ryves are married and support themselves by producing popular songs while he also begins to be accepted as a writer. "Sir Dominick Ferrand" is an absorbing and extremely clever story, and James probably excluded it from the New York Edition because it falls below his highest level as too pat, too clever, too contrived (Edel suggests that one feature was derived from de Maupassant's "Le Chevelure"). The ethical issue is not quite clear, however, since it might well be argued that while the public had no legitimate concern with Sir

Dominick's private scandal, it was entitled to all available information on his performance as a public servant. See the *Notebooks*, pp. 117-18, for James's own account of the origin of the idea.

THE SOLUTION (*New Review*, December 1889-February 1890) is a delightful, perfectly managed trifle, a first-person narrative constituting an Englishman's remembrance of a practical joke he is now much ashamed of having been involved in when he was in diplomatic service in "the slumberous, pictorial Rome of the Popes, before the Italians had arrived or the local color departed." Though nobody really liked Mrs. Goldie, an appalling, though not malevolent, example of James's managing women, with three unattractive daughters to dispose of, "the young men of the diplomatic body" treated her house "almost as a club." Henry Wilmerding, a Carolinian, who was emphatically a gentleman, certainly not a fool, but decidely not a man of the world, was the most innocent among them; Guy de Montant, a French attaché, was the least. When Wilmerding goes off for a little while alone with Veronica Goldie at a picnic, it occurs to de Montant to find out whether he could be persuaded that, according to the custom of the country, he has compromised the girl and must therefore propose to her. Wilmerding, persuaded, does just that, and since he is wealthy, the Goldies jump at him. The narrator, conscience stricken, now persuades Mrs. Rushbrook, the widow of an English naval officer, whom he hopes to marry, to get Wilmerding out of it, and she promises to try, though she is maddeningly secretive as to means. What she does is to arrange for Wilmerding to buy the Goldies off, and then she marries him herself. The story was based on an actual occurence related to James by Fanny Kemble, but in real life the man married the girl. The lovely Roman atmosphere obviously derives from the author's own early visits. In 1891 or 1892 James turned "The Solution" into a play, *Disengaged*, for Ada Rehan, but Augustin Daly dragged his feet on production until the author, disgusted with both producer and star, withdrew it. See Leon Edel's discussion of the matter in *The Complete Plays of Henry James*, pp. 295-99.

THE SPECIAL TYPE (*Collier's Weekly*, June 16, 1900) was suggested by "the circumstances of the W.K. Vanderbilt divorce; his engaging the *demi-mondaine*, in Paris, to *s'afficher* with him in order to force his virago of a wife to divorce him" (*Notebooks*, p. 232), and James never wrote a more touching story nor one that better illustrates his ability to take his materials out of the gutter, if that was where he happened to find them, and make them into something fine. The tale is told by an artist friend who paints Frank Brivet's portrait, and the woman of the "special type" who accommodates Brivet is Alice Dundene, who isn't "so to speak, a lady" nor "professional" either, but who "escapes . . . any classification save as one of the most beautiful and good-natured of women." Brivet goes into the simulated "affair" with no idea of its having any effect on his confederate that his money could not make good. That Mrs. Dundene would fall in love with him any seasoned reader of fiction might have foreseen; the special, characteristically Jamesian turn of the screw is that she should be worth several times the man and the woman he wishes to marry put together. Nobody realizes this except the narrator, to whom she comes at last to beg him to paint Brivet's portrait for her, he having promised her anything she might ask for as a reward for her services and she having refused everything else. She had never, she remarks in passing, been alone with Brivet. The artist gives her the portrait he has painted on a commission from the bride-to-be, which he regards as his masterpiece, and faces the commissioner's wrath with indifference.

THE STORY OF A MASTERPIECE (*Galaxy*, January-February 1868) may well have been influenced by Hawthorne's "The Prophetic Pictures." John Lennox discerns a resemblance between the charming girl he is engaged to marry and a figure in a painting by Stephen Baxter, whose talent so much impresses him that he engages him to paint Marian's portrait. Baxter admits to a previous acquaintance with the girl but does not reveal that he broke with her because he discovered that she had trifled with the affections of two young men. His portrait of her is a masterpiece, and it is not because he is malicious but simply because he is a great painter that Marian's true character is revealed by it. Seriously troubled without being quite able to account for his discomfort, Lennox goes through with the marriage but slashes the portrait to bits. The only serious criticism to be made of this story is that the long flashback devoted to Marian's previous association with Baxter rather disturbs its unity. Originally the tale ended abruptly with the destruction of the portrait; it was at the request of the editor of the *Galaxy* that James added the final paragraph, in which he tells the reader that the marriage did take place and that it is as yet too early to be sure whether it will be successful but refuses to say how Lennox explained the destruction of her portrait to his wife.

THE STORY OF A YEAR (*Atlantic Monthly*, March 1868) was considered James's first published story until "A Tragedy of Error" was discovered. It was the first of James's three Civil War tales, but though there is an interesting resemblance between the war imagery in the elaborate figure in the clouds at the beginning of this tale and that of Stephen Crane in *The Red Badge of Courage*, James deliberately avoids the battlefield to study the effects of the war on the home front. Elizabeth Crowe engages herself to Ford, but when the thrill of his being a soldier wears off, she begins to be interested in Robert Bruce, and when she believes Ford about to die, she engages herself to the other man. Later she changes her mind and tries to live up to her ideal of herself, but Ford, who had always understood her limitations, generously releases her and later accommodatingly dies. Elizabeth is not one of James's vicious heroines; she is simply a shallow, well-meaning girl who has difficulty distinguishing between what she feels, what she would like to feel, and what she thinks she ought to feel. The story is told, loosely and somewhat naively, by the omniscient author.

THE SWEETHEART OF M. BRISEUX (*Galaxy*, June 1873) was derived by Cornelia Kelley from Balzac's *Le Chef d'Oeuvre Inconnu*. The narrator is fascinated by a picture of a girl in a yellow shawl in "the little picture gallery at M——," and when the model, now a white-haired spinster, comes to look at it, he guesses her identity and persuades her (not too convincingly) to tell him her story. She had been a lonely American girl, unhappily engaged to the son of her benefactress, a "perfectly honorable and amiable" but completely empty prig—all surface, with no vices and, unfortunately, no talent—one of James's spoiled mother's boys, who has taken up painting only because he must do something. He had left her alone in a borrowed studio where he was making a hopeless stab at painting her portrait when Pierre Briseux, then poverty-stricken and unknown, wandered in in search of another painter, examined Harold's daub, and by altering it with a few strokes showed her what real painting was like. In "Henry James's Mona Lisa," *Essays in Literature* (Western Illinois University), 8 (1981), 103-108, Adeline R. Tintner finds "that the icon of Mona Lisa" has been suggested in this tale, which makes it an example of James's habit of taking "a classic in art or literature and [making] it serve as a measure of his characters or of their situation."

THÉODOLINDE.   See ROSE-AGATHE.

THE THIRD PERSON   first appeared, without magazine pre-publication, in *The Soft Side* (1900). Except that the statement would give no idea of its sly delicacy, deftness, and sophistication, it might be called James's comic ghost story. Susan and Amy Brush are "two good ladies, [kinswomen] previously not intimate nor indeed more than slightly acquainted," who might be out of *Cranford* except for what would have seemed to the "good ladies" in that work a slight tincture of intellectual perverseness or waywardness. They inherit a charming old house in Rye which, after they have unearthed some family papers, turns out to be haunted by a ghost with his head twisted to one side who is identified by the vicar with a forebear who, in the days when Rye and Winchelsea were important Channel ports, had been hanged for smuggling. Pleased at first to have a man in the house, Amy and Susan almost come to be rivals for his attention, but since he never speaks, they have some difficulty in figuring out the cause of his evident depression, with the result that Susan finally sends her "little all—or almost" to the Chancellor of the Exchequer as "conscience-money," in the hope of giving the ghost peace, while Amy, more daring, becomes a fellow-sinner by smuggling a Tauchnitz novel into England. Since

"The Third Person" is not discussed in James's *Notebooks*, we do not know where he got the idea for it, but it is obviously drenched in the atmosphere of the Lamb House neighborhood that was his final home. See Leon Edel, *The Ghostly Tales of Henry James*, pp. 630-32.

THE TONE OF TIME (*Scribner's Magazine*, November 1900) stretches the long arm of coincidence about as far as it has ever been made to reach, but this merely becomes the means of making a searching study of human character and motives. Mrs. Bridgenorth comes to the painter-narrator for a portrait of an ideal figure she intends to pass off as the husband she never had. He turns the commission over to a painter friend, Mary J. Tredick, who produces a masterpiece in the likeness of the man who had jilted her. But when it turns out that she has painted the portrait of the man who would have married Mrs. Bridgenorth if he had lived and that it was she who took him away from Mary, the latter refuses to relinquish the picture. If Mrs. Bridgenorth could not keep her lover in life, she shall not have him in death. Painting the portrait in hate, Mary Tredick has exorcised her demons and keeps it in joy. For the origin of the idea, almost completely transformed by James, see *Notebooks*, p. 213, and cf. pp. 265-67, 283-84, where it will be seen that at one point he planned to have the two women confront each other but wisely relinquished this idea. In "The Tone of Time" what seems a hopelessly artificial plot is triumphantly handled.

A TRAGEDY OF ERROR (*Continental Monthly*, February 1864), which was obviously inspired by Balzac or Mérimée, was, so far as is now known, James's first published tale. The scene is a French seaport town, the subject matter adultery and murder, and there is a surprise ending suggestive of de Maupassant or O. Henry (the boatman who has been employed to murder the wife's returning husband kills her lover by mistake). Though the twenty-year-old writer has not yet found his proper subject matter, his characterization is sound, and the irony by which the tale is marked is characteristic. See Leon Edel, " 'A Tragedy of Error': James's First Story," *New England Quarterly*, 29 (1956), 291-317; John A. Saverese, "Henry James's First Story: A Study of Error," *Studies in Short Fiction*, 17 (1980), 431-35.

Two Countries. See The Modern Warning.

Travelling Companions (*Atlantic Monthly*, November-December 1870) was, except for "A Tragedy of Error" and "Gabrielle de Bergerac," the earliest of James's European tales. It is told in the first person by the hero, an American living in Europe, to whom James has given his own passion for Italy. The narrator innocently compromises Charlotte Evans by taking her, despite her father's necessary absence, on a sight-seeing trip to Padua, where they miss their last train and are therefore obliged to remain overnight. When he proposes marriage to her, she fears that he has asked her out of chivalry and therefore declines, but ultimately they reach an understanding. Much is said in this tale about Leonardo's *Last Supper* and Tintoretto's *Crucifixion*, and though our hero disclaims "the architectural *coup d'oeil*," there is a rather elaborate and imaginative description of Milan Cathedral. Titian, Giotto, and others are referred to; so is George Sand's *La Dernière Aldini*, and Charlotte reads "Rappaccini's Daughter" in Padua. Her father is James's first portrait of the American businessman on European holiday.

The Visits (*Black and White*, May 28, 1892, as "The Visit"), one of James's most concentrated tales, concerns a girl who literally agonizes herself to death because of the "shame" she feels over having shown a young man who has made no advances to her that she cares for him. The story is told in retrospect by a friend of Louisa's mother, who had found the girl in tears at the house where both chanced to be visiting before they met again in Louisa's own home and who had been sworn to promise that she had never seen her in distress and had kept her word. Suspense as to the cause of the girl's agony is well maintained to the end, but readers can accept her behavior only on the assumption that she is mad. Nor can they claim to have been adequately compensated for the suffering they have been compelled to undergo with her.

The Wheel of Time (*Cosmopolitan Magazine*, December 1892-January 1893) illustrates James's ability to use successfully material that might easily have resulted in an overformalized or mechanical story (see his *Notebooks*, pp. 123-24). The mothers of Fanny Knocker, who has all the gifts of the gods except beauty and is very wealthy besides, and of the impecunious Maurice Glanvil, who has no gifts except his decency and extreme good looks, put their heads together to make a match between the two, but Maurice will not be caught. He marries instead a beautiful Russian girl who dies after a year, leaving him a daughter, Vera, who grows up as plain as the girl from whom he had fled. At forty-nine he again meets Fanny, now the widowed Mrs. Tregent, who has developed into a greatly admired, mature woman of personal distinction and noble character, with a strikingly handsome son. A writer interested primarily in situation would have had Fanny take satisfaction in her son's refusal of Maurice's daughter, but James does nothing of the kind. There is no resentment in Mrs. Tregent, and though she decidedly refuses to marry Maurice when he asks her, she makes no secret of the fact that he was the love of her life and that she has never forgotten him. Of his daughter she makes a protegée, and it is not her fault that her son behaves as Maurice did so long ago. Since the reader is intended to believe in Fanny's charm as a mature woman, her unattractiveness in youth would seem to have been somewhat overplayed, and Vera's death of what used to be called "a broken heart" now seems very Victorian.

Appendix B: *A Chronological List of The Collections of Tales Published by Henry James, with Their Contents*

A Passionate Pilgrim and Other Tales. Boston: James R. Osgood and Company, 1875.

> A Passionate Pilgrim, The Last of the Valerii, Eugene Pickering, The Madonna of the Future, The Romance of Certain Old Clothes, Madame de Mauves.

Daisy Miller: A Study/An International Episode/Four Meetings. Two volumes. London: Macmillan and Company, 1879.

The Madonna of the Future and Other Tales. Two volumes. London: Macmillan, 1879.

> The Madonna of the Future, Longstaff's Marriage, Madame de Mauves, Eugene Pickering, The Diary of a Man of Fifty, Benvolio.

The Diary of a Man of Fifty and A Bundle of Letters. New York: Harper & Brothers, 1880.

Washington Square/The Pension Beaurepas/A Bundle of Letters. Two volumes. London: Macmillan, 1881.

The Siege of London, The Pension Beaurepas, and The Point of View. Boston: Osgood, 1883.

Tales of Three Cities. Boston: Osgood; London: Macmillan, 1884.

The Impressions of a Cousin, Lady Barberina, A New England Winter.

Stories Revived. Three volumes. London: Macmillan, 1885.

The Author of Beltraffio, Pandora, The Path of Duty, A Light Man, A Day of Days, Georgina's Reasons, A Passionate Pilgrim, A Landscape Painter, Rose-Agathe, Poor Richard, The Last of the Valerii, Master Eustace, The Romance of Certain Old Clothes, A Most Extraordinary Case.

The Author of Beltraffio/Pandora/Georgina's Reasons/The Path of Duty/Four Meetings. Boston: Osgood, 1885.

The Aspern Papers/Louisa Pallant/The Modern Warning. Two volumes. London and New York: Macmillan, 1888.

A London Life/The Patagonia/The Liar/Mrs. Temperley. London and New York: Macmillan, 1889.

The Lesson of the Master/The Marriages/The Pupil/Brooksmith/The Solution/Sir Edmund Orme. New York and London: Macmillan, 1892.

The Private Life/Lord Beaupré/The Visits. New York: Harpers, 1893.

The Wheel of Time/Collaboration/Owen Wingrave. New York: Harpers, 1893.

The Private Life/The Wheel of Time/Lord Beaupré/The Visits/Collaboration/Owen Wingrave. London: James R. Osgood, McIlvaine & Co., 1893.

The Real Thing and Other Tales. New York and London: Macmillan, 1893.

The Real Thing, Sir Dominick Ferrand, Nona Vincent, The Chaperon, Greville Fane.

Terminations: The Death of the Lion/The Coxon Fund/The Middle Years/The Altar of the Dead. New York: Harpers; London: William Heinemann, 1895.

Embarrassments. New York: Macmillan; London: Heinemann, 1896.

The Figure in the Carpet, Glasses, The Next Time, The Way It Came.

The Two Magics: The Turn of the Screw/Covering End. New York: Macmillan; London: Heinemann, 1898.

The Soft Side. New York: Macmillan; London: Methuen & Co., 1900.

The Great Good Place, "Europe," Paste, The Real Right Thing, The Great Condition, The Tree of Knowledge, The Abasement of the Northmores, The Given Case, John Delavoy, The Third Person, Maud-Evelyn, Miss Gunton of Poughkeepsie.

The Better Sort. New York: Charles Scribner's Sons; London: Methuen, 1903.

Broken Wings, The Beldonald Holbein, The Two Faces, The Tone of Time, The Special Type, Mrs. Medwin, Flickerbridge, The Story in It, The Beast in the Jungle, The Birthplace, The Papers.

The Finer Grain. New York: Scribners; London: Methuen, 1910.

The Velvet Glove, Mora Montravers, A Round of Visits, Crapy Cornelia, The Bench of Desolation.

NOTES

The following abbreviations are employed in the references given in the notes:

HJ   Henry James
J   James

Publishers

CUP   Cambridge University Press
H   Harper & Brothers (also Harper & Row)
HUP   Harvard University Press
L   J.B. Lippincott Company
M   The Macmillan Company
OUP   Oxford University Press
S   Charles Scribner's Sons
UCP   The University of Chicago Press
UIP   University of Illinois Press
UNCP   University of North Carolina Press
UNP   University of Nebraska Press
YUP   Yale University Press

Periodicals

ABBW   *AB Bookman's Weekly*
AI   *American Imago*
AL   *American Literature*
AQ   *American Quarterly*
ArQ   *Arizona Quarterly*
CE   *College English*
Crit   *Cricitism*
ESQ   *Emerson Society Quarterly*
Exp   *Explicator*
HJR   *Henry James Review*
LP   *Literature and Psychology*
MFS   *Modern Fiction Studies*
MLN   *Modern Language Notes*

MR	*Markham Review*
NCF	*Nineteenth Century Fiction*
NEQ	*New England Quarterly*
NQ	*Notes and Queries*
NS	*Die Neueren Sprachen*
PLL	*Papers on Language and Literature*
PMLA	*Publications of the Modern Language Association*
RSW	*Research Studies of Washington State University*
SAQ	*South Atlantic Quarterly*
SN	*Studies in the Novel*
SSF	*Studies in Short Fiction*
TQ	*Texas Quarterly*
TSL	*Tennessee Studies in Literature*
TSLL	*Texas Studies in Language and Literature*
UKCR	*University of Kansas City Review*

Books are indicated by author (or editor), title, publisher, and date the first time they are cited, thereafter by author and title the first time in any given chapter, and subsequently by the shortest possible intelligible reference.

In "The Uncollected Stories of HJ," *AL*, 21 (1949), 279-91, Bruce McElderry, Jr., included "Pyramus and Thisbe," "Still Waters," and "A Change of Heart" among James's tales; for why this is not admissible see Sidney E. Lind, *AL*, 23 (1951-52), 130-31. The pioneering study of *The Early Development of HJ*, by Cornelia Pulsifer Kelley, was first published in *University of Illinois Studies in Language and Literature*, Vol. 15, Nos. 1-2 (1930) and reprinted in a revised edition by UIP, 1965. James's tales up to 1880 are also covered, some of them skimpily, by James Kraft in *The Early Tales of HJ* (Southern Illinois University Press, 1969). See, further, Krishna Baldev Vaid, *Technique in the Tales of HJ* (HUP, 1964), and Peter Buitenhuis, *The Grasping Imagination* (University of Toronto Press, 1976), neither of which is confined to the early period. Some comment on many of James's tales also appears in such general studies of his work as F.W. Dupee, *HJ* (William Sloane Associates, 1951) and Bruce R. McElderry, Jr., *HJ* (Twayne Publishers, 1965).

Chapter I

1. Like all the older material included, these stories were revised for their appearance in the New York Edition. See Albert Frank Gegenheimer, "Early and Late Revisions in HJ's 'A Passionate Pilgrim,'" *AL*, 23 (1951-52), 233-42: "In general, passages become shorter, excess descriptions are dropped, ornate and flowery language becomes considerably plainer and more precise, and ambiguities are carefully but quietly eliminated." "More concrete and specific images" are also substituted "for what had earlier been vague and even trite comparisons and metaphors," and derogatory references to America are softened.

2. The notion advanced by Van Wyck Brooks in *The Pilgrimage of HJ* (Dutton, 1925) that Clement Searle represents James's own attitude toward England now has no critical standing. The narrator comes closer to James's own early point of view, but he too is a fictional character. Searle himself, before the end, helps a poor man "to get out of this awful England." Ora Segal has the best analysis of the role played by the "Pilgrim" narrator in *The Lucid Interval* (YUP, 1969).

3. Whether the ghost was "real" or not is left for the reader to decide, but as Elizabeth Stevenson points out in *The Crooked Corridor* (M, 1949), the way Searle begins "playfully to exchange his identity for that of the earlier Clement Searle" foreshadows James's late unfinished novel *The Sense of the Past*.

4. A valuable and ingenious article by Michael Ross, "HJ's 'Half-man': The Legacy of Browning in 'The Madonna of the Future,'" *Browning Institute Studies*, 2 (1974),

25-42, argues James's general indebtedness to Browning for his discovery of Italy as literary material and sees the "Madonna" as "an oblique act of homage." Ross relies especially upon "Pictor Ignotus" and "Andrea del Sarto," of which latter he is tempted to see James's tale as "a delicate reversal."

5. See Robert F. Gleckner, "J's 'Madame de Mauves' and Hawthorne's *The Scarlet Letter*," *MLN*, 73 (1958), 580-86; Benjamin C. Rountree, "J's 'Madame de Mauves' and Madame de La Fayette's *Princesse de Clèves*,'" *SSF*, 1 (1963-64), 264-71; John Kenneth Simon, "A Study of Classical Gesture: HJ and Madame de La Fayette," *Comparative Literature Studies*, 3 (1966), 271-83; James Kraft, " 'Madame de Mauves' and *Roderick Hudson*: The Development of James's International Style," *TQ*, Vol. 11, Nos. 3-4 (1969), 143-60; H.A. Bouraoui, "HJ and the French Mind: The International Theme in 'Madame de Mauves,' " *Novel*, 4 (1970-71), 67-76.

6. Though all commentators have chosen to ignore the point, at the time "Madame de Mauves" was written, the possibility of divorce and remarriage was not open to Madame de Mauves under French law. Between 1816 and 1884 she could at best have secured a *séparation de corps*, which would have ruled out remarriage for either her or her husband. My thanks to Professor Sylvère Monod for checking this matter.

7. For Ward see *The Imagination of Disaster* (UNP, 1961); also his "Structural Irony in 'Madame de Mauves,' " *SSF*, 2 (1964-65), 170-82; cf. Louise Dauner, "HJ and the Garden of Death," *UKCR*, 19 (1952-53), 137-43; see also Robert C. McLean, "The 'Disappointed Observer' of 'Madame de Mauves,' " *RSUW*, 33 (1965), 181-96; and "The Completed Vision: A Study of 'Madame de Mauves' and *The Ambassadors*," *MLN*, 38 (1967), 446-61.

8. Kaplan, "J's 'Madame de Mauves,' " *Exp*, 19 (1961), Item 32. For Rountree, see note 5.

9. Other studies of "Madame de Mauves" from various
    points of view (of varying validity) include John O.
    McCormick, "The Rough and Lurid Vision: HJ, Graham
    Greene, and the International Theme," *Jahrbuch für
    Amerikastudien*, 2 (1957), 158-67; Rebecca Patterson,
    "Two Portraits of a Lady," *Midwest Quarterly*, 1 (1960),
    343-61; William P. Safranek, "Longmore in 'Madame de
    Mauves': The Making of a Pragmatist," *ArQ*, 35, (1979),
    293-302. Millicent Bell, *Edith Wharton and HJ: The
    Story of Their Friendship* (George Braziller, 1965), pp.
    250-51, has an interesting comparison between "Madame
    de Mauves" and Mrs. Wharton's "Madame de Treymes."

Chapter II

1. *HJ* (Secker, 1916).

2. John A. Clair, *The Ironic Dimension in the Fiction of HJ*
    (Duquesne University Press, 1965); Leo Gurko, "The
    Missing Word in HJ's 'Four Meetings,' " *SSF*, 7 (1970),
    298-307; Roger Seamon, "HJ's 'Four Meetings': A Study
    in Irritation and Condescension," *SSF*, 15 (1978), 155-63;
    W.R. Martin, "The Narrator's 'Retreat' in J's 'Four
    Meetings,'" *SSF*, 17 (1980), 497-99. Maqbool Aziz,
    "'Four Meetings': A Caveat for J Critics," *Essays in
    Criticism*, 18 (1968), 258-74, has a very able refutation of
    Clair. He also disposes of Leonidas M. Jones, "J's 'Four
    Meetings,'" *Exp*, 20 (1962), Item 53, who sees the story
    as a secular saint's legend, with Caroline as a modern
    martyr of the "new religion of culture," and attacks
    Vincent Tartella, 'Four Meetings': Two Texts Com-
    pared," *NCF*, 15 (1960), 17-28, for his unawareness that
    there are *three* texts of this story. I will comment here
    upon only one item of Clair's alleged evidence. The
    minister's wife does *not* say that the "Countess" has been
    living with Caroline for ten years, thus giving the lie to
    the latter's own statement that she arrived two years and
    four months ago. Understanding and despising the

"Countess," who has victimized Caroline, she merely remarks of the narrator's impending visit, "But *you* don't mean to stay ten years." Obviously "ten" here is a round number, indicating a long period. It does not mean either that the "Countess" has been present for ten years or that the minister's wife knows she intends to stay for that length of time, but simply that she has settled down for an indefinite stay (as she herself tells the narrator) and that there seems to be no reasonable prospect of Caroline's getting rid of her.

3.   Robert J. Griffin, "Notes Toward an Exegesis: 'Four Meetings,' " *UKCR*, 29 (1963), 45-49, and Kermit Vanderbilt, "Notes Largely Musical on HJ's 'Four Meetings,'" *Sewanee Review*, 21 (1973), 739-52, both study James's use of words as leitmotifs, images, allusions, metaphors, etc. Partly because in the New York Edition James changed the name of Caroline's town to North Verona, Vanderbilt sees her as possessing "tendencies which form an American Juliet with a difference."

4.   On the symbolism in both Daisy Miller's name and Frederick Winterbourne's, see William E. Grant, " 'Daisy Miller': A Study of a Study," *SSF*, 11 (1974), 17-24, and Richard A. Hocks, " ' Daisy Miller,' Backward into the Past: A Centennial Essay," *HJR*, 1 (1980), 164-78, both of which touch, often illuminatingly, on many other topics also.

5.   Hocks (see note 4) argues reasonably that the sense of American outrage awakened by "Daisy Miller" has been greatly exaggerated; see also Edmund L. Volpe, "The Reception of 'Daisy Miller,' " *Boston Public Library Quarterly*, 10 (1958), 55-59, and George Monteiro, " 'Girlhood on the American Plan'—A Contemporary Defense of 'Daisy Miller,' " *Books at Brown*, 19 (1963), 89-93. Nevertheless there certainly was much discussion, so that "a Daisy Miller" became almost a generic term. Howells, whose paper on this character in his *Heroines of Fiction* (Harpers, 1901) was the longest and best

known piece she inspired, said the country was divided between pro-Daisy and anti-Daisy factions. See also Elizabeth F. Hoxie, "Mrs. Grundy Adopts Daisy Miller," *NEQ*, 19 (1964), 474-84.

6. See Viola Dunbar, "A Note on the Genesis of 'Daisy Miller,' " *Philological Quarterly*, 27 (1948), 184-87, and Edward Stone, "A Further Note on 'Daisy Miller' and Cherbuliez," *Philological Quarterly*, 29 (1950), 213-16. Motley Deakin, in "Daisy Miller, Tradition and the European Heroine," *Comparative Literature Studies*, 6 (1969), 45-59, is less interested in Daisy's innocence than in the "rebellious independence" that makes her "a champion and martyr to freedom" and would derive her therefore from the heroines of Turgenev, George Sand, and Madame de Staël, but this interpretation flies in the face of James's declared intention, already quoted. In "Frederick Winterbourne, James's Prisoner of Chillon," *SN*, 9 (1977), 35-45, Carl Wood makes a surprisingly strong case for the thesis that Byron's "The Prisoner of Chillon" (Daisy and Winterbourne visit the castle) was an important source. Two articles published almost simultaneously—Jeffrey Meyers, "Velázquez and 'Daisy Miller,' " *SSF*, 16 (1979), 171-78, and Adeline R. Tintner, "Two Innocents in Rome: 'Daisy Miller' and Innocent the Tenth," *Essays in Literature*," 6 (1979), 71-78—see the juxtaposition of true and false innocence in the scene toward the end where Daisy is placed over against the famous portrait of the pope, and Meyers goes so far as to compare the appearance of the pontiff, which has sometimes been described as satanic, with that of Mrs. Costello and Mrs. Walker! He also sees what he regards as Daisy's affinity to the Romantic poets "reinforced when she is buried in the 'little Protestant cemetery' where Keats and Shelley had also been buried," but since the point has often been made that the inability of Winterbourne and others correctly to understand Daisy has been conditioned by their residence in Calvinistic Geneva, there are others who see her interment as an indication that she could not escape from Protestant proprieties even in death.

7. See Leon Edel, ed., *HJ Letters* (HUP, 1974 ff.), II, 303-304.

8. As used in this tale, "flirt" is only mildly pejorative. A girl who "flirts" with men keeps them at a distance. Though she may lead them on, she allows them no unseemly liberties.

9. Winterbourne has come in for a good deal of study during recent years, which has sometimes been carried to the fantastic length of finding in him, not Daisy, the focus of the story. For various points of view see R.P. Draper, "Death of a Hero? Winterbourne and Daisy Miller," *SSF*, 6 (1959), 601-608; James W. Gargano, " 'Daisy Miller': An Abortive Quest for Innocence," *SAQ*, 59 (1960), 114-20; John H. Randall III, "The Genteel Reader and "Daisy Miller,' " *AQ*, 17 (1968), 568-81; Ian Kennedy, "Frederick Winterbourne: The Good Bad Boy in 'Daisy Miller,' " *ArQ*, 29 (1973), 939-50; Cathy N. Davidson, " 'Circumsexualocution' in HJ's 'Daisy Miller,' " *ArQ*, 32 (1976), 353-66.

10. See note 6.

11. Far too many articles have been published about "Daisy Miller" to make it possible to list them all here, but the reader's attention may at least be called to some representative examples not mentioned elsewhere: Viola R. Dunbar, "The Revision of 'Daisy Miller,' " *MLN*, 65 (1950), 311-17; Annette Kar, "Archetypes of American Innocence: Lydia Blood and Daisy Miller," *AQ*, 5 (1953), 31-38; Bruce R. McElderry, Jr., "The 'Shy, Incongruous Charm' of 'Daisy Miller,' " *NCF*, 10 (1955-56), 162-65; Tristram P. Coffin, "Daisy Miller, Western Hero," *Western Folklore*, 17 (1958), 273-75; Peter Buitenhuis, "From Daisy Miller to Julia Bride: A Whole Panorama of Literary History," *AQ*, 11 (1959), 136-46; Carol Ohman, " 'Daisy Miller': A Study in Changing Intentions," *AL*, 36 (1964-65), 3-11; John B. Humma, "The 'Engagement' of Daisy Miller," *RSW* 39 (1971), 154-55; David Galloway, "HJ, 'Daisy Miller,' and the International Novel," *Dutch*

Quarterly Review of Anglo-American Letters, 6 (1976), 304-17; Louisa K. Barnett, "Jamesian Feminism: Women in 'Daisy Miller,'" *SSF*, 16 (1979), 281-87; Janet G. Tassel, "The Sick and the Well: Playing at Life in 'Daisy Miller,'" *Studies in the Humanities*, 8 (1981), 18-20. See also William T. Stafford, ed., *J's* Daisy Miller: *The Story, The Play, The Critics* (S, 1963), which, besides the Jamesian texts, reprints a number of critical articles, along with samples of contemporary opinion, etc.

12. Ms. Tintner's article, " 'An International Episode': A Centennial Review of a Centennial Story," appeared in the first number of *HJR*, 1 (1980), 24-60. The author, who sees the story as inaugurating "the battle for the independence from the myth of marrying into the British aristocracy" and "a declaration of America's social independence from the standards of Great Britain," also traces influences from de Tocqueville, who seems to have supplied the name Beaumont, and from Fenimore Cooper. For the English reaction to James's way of portraying a lord, see his letter to Mrs. F.H. Hill, in Edel, ed., *HJ Letters*, Vol. II, pp. 219-23, where his defense seems more conciliatory than minutely truthful. See also Howell Daniels, "Henry James and 'An International Episode,' " *British Association for American Studies Bulletin*, N.S. 1, September 1980, pp. 3-35, who believes that the tale was occasioned in part by Laurence Oliphant's novel *Tender Recollections of Irene Macgillicuddy* and suggests that Lord Lambeth may owe something to Lord Rufford in Trollope's *The American Senator*. Curtis Dahl, "The Swiss Cottage Owner: A Model for J.L. Westgate in James's 'An International Episode,' " *American Notes and Queries*, 17 (1979), 58-60, suggests plausibly that Westgate and his Newport home (and possibly his wife) were modeled after one Colonel George M. Davis. The visit of the Englishmen to Westgate's office represents, I believe, James's only fictional excursion into the downtown New York business district, and there is much Newport local color.

13. Maqbool Aziz, "Revising 'The Pension Beaurepas': The

Tale and its Texts," *Essays in Criticism*, 23 (1973), 269-82, is a valuable study. See further, on all three of these stories, Adeline R. Tintner, "HJ's Balzac Connection," *ABBW*, April 27, 1968, pp. 3219 ff.

Chapter III

1. George Monteiro, "Geography in 'The Siege of London,' ", *HJR*, 4 (1982-83), 144-45, points out James's mistakes in Western geography, corrected in the New York Edition.

2. See Edel, *HJ: The Middle Years*, (L, 1962), p. 125; Lubbock, *The Letters of HJ*, (S, 1920), I, 103. In "Lady into Horse: J's 'Lady Barberina' and *Gulliver's Travels*, Part IV," *Journal of Narrative Technique*, 8 (1978), 79-86, Adeline R. Tintner brilliantly demonstrates that the metaphor of horse trading is used in this tale as "an eloquent and appropriate figure in which to analogize the Anglo-American marriage market." The Barb is the name of a thoroughbred horse brought into England by the Crusaders, and Lady Barb is called "a daughter of the Crusaders." Her father is Lord *Canter*ville; their house is *Pasterns*, etc. "The way in which James weaves the vocabulary of horsemanship, the care, the anatomy, and the feeding of horses into the figures of speech, the names of the characters, the content of their idioms and particularities of speech, their puns and their observations, makes the story a kind of prose poem in which the words are all connected to the basic metaphor dependent upon associations connected with many aspects of the traditional English aristocratic obsession, horses and hunting." Ms. Tintner not only points out interesting parallels between James's story and *Gulliver* but also finds real life originals for Lord Canterville, his family, and his estate in Lord Portsmouth and Eggesford House in North Devon, which James had visited. Since James seems to have invented the title Canterville, she concludes further that Oscar Wilde's "The Canterville

Ghost" was probably indebted to "Lady Barbarina." See also Herbert Ruhm's edition of *Lady Barberina and Other Tales and Variants* (Vanguard Press, 1961). Both Ora Segal, *The Lucid Reflector*, and Mary Doyle Springer, *A Rhetoric of Literary Character: Some Women of HJ* (UCP, 1879) treat "Lady Barbarina" at some length.

3. F.O. Matthiessen and Kenneth B. Murdock, eds., *The Notebooks of HJ* (OUP, 1947), pp. 57-59; cf. Edel, *HJ Letters*, III, 71-72.

4. "The Artist and the Man in 'The Author of Beltraffio,' " *PMLA*, 63 (1983), 102-108.

5. "In fact," says Ms. Winner, "Ambient virtually expresses the central precepts of [James's essay] 'The Art of Fiction.' " This point is also stressed by Samuel F. Pickering, "The Sources of 'The Author of Beltraffio,' " *ArQ*, 29 (1973), 177-90, which is especially valuable in connection with what he considers the painterly sources of the story. See also Adeline R. Tintner, "Another Germ for 'The Author of Beltraffio,' " *Journal of Pre-Raphaelite Studies*, 11 (1980), 14-20.

6. Ora Segal, *The Lucid Reflector*, pp. 116-24, discusses the details she thinks James added to the story "designed primarily to extend our sympathy to the wife by making her position appear somewhat less monstrous and more understandable."

7. Ms. Winner states the case against him, rather gently and tentatively, at the end of her article; see also Donald H. Reiman, "The Inevitable Imitation: The Narrator in 'The Author of Beltraffio,' "*TSLL*, 3 (1961-62), 503-509, and James Scoggins, " 'The Author of Beltraffio,': A Reapportionment of Guilt," *TSLL*, 5 (1963-64), 265-70.

8. Robert L. Gale, in " 'Pandora' and Her President," *SSF*, 1 (1963-64), 222-24, dates the Bonnycastle party at which Count Otto reencounters Pandora in April 1881 and

makes the President Garfield. But James "deliberately blurred the time lines and the Chief Executive's facial features, so that the casual reader might wonder whether Garfield or Arthur—or perhaps even Hayes—was the Bonnycastle guest." See also Charles Vandersee, "James's 'Pandora': The Mixed Consequences of Revision," *Studies in Bibliography*, 21 (1968), 93-108.

9. *Notebooks*, p. 58.

Chapter IV

1. Philip L. Nicoloff's reading of the tale in "At the Bottom of All Things in HJ's 'Louisa Pallant,' " *SSF*, 7 (1970), 409-20, is not without its insights, but I cannot accept his central thesis, that the narrator is "the hidden protagonist" of the story and that its climax is Mrs. Pallant's convincing him that she has denounced her daughter to Archie in order to stand higher in the narrator's own account and confirm his belief that "he himself was a better man than the one she had abandoned him to marry."

2. *The Notebooks of HJ*, pp. 73-74.

3. *HJ Letters*, III, 225-26.

4. Leon Edel, " 'The Aspern Papers': Great-Aunt Wyckoff and Juliana Bordereau," *MLN*, 67 (1952), 392-95; Ora Segal, *The Lucid Reflector*, pp. 79-80; J. Gerald Kennedy, "Jeffrey Aspern and Edgar Allan Poe," *Poe Studies*, Vol. 6, June 1973, pp. 17-18. Kennedy's further suggestion, that since James is known not to have rated Poe's work highly, he wished also to convey the idea that the narrator's high opinion of Aspern was not justified, has not been widely accepted.

5. "What Aspern Papers? A Hypothesis," *CE*, 23 (1961-62), 178-81.

6. One scholar, Barbara Currier Bell, in "Beyond Irony in HJ's 'The Aspern Papers,' " *SN*, 13 (1981-82), 282-93, sees the tale as warning "about the evil attendant upon the human quest for knowledge" and compares and contrasts it with the Eden story, with the narrator cast as the serpent, whom she identifies, Miltonically rather than Biblically, with Satan.

7. "In Defence of the First Person Narrator in 'The Aspern Papers,' " *Centennial Review*, 13 (1969), 215-40. This excellent article replies to Wayne Booth's complaint in *The Rhetoric of Fiction* (UCP, 1961), pp. 354-64, that James did not handle the narrative voice in the tale satisfactorily. Cf. also Mildred Hartsook, "Unweeded Garden: A View of 'The Aspern Papers,' " *SSF*, 5 (1967), 60-68.

8. Schneider, "The Unreliable Narrator: J's 'The Aspern Papers' and the Reading of Fiction," *SSF*, 13 (1976), 43-49; Gargano, " 'The Aspern Papers': The Untold Story," *SSF*, 10 (1973), 1-10; Crowley, "The Wiles of a 'Witless' Woman: Tina in 'The Aspern Papers,' " *ESQ*, 22 (1976), 159-68; Baskett, "The Sense of the Present in 'The Aspern Papers,' " *Papers of the Michigan Academy of Science, Arts and Letters*, 44 (1958), 38-88; Stein, " 'The Aspern Papers': A Comedy of Masks," *NCF*, 14 (1959), 172-78; Graham, *HJ: The Drama of Fulfilment* (OUP, 1975), Ch. 3; Jensen-Osinski, "The Key to the Palpable Past: A Study of Miss Tina in 'The Aspern Papers,' " *HJR*, 3 (1981-82), 4-10. For Barbara Currier Bell, see note 6.

9. Jacob Korg (see note 5) seems to stand alone in the view that there were no Aspern papers, but he pioneered the idea that Tina might be Juliana's daughter rather than her niece, which was developed by Robert C. McLean, " 'Poetic Justice' in J's 'Aspern Papers,' " *PLL*, 3 (1967), 260-66, to which Constance Hunting, "The Identity of Miss Tina in 'The Aspern Papers,' " *Studies in the Humanities*, 5, October 1976, pp. 28-31, added an

unexpected turn of the screw by returning to the view
that she was a niece but by Jeffrey Aspern, and that this
was the way he had treated Juliana badly. This idea was
probably suggested to Korg by his notion that the niece
who lived with Claire Clairmont in Florence was Allegra, her daughter by Byron, but, as Robert S. Phillips
pointed out in "A Note on 'What Aspern Papers? A
Hypothesis," *CE*, 24 (1962-63), 154-55, Korg forgot that
Allegra had died at the age of five. McLean believes that
Tina was ignorant of her true relationship to Juliana until
she read the papers after Juliana's death and that this
accounts for the "rare change" the observer notices in
her and probably for her destruction of them but his only
real piece of evidence is that Tina's small income is sent
to her every quarter from America.

10. Among the many articles that have been published
     about "The Aspern Papers" not cited elsewhere in my
     discussion are James M. Mellard, "Modal Counterpoint
     in J's 'The Aspern Papers,'" *PLL*, 4 (1968), 299-307; Paul
     C. Rodgers, Jrs., "Motive, Agency, and Act in J's 'The
     Aspern Papers,'" *SAQ*, 73 (1974), 377-87; and Rosemary
     F. Franklin, "Military Metaphors and the Organic Struc-
     ture of HJ's 'The Aspern Papers,'" *ArQ*, 32 (1976),
     327-40. See also Joseph McG. Bottkol's introduction to
     the edition of *The Aspern Papers* published by New
     Directions, 1950, and the section devoted to this story in
     Laurence Bedwell Holland's *The Expense of Vision:
     Essays on the Craft of HJ* (Princeton University Press,
     1964).

11. Robert J. Kane, "Hawthorne's 'The Prophetic Pictures'
     and J's "The Liar,'" *MLN*, 65 (1950), 257-58; Edward M.
     Rosenberry, "J's Use of Hawthorne in 'The Liar,' "
     MLN, 76 (1961), 234-38. There are elements in the
     Hawthorne story of which James made no use, but there
     is certainly a striking resemblance between the closing
     declarations of the wives in the two stories and the
     situations framing them: "But—I loved him!" (Haw-
     thorne); "But you must remember I possess the original!"

(James). I agree with Wayne Booth, *The Rhetoric of Fiction*, pp. 347-54, that the story is far more complex than the *Notebooks*, pp. 61-62, would suggest, but dissent from what seems to me his savage attack on Lyon. "The Liar" has not attracted much commentary, but see Ora Segal's chapter in *The Lucid Reflector*.

12. Cf. "The Story of a Masterpiece" in Appendix A.

13. See *The Notebooks of HJ*, pp. 76-82.

14. *Notebooks*, p. 87.

15. See especially the quotation from James in *The Lucid Reflector*, p. 141.

16. For a fuller discussion of this point, see Peter Barry, "In Fairness to the Master's Wife: A Re-Interpretation of 'The Lesson of the Master,'" *SSF*, 15 (1978), 385-89.

17. In "Iconic Analogy in 'The Lesson of the Master': HJ's Legend of Saint George and the Dragon," *Journal of Narrative Technique*, 5 (1975), 116-27, Adeline R. Tintner develops the idea that the tale is a version of the legend of Saint George and the Dragon, "profaned, burlesqued and converted into a narrative analogue." One of her most telling points is that the color red, which suggests the fire-breathing dragon, is here associated with Marian even more emphatically than with her predecessor. In a writer like James, this is surely not without intention.

18. This is not the place to discuss whether what St. George professes to believe about marriage and the artist has validity. James's way of life worked for James and the kind of art he produced, but there are many mansions in the house of fiction, and he could not occupy them all. Surely we have stopped shuddering elegantly at the spectacle of Anthony Trollope writing his novels, with his watch open on the table before him, at the rate of 250 words every fifteen minutes, and have learned instead to admire his superb control. It would be difficult to prove

that celibates have produced more first-rate art than those who carried the responsibilities of a home and family, and Van Wyck Brooks's interpretation of the "ordeal" of Mark Twain no longer commands attention anywhere. It is related that the wife of Richard Strauss came into his study one day and demanded to be taken for a walk. He replied that he could not go just then because he was composing. She said she would return in twenty minutes, at which time she would require his escort. When she came back, the song he was working on was finished, and he was ready. It was one of his greatest, "Traum durch die Dämmerung."

19. *Notebooks*, pp. 87-90.

Chapter V

1. See also Leon Edel, *HJ: The Treacherous Years*, (L, 1969), pp. 96-100. Adeline R. Tintner, who reads "The Pupil" as an attempt by James "to convince Stevenson and the world that a child's adventure need not only be one involving pirates, but might be a moral adventure," points out a surprising number of resemblances between "The Pupil" and *Treasure Island* and, more especially, *Kidnapped*: "its similes and metaphors built out of terms involving mutiny, shipwreck, and the weather" suggest that psychological adventure may be quite as real as "the islands of the Spanish main." See "J Writes a Boy's Story: 'The Pupil' and R.L. Stevenson's Adenture Books," *Essays in Literature*, 5 (1978), 61-75.

2. Edel, *HJ Letters*, III, 301-302, 307-308, 338-39.

3. Muriel G. Shine, *The Fictional Children of HJ* (UNCP, 1969). For an analysis of the structure of the story, see Vaid, *Technique in the Tales of HJ*, pp. 154-64.

4. Terence Martin, "J's 'The Pupil': The Art of Seeing Through," *MFS*, 4 (1948-59), 335-45, points out that

"moreen" is the name of a fabric that "presents one kind of surface to the eye when underneath it is intrinsically coarse."

5. William Bysshe Stein, " 'The Pupil': The Education of a Prude," *ArQ*, 15 (1959), 13-22, stands alone in finding nothing much wrong with the Moreens except "a certain gaucherie, a trivial fault compared to Pemberton's bigotry." To Stein, Morgan is "an intolerant, opinionated little boy" and Pemberton "swells in monstrous self-righteous scorn."

6. See, for example, Clifton Fadiman, in his anthology, *The Short Stories of HJ* (Random House, 1945), p. 272.

7. Taking his point of departure from Pemberton's unsuccessful management of his own finances, Thomas L. Canavan, "The Economics of Disease in James's 'The Pupil,' " *Crit*, 15 (1973), 253-64, argues that "James wants the reader to condemn Pemberton as a Moreen, one who is part of the family's 'edifice.' " Elizabeth Cummins, " 'The Playroom of Superstition': An Analysis of HJ's 'The Pupil,' " *MR*, 2, May 1970, pp. 13-16, takes off into the blue empyrean of nonsense by arguing that "by resisting Morgan's tutelage while encouraging him to dwell in a 'playroom of superstition,' " the "self-deluding romanticist" Pemberton becomes responsible for his death. Terence Martin (see note 4) sees him as sharing responsibility through passiveness and lack of commitment, and David Eggenschwiler, "J's 'The Pupil': A Moral Tale Without a Moral," *SSF*, 15 (1976), 435-44, who analyzes the relations between the two well, also sees inertia. James V. Hogopian, "Seeing Through 'The Pupil' Again," *MFS*, 5 (1959), 169-71, wrote in reply to Martin, and Pemberton was also defended by William Kenney, "The Death of Morgan in J's 'The Pupil,' " *SSF*, 8 (1971), 317-22, and by John Griffith, "J's 'The Pupil' as Whodunit: The Question of Moral Responsibility," *SSF*, 9 (1972), 257-68. Mary E. Rucker, "J's 'The Pupil': The Question of Moral Ambiguity," *ArQ*, 32 (1976), 301-15,

sees a certain naiveté in Pemberton, and Seymour Lain-off, "A Note on HJ's 'The Pupil,' " *NCF*, 14 (1959-60), 75-77, argues that though "prudential virtue" is "acceptable enough by the world's lights," it is not heroic enough to save Morgan. James is concerned with "the ambiguity of friendship, its tenuousness as well as its adhesiveness."

8. "The Pupil" exercised an important influence upon Forrest Reid's *The Bracknels* (1911), rewritten toward the end of his life as *Dennis Bracknel* (1947) and published posthumously. But Reid's unfortunate boy dies by suicide.

9. See Vaid, *Technique in the Tales of HJ*, pp. 49-55, where there is also an analysis of the structure of the tale. Eddy Dow, "J's 'Brooksmith,' " *Exp*, 27 (1968-69), Item 35, sees Brooksmith's name as a key to his character and function.

10. James's management of the double plot is analyzed by Dale and Chris Kramer, "J's 'The Marriages': Designs of Structure," *UKCR*, 33 (1966-66), 75-80. Bernard Richards, "The Sources of HJ's 'The Marriages,' " *Review of English Studies*, N.S. 30 (1979), 316-22, seeks to derive the tale from a situation involving the Temples of Rutland, Vermont, who were related to the Jameses. In "HJ's Debt to George Meredith," *ABBW*, September 20, 1982, pp. 1811-12 ff., Adeline R. Tintner shows that it was indebted to an episode in *Sandra Belloni*.

11. *HJ, Man and Author* (Houghton Mifflin, 1927), p. 101.

12. *Notebooks*, pp. 70-71.

13. *Notebooks*, pp. 106-108.

14. Just after the London premiere of *The Second Mrs. Tanqueray*, Arthur Wing Pinero urged James to make a play of "The Chaperon." The attempt never got very far, but see Edel, ed., *The Complete Plays of HJ* (L, 1949),

pp. 453-62, 605-39. For a different interpretation of "The Chaperon" than has been given here, see John A. Clair, *The Ironic Dimension*, pp. 103-109.

15. Martha Banta, *HJ and the Occult: The Great Extension* (Indiana University Press, 1972), p. 111.

16. *Notebooks*, pp. 9-10.

17. HJ, *William Wetmore Story and His Friends* (Houghton Mifflin, 1903), II, 88-89.

18. In a notebook entry of August 3, 1891 (*Notebooks*, p. 110), James calls his originals merely "R.B." and F.L.," but the passage already quoted from his biography of Story makes the identification of R.B. with Browning inescapable. "F.L." has generally been interpreted as referring to the great Victorian painter Frederick Lord Leighton. Sidney E. Lind's attempt to discredit James's statements concerning the origin of this story, "J's 'The Private Life' and Browning," *AL*, 23 (1951), 315-22, drew a reply from Earl F. Barbainnier, "Browning, J, and 'The Private Life,' " *SSF*, 14 (1977), 151-58.

19. For various lines of approach, consult Gorham Munson, " 'The Real Thing': A Parable for Writers of Fiction," *UKCR*, 16 (1950), 261-64; Walter F. Wright, " 'The Real Thing,' " *RSW*, 25 (1957), 85-90; Helen Horne, "HJ: 'The Real Thing' (1890), An Attempt at Interpretation," *NS*, 8 (1959), 214-49; Earle Labor, "J's 'The Real Thing': Three Levels of Meaning," *CE*, 23 (1961-62), 376-78; Lavonne Mueller, "HJ: The Phenomenal Self as the 'Real Thing,' " *Forum* (University of Houston), 6 (Spring 1968), pp. 46-50; M.D. Uroff, "Perception in J's 'The Real Thing,' " *SSF*, 9 (1972), 41-46; James D. Pendleton, "The J Brothers and 'The Real Thing': A Study in Pragmatic Reality," *South Atlantic Bulletin*, 38, No. 4 (1973), pp. 3-10; Pauline Lester, "J's Use of Comedy in 'The Real Thing,' " *SSF*, 15 (1978), 33-38. Robert Berkelman's, "HJ and 'The Real Thing,' " *UKCR*, 26 (1959-60), 93-95, is

essentially an appreciation of the Monarchs. Harold Kehler, "J's 'The Real Thing,' " *Exp*, 25 (1966-67), Item 79, sees Miss Churm's name as a play on "charm," which she lacks but can simulate. David Toor, "Narrative Irony in HJ's 'The Real Thing,' " *University Review*, 34 (1967-68), 95-99, sees the painter as an unreliable narrator. In "A Note on HJ's 'The Real Thing,' " *SSF*, 1 (1963-64), 65-66, Robert L. Gale finds a topical reference in the tale to *Black and White*; in "HJ's J.H. in 'The Real Thing,' " *SSF*, 14 (1977), 396-98, he suggests John Hay as the original of the "sterile" critic, Jack Hawley.

20.   Cf. *Notebooks*, pp. 102-105.

21.   Harold T. McCarthy, *HJ: The Creative Process* (Thomas Yoseloff, 1958); Seymour Lainoff, "A Note on HJ's 'The Real Thing,' " *MLN*, 71 (1956), 192-93.

22.   The original suggestion for "Greville Fane" was supplied by the plans and views of Anthony Trollope and Anne Thackeray in this connection. See *Notebooks*, pp. 10-11, 93-95.

23.   *Technique in the Tales of HJ*, pp. 54-60.

24.   *Notebooks*, pp. 118-21.

25.   James later turned "Owen Wingrave" into a one-act play, *The Saloon* (1908); see Leon Edel, ed., *The Complete Plays of Henry James*, pp. 630-74, which includes considerable introductory and historical material, including the letters exchanged between James and Bernard Shaw, who objected violently to what he considered a sickish, sentimental ending that opted for death, not life. These letters juxtapose very effectively the aesthetic convictions of two great writers. Owen himself comes close to Shaw's view that any war in history must have ended at any moment that the soldiers engaged in it developed enough sense to shoot their leaders and go home. James himself had no love for soldiers. He

escaped the Civil War, opposed the Spanish-American War, and rather lost his head over World War I. When Gertrude Kingston produced the play in London in 1911, he objected decidedly to the appearance of the ghost, "a pale, dimly-seen figure," on the stage.

Chapter VI

1. James used this title again for the projected, unfinished third volume of his autobiography, following *A Small Boy and Others* and *Notes of a Son and Brother*. *The Middle Years* was published as he left it by Scribners in 1917. See *Notebooks*, pp. 121-23, for the original idea behind the tale. James did not use the dream element projected, but cf. his "The Great Good Place" (1900).

2. *Notebooks*, p. 148.

3. I cannot, however, accept Gerald Hoag's curious notion that Paraday's greatness exists only in the mind of the narrator, who is "a venal, if not shocking, fraud whose motives and whose very judgment we ought to mistrust." See "The Death of the Paper Lion," *SSF*, 12 (1975), 163-72.

4. *Notebooks*, pp. 152-55, 160-64.

5. P. 373.

6. *Notebooks*, pp. 200-205.

7. *HJ Letters*, III, 507-10.

8. Robert L. Gale, "James's 'The Next Time,' " *Exp*, 21 (1962), Item 35, argues that James was thinking of Thomas Anstey Guthrie and F. Marion Crawford.

9. Forrest Reid, *Walter de la Mare, A Critical Study* (Holt, 1929), Chapter VIII.

10. For details see Mildred E. Hartsock's excellent article, "Dizzying Summit: J's 'The Altar of the Dead,' " *SSF*, 11 (1971), 371-78, and cf. the analysis of structure, with suitable appreciative comments, in Vaid, *Technique in the Tales of Henry James*, pp. 214-23.

11. J.A. Ward, *The Imagination of Disaster*, p. 89; Walter F. Wright, *The Madness of Art* (UNP, 1962), p. 215. Cf. Wright's discussion, pp. 211-19.

12. *Notebooks*, pp. 164-67.

13. *The Short Stories of Henry James*, p. 259.

14. *Notebooks*, p. 223. See pp. 221-24 and 229-30 for James's discussion of the development of the story.

15. *HJ*, p. 122.

16. Parker Tyler, "The Child in 'The Figure in the Carpet,' " *Chicago Review*, 11, Winter 1958, pp. 31-42; Mark Kanzer, "The Figure in the Carpet," *AI*, 17 (1960), 339-48; Seymour Lainoff, "Henry James's 'The Figure in the Carpet': What Is Critical Responsiveness?" *Boston University Studies in English*, 5 (1961), 122-28; Lyall H. Powers, "A Reperusal of James's 'The Figure in the Carpet,' " *AL*, 33 (1961-62), 224-28; Leo B. Levy, "A Reading of 'The Figure in the Carpet,' " *AL*, 33 (1961-62), 457-65; Edward Recchia, "James's 'The Figure in the Carpet': The Quality of Fictional Experience," *SSF*, 10 (1973), 357-65; Shlomith Rimmon, "Barthes' 'Hermeneutic Code' and HJ's Literary-Detective-Plot Composition in 'The Figure in the Carpet,' " *Hebrew University Studies in Literature*, 1 (1973), 183-207; Dorothy M. Boland, "HJ's 'The Figure in the Carpet': A Fabric of the East," *PLL*, 13, (1977), 424-29; Rachel Salmon, "A Marriage of Opposites: HJ's 'The Figure in the Carpet' and the Problem of Ambiguity," *ELH*, 47 (1980), 788-803; J. Hillis Miller, "The Figure in the Carpet," *Poetics Today*, 1, No. 3 (1980), pp. 107-18; Peter W. Lock, " 'The Figure in the Carpet': The Text as Riddle and Force," *NCF*, 36 (1981), 157-75; Adeline R. Tintner, "Hiding

Behind J: Roth's *Zuckerman Unbound*," *Mainstream*,
28, April 1982, pp. 49-53. The articles by Lainoff and
Levy give some references not repeated here. See also
Vaid, *Technique in the Tales of HJ*, pp. 79-89.

17.   Preface to Vol. XVII of New York Edition. See *Notebooks*, pp.xiv, 241-5, for the development of the tale in
the author's mind before it was written down.

18.   Edel, *HJ: The Treacherous Years*, p. 149, and *The Ghostly Tales of HJ* (Rutgers University Press, 1948), p. 396.
Pamela J. Shelden, " 'The Friends of the Friends':
Another Twist to the Screw," *Wascana Review*, 11
(1976), 3-14, sees the story as a kind of rehearsal for "The
Turn of the Screw." "Certainly the principal focus of
both tales is always on the minds of the women who are
victimized by their own obsessions and delusions." But it
is more heroic than convincing to seek to dispose of the
hottest controversy in all James criticism with one word,
"certainly." For "Maud-Evelyn" see Appendix A of this
volume.

Chapter VII

Because of the frequency with which "The Turn of the
Screw" recurs in the titles cited in this chapter, the abbrevia-
tion TS will be employed.

1.   Four books have been published about TS: Eli Siegel, *J
and the Children: A Consideration of HJ's TS*, ed. Martha Bond (Definition Press, 1938); Muriel West, *A
Stormy Night with TS* (Frye & Smith, Ltd., 1964); Thomas Mabry Cranfill and Robert Lanier Clark, Jr., *An
Anatomy of TS* (University of Texas Press, 1965); and
E.A. Sheppard, *HS and TS* (Auckland University Press-
OUP, 1974). The first two are unimportant. The third is a
detailed commentary on the text from the nonapparitionist standpoint. The last, though not lacking in oddi-
ties, is a work of genuine value, the most elaborate single

study that has been made. Robert Kimbrough's Norton Critical Edition, *HJ, TS: An Authoritative Text, Background and Sources, Essays in Criticism* (1966) and Gerald Willen, ed., *A Casebook on HJ's TS*, 2nd ed. (Crowell, 1969) are both useful tools and reprint much material that it is more convenient to consult here than as it originally appeared. No attempt has been made to list here the multitudinous articles that have appeared about TS. Those that most concern my discussion are cited in the following notes; readers who desire more must consult the bibliographies appearing in *AL* and *PMLA*.

2. Miriam Allott, "Mrs. Gaskell's 'The Old Nurses's Story': A Link between *Wuthering Heights* and TS," *NQ*, N.S. 8 (1961), 101-102; Ray L. Ryburn, "TS and *Amelia*: A Source for Quint," *SSF*, 16 (1979), 235-37; Valerie Parton, "J's TS, Chapter 9," *Exp*, 34 (1975), Item 24; Nathan B. Fagan, "Another Reading of TS," *MLN*, 56 (1941), 196-202. Adeline R. Tintner, "HJ's Use of *Jane Eyre* in TS," *Brontë Society Transactions*, 14 (1976), 42-45, supplies additional valuable material. Ronald Schliefer, "The Trap of the Imagination: The Gothic Tradition, Fiction, and TS," *Crit*, 22 (1980), 297-319, attempts to relate the story to both the Gothic tradition and Kierkegaardian speculation.

3. Ignace Feuerlicht, " 'Erlkönig' and TS," *Journal of English and Germanic Philology*, 58 (1959), 68-74; Michael Egan, *HJ: The Ibsen Years* (Vision, 1972). Two writers have seen important influences from art. Since it appeared in the same number of *Black and White* as "Sir Edmund Orme," James must have seen the picture by Tom Griffiths which R.L. Wolff describes in "The Genesis of TS," *AL*, 13 (1941), 1-8, but the resemblances noted are too general to support the weight Wolff rests upon them. More recently, Jean Frantz Blackall, "Cruikshank's *Oliver* and TS," *AL*, 15 (1979-80), 161-78, has entered a much stronger case.

4. Robert B. Heilman, "TS as Poem," *UKCR*, 14 (1948), 277-89; Donal O'Gorman, "HJ's Reading of TS," *HJR*, 1

(1979-80), 125-38, 228-56; Robert M. Slabey, " 'The Holy Innocents' and TS," *NS* 1963, pp. 170-73; Mary V. Hallab, "TS Squared," *Southern Review*, 13 (1977), 492-504. O'Gorman argues specifically for J's use of an article by Arthur F. Leach, "The Schoolboys' Feast," *Fortnightly Review*, January 1, 1896. See also Albert E. Stone, "HJ and Childhood and TS," *John B. Stetson University Bulletin*, 61 (1961), 1-18.

5. Leo B. Levy, "TS as Retaliation," *CE*, 17 (1956), 186-88; Oscar Cargill, "TS and Alice James," *PMLA*, 78 (1963), 238-49, a revision of his "HJ as Freudian Pioneer," *Chicago Review*, 10 (1956), 13-29. For Leon Edel, see *HJ: The Treacherous Years*, pp. 200-214, and his anthology, *The Ghostly Tales of HJ*, p. 430. For Henriette Deluzy-Desportes, see Nathalia Wright, "Hawthorne and the Praslin Murder," *NEQ*, 15 (1942), 5-14, and, for a full account of the case, Stanley Loomis, *A Crime of Passion* (L, 1967). Joseph Shearing's novel, called in England *Forget-Me-Not* and in America first *Lucile Cléry, A Woman of Intrigue* and then *The Strange Case of Lucile Cléry* (Harpers, 1932) takes a dim view of Henriette's character, but her kinswoman Rachel Field wrote a wholly admiring novel about her, *All This and Heaven Too* (M, 1938). "Joseph Shearing" was a pseudonym of the brilliant English historical and sensation novelist Gabrielle Margaret Long, who was also Marjorie Bowen and George R. Preedy. Elliot Schrero's excellent article is "Exposure in TS," *Modern Philology*, 78 (1980-81), 261-74; I dissent only from his closing point that the governess was herself in moral danger through her attraction to Miles. Mark Spilka, on the other hand, is unconvincing when he argues in "Turning the Freudian Screw: How Not To Do It," *LP*, 13 (1963), 105-11, that the governess, like the children, is "the victim of a cultural impasse" in her prurience and sensitivity to "sex-ghosts," and Jane Nardin's attempt to rehabilitate Quint and Miss Jessel in "TS: The Victorian Background," *Mosaic*, 12 (1978), 131-42, is worse than that. Ernest Zimmerman's argument in "Literary Tradition and TS," *SSF*, 17 (1970), 634-37, that the governess is "the quixotic

heroine" of eighteenth-century fiction "who attempts to impose on the external world an imagination shaped by fiction" seems very odd in view of the character's unfamiliarity with this fiction.

6   This influence was first suggested by Dorothy Scarborough in 1917. The pioneering documented account was that of Francis X. Roellinger, Jr., "Psychical Research and TS," *AL*, 20 (1948-49), 401-412; by all means the fullest and most fascinating is Sheppard's Chapter VIII.

7. *Notebooks*, pp. 178-79, 299-300; Lubbock, *Letters*, I, 278-79, 290, 296-301. In her article on *Oliver Twist* (see note 3), Jean Frantz Blackall has recently reported William James, Jr., as having told her that when, in 1910, his mother asked his Uncle Henry why he did not write another story like "The Turn of the Screw," he replied, "My God, Alice, I wish I could!" Critics have been so preoccupied with the meaning of "The Turn of the Screw" that comparatively little attention has been paid to formal technical aspects, but see Hans-Joachim Lang, "The Turns in TS," and Hildegard Domaniecki, "Complementary Terms in TS: The Straight Turning," both in *Jahrbuch für Amerikastudien*, 9 (1964), 110-28, and 10 (1965), 206-14, respectively. See also Robert M. Slabey, "TS: Grammar and Optics," *CLA Journal*, 9 (1965-66), 68-72; Barbara Bengels, "The Term of the 'Screw': Key to Imagery in HJ's TS," *SSF*, 15 (1978), 323-27. Michael Egan, who is excellent on imagery and symbolism, analyzes the structure of the tale in terms of a five-act play, in my opinion overstressing the influence of Ibsen's *Ghosts*. See also Sheppard, *HJ and TS*, Ch. 3. There is no space in this volume to consider dramatic adaptations of "The Turn of the Screw," but William Archibald's play, *The Innocents* (1950), has enlisted, among others, the talents of Beatrice Straight, Flora Robson, Ingrid Bergman, Deborah Kerr, and Claire Bloom. Thomas M. Cranfil and Robert Clark, Jr., "The Provocativeness of TS," *TSLL*, 12 (1970), 93-100, contains the best account of the tale's vogue and adaptations. For Benjamin Britten's opera see, S. Corse, "From Narrative to Music:

Benjamin Britten's TS, "*University of Toronto Quarterly*, 51 (1981-82), 161-74. Jennifer Vyvyan was the governess, Joan Cross Mrs. Grose, Peters Pears the Prologue and Quint, and Ada Mandikian Miss Jessel, and there was a recording by Decca-London.

8.   Harold C. Goddard, "A Pre-Freudian Reading of TS," pref. n. by Leon Edel, *NCF*, 2 (1957), 1-36; Edna Kenton, "HJ to the Ruminant Reader," *Arts*, 6 (1924), 347-52; Edmund Wilson, "The Ambiguity of HJ," *Hound and Horn*, 7 (1934), 385-400, reprinted with additions, retractions, and reaffirmations in Willen. Among the replies called forth by Wilson, see N.B. Fagin (see note 2); A.J.A. Waldock, "Mr. Edmund Wilson and TS," *MLN*, 62 (1947), 331-34; Robert B. Heilman, "The Freudian Reading of TS," *MLN*, 62 (1947), 433-45; Glenn A. Reed, "Another Turn on J's TS," *AL*, 20 (1948-49), 413-23; Oliver Evans, "J's Air of Evil: TS," *Partisan Review*, 16 (1949), 175-89; Normal Mukerji, "The Problem of Evil in TS—A Study in Ambiguity," *Calcutta Review*, 168 (1963), 63-70. Heilman developed his own somewhat allegorical interpretation of the meaning of the tale in 1948 (see note 4); his most recent word on the subject is "The Lure of the Demonic: J and Dürrenmatt," *Comparative Literature*, 13 (1961), 346-57. Dorothea Krook, *The Ordeal of Consciousness in HJ* (CUP, 1963) does not go as far as Heilman, but she does see the tale as a kind of morality play, "a fable about the redemptive power of human love," even though sometimes at the cost of human life. Joseph J. Firebaugh, "Inadequacy in Eden: Knowledge and TS," *MFS*, 3 (1957), 57-63, had already achieved a kind of unorthodox variation on Heilman; to him the tale concerns "denial of knowledge." Miles and Flora represent humanity. Quint and Miss Jessel play the role of the serpent. The uncle is "the irresponsible deity of the Old Testament" and the governess his inadequate priestess and "agent of denial." I take no stock in the view of Kevin Murphy, "The Unfixable Text: Bewilderment of Vision in TS," *TSLL*, 20 (1972), 538-51, that the tale is opaque and that James intended it to be so, nor in those of E.C. Kurtsinger, "TS

as Writer's Parable," *SN*, 12 (1979-80), 344-58, and David A. Cook and Timothy J. Corrigan, "Narrative Structure in TS: A New Approach to Meaning," *SSF*, 17 (1980), 55-65, who see it as a study of the nature of fiction. A.W. Thomson, "TS: Some Points on the Hallucination Theory," *Review of English Literature*, 6, October 1965, pp. 26-36, attempts to refute Dorothea Krook's arguments against Wilson, and Fred L. Milne's "Atmosphere as Triggering Device in TS," *SSF*, 18 (1981), 293-99, is a late attempt to bolster Wilson by a study of the conditions under which the ghosts manifest. John Lydenberg, "The Governess Turns the Screw," *NCF*, 12 (1951), 37-58, proves that it is possible to be both anti-Wilson and anti-governess. Rictor Norton, 'TS: Coincidental Oppositorium," *AI*, 28 (1971), 373-90, though committed to the psychoanalytical approach, writes that "although I sometimes question the governess' abhorrence of the apparitions, I never question their objective existence as demons, ghosts, or fairies." Alexander E. Jones, "Point of View in TS," *PMLA*, 74 (1959), 112-22, gives an excellent account of the Freudian controversy to the date of its publication, with sensible interpretation. See also Martin Slaughter, "Edmund Wilson and TS," in the Norton Critical Edition. In "An Illustrator's Literary Interpretation," *ABBW*, March 26, 1979, pp. 2275-80, 2282, Adeline R. Tintner finds in the headings John La Farge did for the serial version of TS in *Collier's Weekly* evidence that he anticipated the Freudian view.

9. See Edward Stone, "Edition Architecture and TS," *SSF*, 13 (1976), 9-16, where the refutation is complete.

10. "The Structure of TS," *MLN*, 75 (1960), 312-21.

11. For James's only extended discussion of such matters in propria persona, see his article, "Is There a Life After Death?" originally in *Harper's Bazar*, January-February 1910, reprinted in the symposium *In After Days* (Harpers, 1910) and in F.O. Matthiessen, ed., *The James Family* (Knopf, 1947), pp. 602-614.

12.   James is perhaps somewhat confusing when he writes in
       his preface "that Peter Quint and Miss Jessel are not
       'ghosts' at all, as we now know the ghost, but goblins,
       elves, imps, demons as loosely constructed as those in
       the old trials for witchcraft; if not, more pleasingly,
       fairies of the legendary order, wooing their victims forth
       to see them dance under the moon," but this may seem
       less like a lumping together of dissimilar creatures to
       those who think of the fairies in terms of the old Scottish
       ballads or such German poems as Goethe's "Erlkönig",
       Heine's "Die Loreley," or Josef von Eichendorff's "Wal-
       desgespräch." We must remember too that James called
       the ghost story "the most possible form of fairy tale." He
       surely cannot have intended to dissociate the psychic
       manifestations at Bly from the Quint and Miss Jessel who
       had lived there, for whatever his intention in the "Screw"
       may have been, this would have been to throw away half
       the story. In Shakespeare's time, Catholics generally
       thought of ghosts as spirits of the dead allowed for some
       reason to escape from purgatory, but for Protestants,
       who had rejected purgatory and who thought of the
       saved in heaven and the damned in hell, this view was
       impossible; they tended therefore to believe "that ghosts,
       while occasionally they might be angels, were generally
       nothing but devils, who 'assumed'—such was the tech-
       nical word—the form of departed friends or relatives, in
       order to work bodily or spiritual harm upon those to
       whom they appeared" (J. Dover Wilson, *What Happens
       in Hamlet*, Macmillan, 1935, p. 62). Whether James was
       familiar with these views I cannot say, nor how much he
       knew about the elaborate Swedenborgian supernatu-
       ralism that his father must have known from A to Z.
       Possibly, by saying that Quint and Miss Jessel "are not
       'ghosts' at all, as we now know the ghost," he may simply
       have meant as we know ghosts in modern literature or in
       the reports of the Society for Psychical Research, with
       which he *was* familiar. Many persons in the nineteenth
       century (I am not suggesting that James was one of
       them) seem to have entertained the theologically wild
       notion that the redeemed became angels after death and
       the damned devils; witness the epitaph that Dickens

composed for his adored young sister-in-law, Mary
Hogarth: "Young, beautiful, and good, God numbered
her among his angels at the early age of seventeen."
Longfellow, too, speaks of his first wife as

> the Being Beauteous,
> Who unto my youth was given,
> More than all things else to love me,
> And is now a saint in heaven.

The "saint" may, in a measure, save him theologically,
but the poem from which these verses are taken is called
"Footsteps of Angels."

13. Stanley Trachtenberg, "The Return of the Screw," *MFS*,
11 (1965), 180-181; Mary Doyle Springer, *A Rhetoric of
Literary Character*, pp. 89-111. Ms. Springer's is the most
extensive study of Flora and also, I fear, one of the most
wrong-headed. To her the governess is "mad" and "a
dead soul" and Flora, ironically, the most normal character in the story and the only one steady enough to resist
the governess' pressure, which is a curious thing indeed
to say of an eight-year-old. It is interesting that all three
of Flora's warmest defenders—Ms. Springer, Dorothea
Krook, and Muriel G. Shine—should be women.

14. Carl Van Doren's opinion was stated in his introduction
to the edition of TS published by The Limited Editions
Club in 1949. Donal O'Gorman invokes "Rumpelstilt-
skin" and "the folk tradition according to which a spirit's
power is broken the moment its name is pronounced by
the victim," and Martha Banta (*Henry James and the
Occult*, pp. 123-4, 256, note 46) has some interesting
remarks on how, until we come to the final scene, Miles
is less a human boy than the kind of angel Mark Twain
presents in *The Mysterious Stranger* (which she does
not, however, mention). John R. Byers, Jr., who achieves
the most hysterical attack on the governess yet recorded
in his "TS: A Hellish Point of View," *MR* 2 (1971), 101-
104, thinks Miles's heart is "dispossessed of grace and
innocence" so that he "becomes a companion for our

governess in hell." Quint and Miss Jessel work on the children because they are the only members of the household whom these predators could *not* corrupt while they were in the body, and the devil sends the governess as his agent to complete their work. Byers adds that James used the name Douglas in the prologue to remind the reader of Lord Alfred Douglas! It seems clear that Quint appears and reappears in the final scene to try to prevent Miles's confession. Miles's conjectural mention of Miss Jessel where one would expect "Quint" is puzzling, and his final "Peter Quint—you devil" is ambiguous. If Quint is here addressed, Miles would seem to be renouncing him and the devil with him, but if he is calling the governess a devil, he is apparently turning away from his salvation. There has also been speculation, much of it silly, about the physical cause of Miles's death. Terence J. Matheson, "Did the Governess Smother Miles?" *SSF*, 19 (1982), 172-75, answers his own question in the affirmative: "James may well be hoping his readers will take into account the great strength the insane are said to possess." Susan Clark, "A Note on TS: Death from Natural Causes," *SSF*, 15 (1978), 110-12, goes beyond the text to suggest that Miles was dismissed from school because he had a rheumatic heart, which the headmaster's letter failed to specify "from a Victorian aversion to the indelicacies of sickness and death."

15.   The quotations are from E.A. Sheppard and Jean Frantz Blackall; see further, on this point, Charles Thomas Samuels, *The Ambiguity of Henry James* (UIP, 1971), p. 18. C.B. Ives, "J's Ghosts in TS," *NCF*, 18 (1963), 183-89, finds the inactivity of Quint and Miss Jessel, who only stand and look, more like that of the "recorded and attested" ghosts of psychical research that James promised to abjure than that of the "figures of action" in the wonder tales. But how do we know that they are inactive? If the governess is right in believing that they are often with the children when she cannot see them, they may be very active indeed. James's preface calls them "agents in fact" who "reek with the air of Evil" and achieve a "dreadful, . . . designed horror." See George

Knox, "Incubi and Succubi in TS," *Western Folklore*, 22 (1963), 122-23.

16. The quotation from James is from the preface to the New York Edition, p. xix. For convincing refutations of the views, previously advanced elsewhere, to the effect that James's revision of the tale for the New York Edition made the governess's reports more subjective, see Sheppard, Appendix A, and David Timms, "The Governess' Feelings and the Argument from Textual Revision of TS," *Yearbook of English Studies*, 6 (1972), 194-201.

17. Mrs. Grose has her affinities with Mrs. Wix in *What Maisie Knew*, though she is considerably less complicated. In an excellent article called "Mrs. Grose's Reading of TS," *Studies in English Literature, 1500-1900*, 14 (1972), 619-35, Arthur Boardman establishes her importance in the tale by analyzing her words and actions in detail as a check on the governess, her own inability to see, and her scepticism followed by final conviction establishing the point that the evil in the story does not come from the governess but from "the universe itself." But we should not deny ourselves whatever entertainment we may derive from noting that C. Knight Aldrich's "Another Twist to TS," *MFS*, 13 (1967), 167-78, which argues that Mrs. Grose is the mother of the children by the master and the engineer of a plot to drive the governess mad, had the bad luck to appear *after* Eric Solomon had "demonstrated" much the same thing in a brilliant burlesque of "Screw" pseudo-scholarship, applying the methods of Sherlock Holmes, "The Return of the Screw," *University Review*, 30 (1964), 205-11. "This article is definitive and provides the one, incontrovertible explanation of the strange happenings at Bly. Never again need there be another explanation of 'The Turn of the Screw.' "

18. See Preface to Volume XII of the New York Edition, pp. xviii-xix; Lubbock, *Letters*, I, pp. 298-99. Pelham Edgar went along with all this as late as 1927 (*HJ, Man and Author*, p. 159), writing of the governess that "save for

courage and devotion, she has no discernible attributes."
But cf. Dorothea Krook, "Intentions and Intentions: The
Problem of Interpretation and HJ's TS," in John Hal-
perin, ed., *The Theory of the Novel* (OUP, 1974), pp.
353-72, a devastating refutation of the Wilson thesis that
culminates in a conjectural reconstruction of how the
governess figure was developed.

19. James's foot slips, I think, when he permits the governess
to say "how the deuce" and to compare the "hard spaces
and scattered dead leaves" of autumn to "a theatre after
the performance—all strewn with crumpled playbills."

20. See Carvel Collins, "J's TS," *Exp*, 13 (1954-55), Item 49;
Louis D. Rubin, Jr., "One More Turn of the Screw,"
MFS, 9 (1963-64), 314-28; Stanley Trachtenberg (n. 13).
One may hope that Marcella M. Holoway's "Another
Turn to J's TS," *CEA Critic*, 41 (January 1949), pp. 9-17,
records the ultimate turn. Her notion is not only that the
governess loves Douglas but also that he "reflects
James's own personal problems." See further Walter
Stepp, "TS: If Douglas is Miles . . . ," *Nassau Review*, 3,
No. 2 (1976), 76-82.

21. The fullest examination of the prologue is in John J.
Allen's "The Governess and the Ghosts in TS," *HJR*, 1
(1979-80), 73-80, which also treats the final scene and
enlarges the list of incidents in the tale previously noted
as inexplicable upon the hallucination theory. Sidney E.
Lind's objection in "TS: The Torment of Critics," *Centennial Review*, 14 (1970), 225-40, that Douglas's testimony is irrelevant because he only knew the governess
at a later date, is unconvincing not only because it is
inconceivable that a hysterical or lunatic girl could have
developed into the poised and gracious woman he knew
but, also because it leaves the prologue without function.
Though Peter A. Obuchowski, "Technique and Meaning
in J's TS," *CLA Journal*, 21 (1977-78), 380-89, says much
of value, when he argues that the prologue is misleading
because it puts the reader off guard about the
governess, he blames James for securing his own effect

rather than the critic's. It is worth noting also that the governess herself supplies all the data about her youthful shortcomings by which some critics have been so much impressed. Michael J.B. Taylor, "A Note on the First Narrator of TS," *AL*, 53 (1981-82), 717-22, makes a strong case for identifying the first narrator as a woman. See also Anthony J. Mazzella, "An Answer To The Mystery of TS," *SSF*, 17 (1980), 327-33, and William B. Goetz, "The 'Frame' of TS: Framing the Reader In," *SSF*, 18 (1981), 71-6.

22. Brenda Murphy, "The Problem of Validity in the Critical Controversy over TS," *RSW*, 47 (1979), 191-201, contains a valuable classification of and commentary upon the varieties of interpretation that have been offered. Goddard not only saw the insanity of the governess as the "theme" of the story, but because James called her father "eccentric" suggested that the latter was insane also, which sets Cranfill and Clark off on describing him as fully as if they had read his life and letters. But Goddard's admission that he interpreted the story in terms of a childhood experience of his own with an abnormal domestic makes his interpretation about as valuable as Bernard Shaw's persistent disparagement of Sarah Bernhardt's acting because, as he later admitted, she reminded him of an aunt whom he disliked. (In any case, James softened "eccentric" to "whimsical" in the New York revision). It has also been suggested that the governess is sexually attracted to Miles, that she writes her story as a piece of fiction, that she wishes to kill the children, and that she has an affinity of spirit with the ghosts. One writer has not even been content to stop short of arguing that the uncle, Miles, Flora, the governess, Peter Quint, and Miss Jessel all resemble one another so strongly "that the governess substitutes one figure for another." In addition to references already cited, see Katherine Anne Porter (Willen, *Casebook*, p. 161); Bernardine Brown, "TS: A Case of Romantic Displacement," *Nassau Review*, Vol. 2, No. 5 (1974), 75-82; Paul N. Siegel, "Miss Jessel, Mirror Image of the Governess," 18 (1968), 30-38; E. Duncan Aswell, "Reflec-

tion of a Governess: Image and Distortion in TS," *NCF*, 23 (1969), 49-63; Juliet McMaster, "The Full Image of Repetition in TS," *SSF*, 6 (1969), 377-82.

23. See John Lydenberg, (note 8); Ernest Tuveson, "TS: A Palimpsest," *Studies in English Literature, 1500-1900,* 12 (1972), 783-800. Cf. Dennis Gruner, "The Demonic Children in TS," *Psychocultural Review*, 2 (1978), 221-39: "For James's governess proof of the corruption of her charges is the hell that must be harrowed before the break of grace. When they confess, she believes, they will be saved and she will be saved, and the goodness of all will be reinstated in the eye of God." See also Walter F. Wright, *The Madness of Art*, pp. 181-85, a valuable discussion.

24. James W. Gargano, "TS," *Western Humanities Review*, 15 (1961), 173-79.

25. The quotation from Wright is in *The Imagination of Disaster*, p. 173, and those that follow are from Tony Tanner's discussion of "In the Cage" in *The Reign of Wonder: Naivety and Reality in American Literature* (CUP 1965), pp. 310-19. Though Tanner describes the telegraphist as "a comic parody of the Jamesian artist," he adds that "James has subjected the habits of her imagination to a scrutiny which lifts the book above parody," making it "a genuine exploration onto the activities of the speculative imagination, not a joke." Aswell's broadside is delivered in his "James's 'In the Cage': The Telegraphist as Artist," *TSLL*, 6 (1966), 274-84; for Samuels, see *The Ambiguity of Henry James*, Ch. VII. Attacks on the governess of the "Screw" have been documented in this chapter; for *The Sacred Fount*, see the present writer's *The Novels of H.J.*, Ch. VII. On the general matters under consideration, consult also Heath Moon, "More Royalist Than the King: The Governess, The Telegraphist, and Mrs. Gracedew," *Crit*, 25 (1982), 16-35.

26. Jean H. Frantz, "H.J. and Saintine," *NQ*, N.S. 7 (1960),

266-68; William B. Stone, "On the Background of J's 'In the Cage,'" *American Literary Realism, 1870-1910*, 6 (1973), 243-7; Albert C. Friend, "A Forgotten Story by HJ," *SAQ*, 53 (1954), 100-108. Zabel's collection was published by Norton in 1958.

27. See especially Stuart Hutchinson, "J's 'In the Cage': A New Interpretation," *SSF*, 19 (1982), 19-26, who argues that the telegraphist "is afraid of any life beyond the control of her consciousness" and sees the ending of the tale as "potential." Cf. also Jean Frantz Blackall, "J's 'In the Cage': An Approach Through the Figurative Language," *University of Toronto Quarterly*, 31 (1961-62), 164-79. Mrs. Blackall finds Captain Everard rather like Sir Claude in *What Maisie Knew*, "charming but rather weak, subject to Lady Bradeen as Sir Claude is to Mrs. Beale and like Sir Claude impecunious."

28. The brave scholar is Ralf Norman in "The Interpretation of the Telegram Plot in HJ's 'In the Cage,'" *NQ*, N.S. 24 (1977), 425-27. The quotation from Edel is in *HJ: The Treacherous Years*, p. 259. For James's remark see Simon Nowell-Smith, *The Lesson of the Master* (S, 1948), p. 122.

29. James's treatment of Mudge, in himself and in the contrast he affords to the flashy and uncertain Everard, would alone refute, if refutation is still needed, the common misapprehension that the author's own sympathies were limited by the boundaries of Mayfair. If Mudge has waited long for an adequate exposition of his virtues, Joel Salzberg has now splendidly supplied it in "Mr. Mudge as Redemptive Fate in J's 'In the Cage,'" *SN*, 11 (1979-80), 63-76. See further Wilhelm Füger, "'In the Cage': Versuche zur Deutung einer umstrittenen HJ Novelle," *NS*, 15 (1966), 506-13.

30. See *Notebooks*, pp. 190-91, and preface to Vol. XVI of the New York Edition, pp. x-xii. There are studies of structure and imagery in Vaid, *Technique in the Tales of*

Henry James, pp. 42-47, and in Buitenhuis, *The Grasping Imagination*, pp. 173-77.

31. T.M. Segnitz, "The Actual Genesis of H.J.'s 'Paste,' " *AL*, 36 (1964-65), 216-19, argues the possible influence of another de Maupassant story, "The Jewelry."

32. *Notebooks*, pp. 265-66.

Chapter VIII

1. Adeline R. Tintner, "The Influence of Balzac's *L'Envers de l'Histoire Contemporaine* on J's 'The Great Good Place,' " *SSF*, 9 (1972), 343-51; Robert E. Whelan, Jr., "God, HJ, and 'The Great Good Place,' " *RSW*, 47 (1979), 212-20. Ms. Tintner cites "Benvolio," *Roderick Hudson*, and *Guy Domville*, as well as "figures of speech in stories written during the eighteen-nineties" to establish James's "lifelong yearning . . . for some form of retreat like that provided by the Catholic Church." Mr. Whelan writes: "All James's characters of fine conscience are . . . like Dane in that they must renounce their respective forms of egotism if they are to find ease and space for their souls." Harry Silverstein has another good critical essay, "The Utopia of HJ," *NEQ*, 35 (1962), 458-68. Joseph M. DeFalco essays a psychoanalytical interpretation of the tale in " 'The Great Good Place': A Journey into the Psyche," *LP*, 6, Spring 1958, pp. 18-20, and Mary Ellen Henx, "The Monomyth in 'The Great Good Place,' " *CE*, 24 (1963), 439-43, reads it as summarizing "the archetypal pattern of the adventures of a 'hero' "—departure, initiation, and return. Leon Edel's introduction to the story in *The Ghostly Tales of HJ* is suggestive but highly speculative.

2. *The Short Stories of Henry James*, pp. 413-15.

3. *The Madness of Art*, p. 190.

4. *Sweet Rocket* was published by Harper and Brothers in 1920 and reprinted in *Six Novels of the Supernatural*, ed. Edward Wagenknecht, (Viking Press, 1944). Mary Johnston is known greatly to have admired HJ, and if this does not show in the historical romances for which she is best known, it does not seem fanciful to discern traces of his influence and especially of "The Great Good Place" in the mystical novels of her later years.

5. Edgar, *HJ, Man and Author*, p. 192; Stevenson, *The Crooked Corridor*, p. 74; Ward, "Silence, Realism, and 'The Great Good Place,'" *HJR*, 3 (1981-82), 129-32.

6. *Notebooks*, pp. 189-90.

7. *Notebooks*, p. 289.

8. Samuel Irving Bellman's article, "HJ's 'The Tree of Knowledge': A Biblical Parallel," *SSF*, 1 (1963-64), 226-28, in which he argues that the relation between the Master and Peter Brench suggests that between Jesus and Peter in the New Testament and that the story is "a kind of parody of Christian theology," which reveals its author's "morbid, negative veiw of art and life" does not merit serious consideration.

9. There can be no question, however, that this is what James intended the reader to believe. Robert L. Gale's article, "The Abasement of Mrs. Warren Hope," *PMLA*, 68 (1963), 98-102, which presents Mrs. Hope as "the demented wife of an unexceptional, long-suffering man" who is herself wrong about both her husband and Lord Northmore, presents a different interpretation of the story from that which has been offered in these pages; but though it is ingeniously argued, I am not convinced.

10. *Notebooks*, pp. 296-97.

11. See Lubbock, *Letters*, II, 260-61.

12. The language is J. Peter Dyson's in his admirable article, "Perfection, Beauty, and Suffering in 'The Two Faces,'" *HJR*, 2 (1980-81), 116-25, the most important study of the tale that has been made, relating it to J's other works and viewing it in the context of his thought and moral outlook. Dyson praises Eleanor M. Tilton's introduction to her 1961 Signet edition of *The Marriages and Other Tales*, which is now out of print and unavailable to me. Madame Merle is of course Isabel Archer's bad angel in *The Portrait of a Lady*. See also Richard Amacher, "J's 'The Two Faces,'" *Exp*, 12 (1954), Item 20, and Henry R. Rupp's commentary on it under the same title in *Exp*, 14 (1955), Item 30. Stanley Kozikowski's "Unreliable Narration in HJ's 'The Two Faces' and Edith Wharton's 'The Dilettante,'" *ArQ*, 35 (1979), 357-72, is a critical and comparative study of the two tales.

Chapter IX

1. See *Notebooks*, pp. 265, 267, 278-79, 292, 295.

2. "The Sources of HJ's 'Mrs. Medwin,'" *NQ*, N.S. 27 (1980), 226-30. Richards also, rather startlingly, identifies Miss Cutter's disreputable half-brother Scott Homer with Robert Temple, brother of Minny Temple, whom James revered and immortalized as Milly Theale in *The Wings of the Dove*.

3. All this is beautifully demonstrated by Kenneth Bernard in "HJ's Broken Discourse in 'Mrs. Medwin,'" *Discourse*, 6 (1963), 310-14.

4. *Notebooks*, pp. 290-91.

5. Adeline R. Tintner, "The Real-Life Holbein in J's Fiction," *ABBW*, January 8, 1979, pp. 278-87, identifies the particular Holbein painting James had in mind as the portrait of Lady Butts (Margaret Bacon, lady-in-waiting to Catherine Howard), which was purchased by Mrs.

"Jack" Gardner and is now in the Isabella Stewart Gardner Museum in Boston (see the reproduction of the painting in the article). James makes a point of there being in Mrs. Brash's appearance "nothing . . . of the ascetic or the nun. She was a good hard sixteenth-century figure, not withered with innocence, bleached rather by life in the open." Ms. Tintner also finds a reference to Mrs. Gardner's purchase of Titian's "The Rape of Europa" in the comparison of Lady Beldonald's beauty to that of a Titian painting and explores other possible references to Mrs. Gardner in this story and elsewhere in James, especially in "A New England Winter" and *The Spoils of Poynton*. In another article, "J's 'The Beldonald Holbein' and Rollins' 'A Burne-Jones Head': A Surprising Parallel," *Colby Library Quarterly*, 14 (1978), 182-90, the same writer makes it seem likely that James also took important suggestions from a story by the twenty-year-old Clara Sherwood Rollins, published in *A Burne-Jones Head and Other Sketches* (1884).

6. Gargano, "J's Stories in 'The Story in It,' " *Notes on Modern American Literature*, 1 (1976), Item 2; see also Ellen Tremper, "HJ's 'The Story in It': A Successful Aesthetic Adventure," *HJR*, 3 (1981-82), 11-16.

7. Adeline R. Tintner, "HJ's 'The Story in It' and Gabriele D'Annunzio," *MFS*, 28 (1982), 201-14, studies the tale in connection with D'Annunzio's novels, especially *Il Piacre*, and James's own essay on that writer, whose art he admired and whom he criticized not because of his eroticism as such but because he left "the romance inherent in a passion involving the senses" without relationship to the rest of life. "James prevents the embroilment between Maud and Voyt because Jamesian people do not live only in their erotic and plastic senses."

8. *Notebooks*, pp. 275-78; cf. the preface to the New York Edition, Vol. XVIII, p. xxii.

9. In *The Novels of HJ* (Ungar, 1983).

10. Lubbock, *Letters*, II, 487-89.

11. *Notebooks*, pp. 286-89.

12. Anderson's comments are in his introduction to *HJ: Selected Short Stories* (Rinehart, 1950), Holleran's in "An Analysis of 'The Birthplace,' " *PLL*, 2 (1966), (1966), 76-80, and Ross's in "J's 'The Birthplace,': A Double Turn of the Narrative Screw," *SSF*, 3 (1966), 321-28. George Arms has an interesting study of the religious symbolism in the story in "J's 'The Birthplace': Over a Pulpit-Edge," *TSL*, 8 (1968), 61-69, but seems to me to allow insufficiently for the ironical element in James's application of it. In "J Examines Shakespeare: Notes on the Nature of Genius," *PMLA*, 73 (1958), 123-28, William T. Stafford analyzes the story in detail against the background of what we know about James's knowledge of and attitude toward Shakespeare. See also Clifton Fadiman's note on "The Birthplace" in his *The Short Stories of HJ*. Mildred E. Hartsook, "The Conceivable Child: J and the Poet," *SSF*, 8 (1971), 569-74, and William McMurray, "Reality in HJ's 'The Birthplace,' " *Exp*, 35 (1976), 10-11, both support the view of Gedge as artist.

13. *Notebooks*, pp. 306-307.

14. This is well analyzed in Vaid, *Technique in the Tales of HJ*, pp. 192 ff., where due attention is also given to the differences between the two central characters. On the second aspect, see also J. Peter Dyson, "Death and Separation in 'Fordham Castle,' " *SSF*, 16 (1979), 41-44. Kermit Vanderbilt, " 'Complicated Music of Short Order' in 'Fordham Castle,' "*HJR*, 2 (1980-81), 61-66, sees the tale as an adaptation of "some of the tonal patterns and ordered counterpoint of musical composition." The development of the basic idea can be traced through the *Notebooks* (pp. 116, 267-68, 274-75, 292-94).

Chapter X

1. *Notebooks*, p. 322; Hoffmann, *The Short Stories of*

HJ, p. 99; Jessie R. Lucke, "The Inception of 'The Beast in the Jungle,' " *NEQ*, 26 (1953), 529-32 (cf. George Monteiro, "Hawthorne, J, and the Destructive Self," *TSLL*, 4 [1962-63], 58-71); Leon Edel, in *HJ: The Master* (L, 1972), pp. 13-39, and elsewhere; William Nance, " 'The Beast in the Jungle': Two Versions of Oedipus," *SSF*, 13 (1976), 433-40; Ellen Tremper, "HJ's Alter Ego: An Examination of the Psychological Double in Three Tales," *TQ*, 19, No. 3 (1976), 59-75; Milton H. Mays, "HJ, or, The Beast in the Palace of Art," *AL*, 39 (1967-68), 467-87. In a superlative article, "The Idea of 'Too Late' in J's 'The Beast in the Jungle,' " *HJR*, 4 (1982-83), 128-39, Michael C. Berthold demonstrates more affinities with Hawthorne than had previously been noted and also shows that James "exploited the idea's possibilities as a structural device in a way evidently unperceived by Hawthorne."

2. "The Beast in the Jungle" has inspired far more commentary, much of it psychological or psychoanalytical, than can be listed here. The following items will indicate the wide variety of interpretations that have been entered: Betsy Miller, "Miss Savage and Miss Bartram," *Nineteenth Century and After*, 144 (1948), 285-91; David Kerner, "A Note on 'The Beast in the Jungle,' " *UKCR*, 17 (1950-51), 100-118; Robert Rogers, "The Beast in HJ," *AI*, 13 (1956), 427-53; Courtney Johnson, "John Marcher and the Paradox of the 'Unfortunate' Fall," *SSF*, 6 (1968-69), 121-35; James Kraft, "A Perspective on 'The Beast in the Jungle,' " *Literatur in Wissenschaft und Unterricht*, 2 (1969), 20-26; Peter J. Conn, "Seeing and Blindness in 'The Beast in the Jungle,' " *SSF*, 7 (1970) 472-75; Ronald Beck, "J's 'The Beast in the Jungle': Theme and Metaphor," *MR*, 2, February 1970, unpaged; Jane P. Tompkins, " 'The Beast in the Jungle': An Analysis of J's Late Style," *MFS*, 16 (1970-71) 185-91; Joseph Kau, "HJ and the Garden: A Symbol Setting for 'The Beast in the Jungle,' " *SSF*, 10 (1973), 187-98; Joseph R. Kehler, "Salvation and Resurrection in J's 'The Beast in the Jungle,' " *Essays in Literature* (University of Denver), 1 (1973), 13-28; Randall H. Waldron, "Prefiguration in 'The Beast in the Jungle,' " *Studies in American*

Fiction, 1 (1973), 101-104; Vern Haddock, "Fear and
Growth: Reflections on 'The Beast in the Jungle,' "*Journal of the Otto Rank Association*, 9, No. 2 (1974-75),
38-42; Francis E. Crowley, "HJ's 'The Beast in the Jungle' and *The Ambassadors*," *Psychoanalytic Review*, 9
(1975-76), 153-63; Mark L. Krupnick, " 'The Beast in the
Jungle' and the Dilemma of Narcissus," *Southern Review*
(University of Adelaide), 9 (1976), 113-20; Anthony
B. Dawson, "The Reader and the Measurement of
Time in 'The Beast in the Jungle,' " *English Studies
in Canada*, 3 (1977), 458-64; O. P. Jones, "The Cool
World of London in 'The Beast in the Jungle,' " *Studies in American Fiction*, 6 (1978), 227-35; Elizabeth
Shapland, "Duration and Frequency: Prominent Aspects
of Time in HJ's 'The Beast in the Jungle,' " *PLL*, 17
(1981), 33-47; Rachel Salmon, "Naming and Knowing in
HJ's 'The Beast in the Jungle': The Hermeneutics of a
Sacred Text," *Orbis Literarum*, 36 (1981), 302-22; Janice
H. Harris, "Bushes, Bears, and 'The Beast in the Jungle,'"
SSF, 18 (1981), 147-54; David Smit, "The Life of the
Beast: The Dramatic Style of Henry James's 'The Beast
in the Jungle,' " *Henry James Review* 4 (1983), 219-306.
See also the discussions of the tale in Wayne C. Booth,
The Rhetoric of Fiction; Walter F. Wright, *The Madness
of Art*; Krishna Baldev Vaid, *Technique in the Tales of
HJ*; and Ora Segal, *The Lucid Reflector*.

3. Peter Buitenhuis, "From Daisy Miller to Julia Bride, 'A
Whole Passage of Intellectual History,' " AQ 11 (1959),
136-46, the substance of which was taken up into his
book, *The Grasping Imagination*; Adeline R. Tintner,
"Landmarks of 'The Terrible Town': The New York
Scene in HJ's Last Stories," *Prospects, An Annual of
American Cultural Studies*, 2 (1976), 399-435; F.W.
Dupee, *HJ*, p. 276; Bruce McElderry, Jr., *HJ*, p. 144;
Charles G. Hoffmann, *The Short Novels of HJ*, pp.
110-11; Pelham Edgar, *HJ, Man and Writer*, p. 74.

4. Leon Edel, *HJ: The Master*, pp. 312-16.

5. Edward Honig, "The Merciful Fraud in Three Sto-

ries by HJ," *The Tiger's Eye*, No. 9 October 1949, pp. 83-96; James F. Rosenblatt, "Bridegroom and Bride in 'The Jolly Corner,'"*SSF*, 14 (1977), 282-84; Mildred K. Travis, "Hawthorne's 'Egotism;' and 'The Jolly Corner,'" *ESQ*, No. 63 (1971), 13-18; M.E. Grenander, "Benjamin Franklin's Glass Armonica and HJ's 'The Jolly Corner,' " *PLL*, 11 (1975), 415-17, which concerns Brydon's feeling about the house, "in the likeness of some great glass bowl, all precious concave crystal, set delicately humming by the play of a moist finger round its edge." Franklin did not invent the glass armonica but he did help perfect it, and Mesmer played it as background music during his hypnotic sessions. "If the house acted on Spencer Brydon as the glass armonica operated on Mesmer's subjects, then Brydon's continued trips to his old house would eventually have helped to induce in him a state of autohypnosis in which he saw what he had all along been willing himself to see." Jesse Bier, "HJ's 'The Jolly Corner': The Writer's Fable and the Deeper Matter," *ArQ*, 35 (1979), 321-34, sees James striving "for a delicate amalgam" of Hawthorne and Poe, but with "the Hawthornian side" remaining "dominant, quite overbalancing the other."

6. As by Saul Rosenzweig in his once-influential but wrong-headed article, "The Ghost of HJ," *Character and Personality*, 12 (1943), 79-100, accepted and summarized by Clifton Fadiman, *The Short Stories of HJ*, pp. 241-42. James recorded his Galerie d'Apollon nightmare in *A Small Boy and Others* (S, 1912), pp. 347-49. See Adeline R. Tintner's *Prospects* article (cf. note 3), pp. 408-09, for her identification of Brydon's haunted house with 21 East 11 Street.

7. The usual interpretation of "The Jolly Corner" is that Brydon confronts what he had been seeking, the ghost of himself as he might have been had he remained in New York, but Floyd Stovall, "HJ's 'The Jolly Corner,'" *NCF*, 12 (1957-58), 72-84, thinks that the ghost that frightens him in the hall is not the one whose confrontation he had funked upstairs but rather the ghost of himself as he

actually is, after having been false to himself for thirty-three years. Stovall's article, which is persuasively developed, contains valuable insights (whatever we may make of its central thesis), but it seems doubtful that we need two ghosts in the story or that had he intended this, James would have indicated it so obscurely that no reader should have perceived it until 1957. For further comment on this point, see Buitenhuis, *The Grasping Imagination*, p. 216. See also Joan Delfattore, "The 'Other' Spencer Brydon," *ArQ*, 35 (1979), 335-41.

8. *The Ordeal of Consciousness in HJ*, pp. 334-48. See also, in addition to Edward Honig's article (note 5), Courtney Johnson, "HJ's 'The Jolly Corner': A Study in Integration," *AI*, 24 (1967), 344-60; Ernest Tuveson, " 'The Jolly Corner': A Fable of Redemption," *SSF*, 12 (1975), 271-80; John J. Byers, Jr., "Alice Staverton's Redemption of Spencer Brydon in J's 'The Jolly Corner,' " *South Atlantic Bulletin*, 41 (1976), 90-99.

9. "Universality in 'The Jolly Corner,' " *TSLL*, 4 (1962-63), 12-15.

10. Allen F. Stein, "The Beast in 'The Jolly Corner': Spencer Brydon's Ironic Rebirth," *SSF*, 11 (1974), 61-66.

11. In addition to the articles about "The Jolly Corner" cited elsewhere, see Maurice Beebe, "The Turned Back of HJ," *SAQ*, 50 (1954), 521-39, and Earl Rovit, "The Ghosts in J's 'The Jolly Corner,' " *TSL*, 10 (1965), 65-72. Fred C. Thomson has an interesting analysis of Chapter II, paragraph 20, in "J's 'The Jolly Corner,' " *Exp*, 22 (1963-64), Item 28. Among the books that include comparatively detailed discussions of this story are Martha Banta, *HJ and the Occult*; John A. Clair, *The Ironic Dimension in HJ*; Mary Doyle Springer, *A Rhetoric of Literary Character*; Krishna Baldev Vaid, *Technique in the Tales of HJ*; and Walter F. Wright, *The Madness of Art*.

Chapter XI

1. The "blurb" seems to have been used only in part on the jacket but was printed in its entirety by E.V. Lucas in his *Reading, Writing, and Remembering* (Methuen, 1932), Adeline R. Tintner, who is the principal authority on James's last stories, and to whom this chapter is deeply indebted, quotes the whole in "The Metamorphoses of Edith Wharton in HJ's *The Finer Grain*," *Twentieth Century Literature*, 21 (1975), 355-79. In addition to this article and the one cited in Chapter X, note 3, Ms. Tintner has also published "J's Mock-Epic: 'The Velvet Glove,' Edith Wharton, and Other Tales," *MFS*, 17 (1971-72), 483-99; "HJ at the Movies: Cinematograph and Photograph in 'Crapy Cornelia,'" 6 (Fall 1976), pp. 1-8; "An Interlude in Hell: HJ's 'A Round of Visits' and *Paradise Lost*," *Notes on Modern American Literature*, 5 (1981), Item 12. See also J. Peter Dyson, "Romance Elements in Three Tales by HJ: 'Mora Montravers,' 'The Velvet Glove,' and 'The Bench of Desolation,'" *English Studies in Canada*, 5 (1979), 66-77.

2. Joseph Milicia, "HJ's *The Winter's Tale*: 'The Bench of Desolation,'" *Studies in American Fiction*, 6 (1977), 141-56.

3. Ms. Tintner sees the "Glove" corresponding to a "*Scène de la vie de parisienne*"; "Mora" to a "*Scène de la vie de Provence*"; and "Bench" to a "*Scene de le vie de Campagne*" or "*Les Paysans*," while "Cornelia" and "Visits" are "reworkings in miniature of *Les Parents pauvres*."

4. Thus in "Crapy Cornelia" Mrs. Wharton in her fashionable aspect "stands behind" Mrs. Worthingham and her sister-in-law, Mary Cadwalader Jones, in whose much plainer abode James felt much more at home than with Edith, behind Cornelia herself. Mrs. Wharton's up-to-dateness appears again in Mrs. Folliott of "A Round of Visits," while her matrimonial problems are suggested

in Mrs. Ash. But it is in Kate Cookham of "The Bench of Desolation" that we have "the complete periodic embodiment of the extremes of Edity Wharton's persona. She manifests both the difficult as well as the saving aspects of her cleverness, generosity, and wealth." When Mrs. Wharton's lover, Morton Fullerton, was being threatened by a woman he had abandoned, Edith offered to buy her off, thus suggesting Kate's later aspect—"an interesting coalescence of an angel of mercy and an angel of devastation and desolation." In *The Finer Grain* the tales are printed in the following order: "Glove," "Mora," "Visits," "Cornelia," "Bench," thus presenting Mrs. Wharton "moving from a goddess to 'an angel of desolation,' sitting on the bench of desolation with the hero whom she has first defeated and then succoured." "The Angel of Desolation" was one of the terms James applied to Edith when she swept down upon him from time to time with her Panhard and all the other appurtenances of wealth, generosity, and executive competence to entertain him royally and impose a schedule upon him more strenuous than he cared to face. For further material on James's relations with Mrs. Wharton see Leon Edel, *HJ: The Master*, pp. 352-59, and for a full-length study, Millicent Bell, *Edith Wharton and HJ: The Story of Their Friendship* (George Braziller, 1965).

5. (Appleton-Century, 1934), pp. 308-309.

6. Like Lambert Strether in *The Ambassadors*, Berridge is not sure he has "lived" enough, and this feeling is shared by Sidney Traffle in "Mora Montravers."

7. Allen F. Stein, "The Hack's Progress: A Reading of J's 'The Velvet Glove,' " *Essays in Literature* (Western Illinois University), 1 (1974), 219-26, argues among other things that in James dazzling current success is not generally the hallmark of a great writer. E.C. Curtsinger, Jr., "HJ's Farewell in 'The Velvet Glove,' " *SSF*, 18 (1981), 163-69, is probably unique in seeing the Princess as "the embodied imagination of James's writer" and in Ber-

ridge's parting from her "a beauty unbearable for all true lovers of James."

8. *Notebooks*, pp. 309-10. For *The Saloon* see Chapter V, note 34. J. Peter Dyson, "Bartolozzi and HJ's 'Mora Montravers,' " *HJR*, 1 (1979-80), 264-66, interprets illuminatingly the reference to the stipple engraver Francesco Bartolozzi (1727-1813) in the second paragraph.

9. In her "HJ at the Movies" (see note 1), Adeline Tintner shows that White-Mason's view of Cornelia's head and hat "that came nearer and nearer, while it met his eyes, after the manner of images in the cinematograph" toward the end of Chapter II probably reflects James's memory of the famous film of the Corbett-Fitzsimmons prize fight, which we know he saw. She also notes that the quotation from the *Aeneid* in the fourth paragraph of Chapter III is the only Latin quotation of any length in any of James's stories and points out what she considers echoes of this in "Crapy Cornelia."

10. "Language as Art: The Ways of Knowing HJ's 'Crapy Cornelia,' " *Style*, 1 (1967), 130-49. Purdy's special point, however, is that the tale represents "a kind of final climax to the word-and conversational play to which James devoted so much of his art."

11. *Notebooks*, pp. 330-32.

12. See note 2.

13. Krook, *The Ordeal of Consciousness in HJ*, pp. 347, 349; Vaid, *Technique in the Tales of HJ*, pp. 271-93; Springer, *A Rhetoric of Literary Character*, Chapter II.

14. Ora Segal, "The Weak Wings of Pride: An Interpretation of J's 'The Bench of Desolation,' " *NCF*, 20 (1965), 145-54.

15. W.R. Martin and Warren H. Ober, "Dantesque Patterns

in HJ's 'A Round of Visits,' " *Ariel* (University of Cal-
gary), 12, October 1981, pp. 45-54. For Ms. Tintner's
article consult note 1. See also Strother B. Purdy,
"Conversation and Awareness in HJ's 'A Round of Visits,' " *SSF*, 6 (1968-69), 421-32.

16. *Notebooks*, pp. 251, 158-60, 266-67, 280-82.

17. See Sara S. Chapman, "The Obsession of Egotism
in HJ's 'A Round of Visits,' " *ArQ*, 29 (1973), 130-38,
who sees the story as basically "an account of the protagonist's own spiritual development from an almost
completely self-indulgent egotism to a beginning recog-
nition of the need to react beyond the power of ego
toward the walled-in personalities of other people."

18. It is an interesting testimonial to James's awareness
of the complexity of human character and experience
that as Chad Newsome should have been refined by
what was technically an illicit love affair, Winch has
grown in spirit and sensitivity through becoming a
criminal!

19. The critics quoted are in order McElderry, *HJ*, p.
144; Buitenhuis, *The Grasping Imagination*, p. 236;
Ward, *The Imagination of Disaster*, p. 162. The most
curious and high-flown interpretation is that of Martin
and Ober, who, though they would think Winch's
pistol shot more at home in an Ibsen play than a James
story, somehow manage to make his suicide an act of
affirmation. By forgiving Bloodgood, Monteith has
demonstrated to Winch "that human sympathy and
forgiveness can reach him too," thus giving him courage
to "escape from Hell to appear before a God who will
not be less sympathetic." Mark understands all this,
and his final sentence "is spoken with more gladness and
pride than regret." The authors comment, not too rele-
vantly: "For James damnation was not, it seems, an
eternal and irrecoverable state."

Index of Names

Index of James's Writings